Contents

Death Dreams

*Unveiling Mysteries of the
Unconscious Mind*

Kenneth Paul Kramer

With John Larkin

PAULIST PRESS
New York/Mahwah, N.J.

The publisher gratefully acknowledges use of excerpts from the following sources: *The Basic Writings of Sigmund Freud,* copyright 1938, copyright renewed 1964 by Gioia B. Bernheim and Edmund Brill. Reprinted by permission; *The New World of Dreams,* Ralph L. Woods and Herbert B. Greenhouse, editors (New York: Macmillan, 1974). Full credit must be given to author and publisher on every copy reproduced. Reprinted by permission; *Leaves of Grass,* Walt Whitman (New York: Signet, 1980). *The Portable Walt Whitman,* Walt Whitman, edited by Mark van Doren (New York: Viking Press, 1945). Reprinted by permission; Artemidorus, *The Interpretation of Dreams,* translated by Robert J. White (Noyes Press: Park Ridge, N.J. 1975); *The Meaning of Death,* copyright 1959, by H. Feifel (New York: McGraw-Hill, Inc.); Excerpt from *The Unbearable Lightness of Being* by Milan Kundera. Copyright © 1984 by Harper & Row, Publishers, Inc. Reprinted by permission of HarperCollins Publishers; Excerpt from *The Spiral Dance* by Starhawk. Copyright © 1979 by Miriam Simos. Reprinted by permission of HarperCollins Publishers; *Life After Life* and *Reflections on Life After Life,* by Raymond A. Moody (Mockingbird Books Inc., St. Simons Island, Georgia); From *Dreamtime & Inner Space,* by Holger Kalweit, © 1984 by Holger Kalweit and Scherz Verlag, Bern and Munich. Translation © 1988 by Shambhala Publications, Inc. Reprinted by arrangement with Shambhala Publications, Inc., 300 Massachusetts Avenue, Boston, MA 02115; From *Myths, Dreams, and Religion,* by Joseph Campbell. Copyright © 1970 by the Society for the Arts, Religion, and Contemporary Culture. Used by permission of the Publisher, Dutton, an imprint of New American Library, a division of Penguin Books USA Inc.; Reprinted with permission of Charles Scribner's Sons, an imprint of Macmillan Publishing Company, from *The Short Stories of Ernest Hemingway.* Copyright 1936 by Ernest Hemingway; renewal copyright © 1964 by Mary Hemingway.

Library of Congress Cataloging-in-Publication Data

Kramer, Kenneth, 1941–
    Death dreams : unveiling mysteries of the unconscious mind / Kenneth Paul Kramer with John Larkin.
        p. cm.
    Includes bibliographical references and index.
    ISBN 0-8091-3349-0 (pbk.)
    1. Death in dreams. I. Larkin, John (John S.) II. Title.
BF1099.D4K73 1992
154.6'32—dc20   92-29605
                                                                                    CIP

Published by Paulist Press
997 Macarthur Boulevard
Mahwah, New Jersey 07430

Printed and bound in the United States of America

CONTENTS

III

I find it's kind of funny,
I find it's kind of sad,
The dreams in which I'm dying,
Are the best I've ever had.

—Tears for Fears from "Mad World"

Dedicated to
Linda Therese Garcia

A CASTILIAN ROSE
WHERE NO OTHERS BLOOM

ACKNOWLEDGEMENTS

More than anyone else, I would like to acknowledge John Larkin, a San Jose State University undergraduate extraordinaire who has worked with me on this project since its inception. John has provided untold logistical and creative assistance. Clearly, John's contributions—his questions, curiosity and diligence—propelled the book to another level.

I also wish to thank the following students who contributed research and written suggestions for specific sections of the book: Susanna Marsch and Glenda Cresap (Chapter 1); Diane B. Kershaw and Alfred Brinnand (Chapter 2); Cheryl Woods (Chapter 3); Deidre Jordy (Chapter 7); Mary Jane Sullivan (Chapter 8); and Karen Siry (Chapter 9). As well, I would like to express appreciation to all of the students who contributed their death dreams in the 1988–1990 semesters at San Jose State University in my "Death, Dying & Religions" course.

To the typists Leslie Rogers and Rita Kokin, who put up with my handwriting, I am thankful for their almost eager willingness to plunge into the project, and to see it through. Also, I am grateful to Wendy Donaldson who made valuable suggestions toward a Glossary, and who contributed several computer graphics.

At the center of the whole project is the person whose technical expertise, stylistic and layout abilities, as well as constant support, encouragement and echoes of death, animated, and re-animated, the book. To Linda Garcia, I offer a deep bow of profound gratitude. While insufficient, it is all that these words can offer.

Then, too, special thanks to our illustrators—Sharon Sullivan, Katherine Massucco, Colleen Connery and David Perry—who got hooked on the project as the rest of us did, and whose artistry makes the book a pleasure to read. As well, I would like to thank Bill Adrian for his computer support, and Jeff Kaufman for helping with the surveys.

To Henry Maestas and John Williamson I owe special gratitude for their profound insight as long-time students of dreams and meditation, for their willingness to be interviewed, and for their provocative disclosures.

I would also like to thank San Jose State University, the School of Humanities and the Arts and the Religious Studies Program for a California State University Research Grant (awarded in 1988) which funded the initial research.

August 14, 1991
Kenneth Paul Kramer

INTRODUCTION:
NOT WAITING FOR DEATH

Was I sleeping, while the others suffered? Am I sleeping now?
... Astride of a grave and a difficult birth. Down in the hole,
lingeringly, the grave-digger puts on the forceps. We have
time to grow old. The air is full of our cries. (He listens.) But
habit is a great deadener. (He looks again at Estragon.) At me
too someone is looking, of me too someone is saying, He is
sleeping, he knows nothing, let him sleep on. (Pause.) I can't
go on! (Pause.) What have I said?[1]

OPENING THE SUBJECT

"How do we open up the subject of death and dying for westerners?" she asked. Merle was lying on the hospice bed with only
a short time left to live. Diagnosed months earlier with terminal
brain cancer, Merle had come to grips with her own death and
was facing it willingly and acceptingly. In response to a question
about her self-image she had once said, "I have a pair of almost
black eyes that won't let go. I guess you could say I have short,
dark brown hair (though it used to be longer and curly) and am
tall and slender with an athletic body. My aunt Eva used to say
that I had question mark eyes."

As she lay on her back, ever paler, my first thought was to
respond to her question with the notion that we had to become as
children in the face of death. That is, we had to become more
curious, more fascinated, and more willing to be innocent in its
presence. But that didn't seem right, or rather it felt too much like
a left brain idea. And then it struck me: "Of course, Merle,
through dreams! That's the way the subject needs to be opened
up—through the doorway of the unconscious." At that, she slowly told me what she had dreamed the night before:

I am in a very large, inelegant drawing room with much furniture (tables, chairs, lamps) and insignificant individuals. It
was like a picture in a frame that was not going anywhere,

1

like a moving picture that was not going anywhere. It was an energy picture. People walked in and took care of their business. One man zipped up his pants and then hiked them up. The picture was alive with visual life. I recognized it. I became it. The next picture was of an airplane over the Bay Area, over my house, hovering, energized. I was all of the energy of these pictures, every animate and inanimate object in the picture. It was utterly, palpably, the life energy called US, and I knew I was going to die into US, or live into US.

She paused. Her mouth was dry. I could see that she was more excited by the dream than she could show.

"How did you feel in the dream?" I asked her. "Do you remember your feelings at the time of the dream?"

"It's so palpitating," she responded. "You know, Ken, that I was almost positive that I'm not going anywhere when I die. I am slipping someplace like when you have your bathrobe on and you walk down the front walk to pick up the morning paper and you are dressed ready to go downtown. It's like that, like a space warp."

"Was that the actual image," I asked, "or one that you had thought of earlier?"

"It's an image I had at a specific time," she answered,"also a mocked-up image. The funny thing was the restlessness of the dying. It was an energy picture which didn't move. The active part, the dying part, by the time you get to the death country, by that time the picture opens up. Let me explain it to you. You are about to run a race. You stretch to prepare yourself. So you are getting ready to run, but you are not running it yet. It's like that."

She broke off to shift her body weight in the bed. "In this period of time, death and dying has been opened to me," she continued. "Death has been making itself known. I am not imagining it."

"What is it showing you about itself?" I asked.

"Its existence for me," she said. "I'm not thinking, I wonder what death is like. It's like this or that. It's just that I'm in a death country. But this is just the thinnest part of it."

At this point the nurse entered the room with Merle's medication and asked her if she was ready for it. "Let's not stop the wheels of progress," she said. After she had taken her medicine, I asked her if there was anything she especially wanted to say about her experience of dying.

"I really want to let everyone know something," she said. "C.S. Lewis once said that life is a public performance where you learn about life as you go along. This is a model for me. We learn the way to be as we do it. We make mistakes. We keep missing life. We learn that we die as we live, but our expectations are in death. We bring forth the expectations we have about death in our dying. If we expect them to be shitty and full of suffering, that's how they will show up. It's the mood and tone and pattern that we're supposed to have sex in. The real sex is the sex between two people as they invent it right then. Mostly, I say, like sex death is not the way we expect it to be. Unfortunately, we act it out the way we have been taught (both in sex and in death). It's too bad because it could be quite spectacular, quite amusing. The fact is we should leave ourselves open to see what's possible with death. Otherwise, it's such a cliché. So here's the thing and it's rife, and there's plenty of opportunity to do it wrong. I've learned so much, in actual fact, about my living and dying and about my to-be death. My death is right on schedule. It's me who isn't."

She closed her eyes and rested. After a few moments had passed, I asked, "How would you describe yourself now?" She smiled. "If I can get this right," she said, "I can go to bed and die tonight. I've sensed I had a purpose in life, yet I haven't known what it is. On the one hand, it is important for me to see myself as an ordinary human being because that's what I am, and because it's that body of lore with which I am most centrally identified. I'm not a creative artist, scientist, teacher, or inventor, someone bringing a new discipline to the floor. On the other hand, my life's path has been odd, but not just odd—I'd say seeking in a special way to resolve basic life issues for myself and for others as well. I haven't had a clue what my life has been like; only my life has had a clue. I brought my own poetry to my own life," she said softly. She smiled as she whispered: "Otherwise, it would have been as mundane as anybody's could have been. Do you know what I mean? Life is a certain timetable. It's amazing how banal and repetitive it can be. It's only the stories you tell about your life that ever invest it with any poetic particularity."

Again she shifted herself in a vain attempt to find comfort. "Merle, do you feel fully ready to die?" I asked.

"When I die," she said, "I'm not going off to play pro basketball, and I don't think the earth is going to lose sight of me quickly. But I don't know how it is going to be done. In that sense, I am not ready to retire. I certainly have an active future set out for myself. At the same time I'm ready to go. As far as I can see, there is no end to the ways in which we can go. From the time that I got sick, I noticed that we are simply using too much effort. I could hear people on the phone—the improper estimation of effort."

At this her daughter Jill returned with a special lunch which Merle had requested from a local deli, and we gathered round her bed for an indoor picnic. Merle died peacefully a week later.

DEATH'S FUTURE

But why did Merle ask that question—"How do we open up the subject of death and dying for westerners?"—just before she died? One reason, among others, is because she knew the subject of death is easy to forget, to ignore, to dread, to deny. From earliest consciousness, we are conditioned to defer its significance from our lives and not think of it because of the pain and dis-ease it often brings. But perhaps we have learned to fear death without considering that death might be the unfortunate victim of having been constantly associated (and perhaps mistakenly) with pain. In American culture, if not internationally, death is often viewed as the final extinguisher of life. And since we want to live and continue to have "good times," we fear anything that will take those good times away from us, or at least stop us from continuing to experience them. This fear of death has continued through the ages, and has brought with it a great danger—to ignore or deny death as if it will not happen to us. Even though death is perhaps the single most important unknown in life, we find ourselves in the habit, often enough, like the characters in *Waiting for Godot,* of psychologically "deadening" ourselves to its potential message.

If death can be said to have a message, what might it be? Is it possible to imagine death in a way that creates an entirely new context within which to perceive it? Is it possible that the experience of death offers hints for picturing a future not necessarily conditioned by past formulations and religious beliefs? What if in the night, when we turn off, so to speak, our conscious awareness and enter into the silent house of sleep and dreams, we are presented with data relevant to the possibility of an afterlife? And what if, contained in the images and symbols of our dreams, one can discover pathways, or spirit guides, or clues, which can be brought back into consciousness, and which throw new light on death's future presence?

Convinced that facing death is the single most significant task in life, and aware that religious answers to the threat it poses are often unaccessible, or have atrophied, we turn here to the unconscious as a largely untapped resource in current death studies. While the primary subject in this book is dreams of death, like spokes on a wheel we will examine these death dreams from multiple vantage points to open up possibilities not before realized, and to refocus our attitudes toward death. Our principal concern will be to investigate unconscious imagery of death in ways which make it available to ordinary consciousness. Chapter by chapter, through cross-cultural traditions, through myths, stories and interpretations, an edifice will come into being whose doors and windows will be left unlocked. You the reader are as welcome here as you are in your own home, perhaps more so.

BUT WHY DREAMS?

Our investigation begins with the unconscious because that is the domain in which unadulterated (or as close as possible) expressions of the death-instinct can be seen to interact with awareness. Dreams are the most essential part of any study of this sort since we have a tremendous consistency of recorded dream information from virtually every part of the world, and at every possible time. We have more recorded accounts of dreams through history than of any other altered state of consciousness.

The dream is also ideal because sleep affords the one time in which death is quite commonly expressed against our wills (who wants a nightmare, for instance?).[2] It is quite evident that something in us knows that death is, under certain conditions, as integral to our lives as life itself. And clearly, the instinctual processes which are active within us during sleep have some great meaning to our psyche and/or physiology. In the words of Dr. Alan Rechtschaffen, of the University of Chicago:

> We think that sleep has an absolutely vital function because we sacrifice so much to sleep—meaning we don't protect our young, we don't gather food, we don't do all of the things that we don't have enough time to do when we're awake. . . . Sleep is so expensive that if it doesn't have a vital function, it's probably one of the greatest mistakes that evolution has ever made.[3]

Our intent here will be, at least partially, to speculate on that vital functioning of sleep and to explore the connection between sleep, dream states and death. Once we have discarded our social fears or biases, can the dream state tell us anything about the nature of death? Is it, as Marie-Louise von Franz suggests in her *On Dreams and Death,* that dreams of the dying, especially death dreams, are nature's way of preparing us for our own death? And if so, is one not to be reassured and intellectually enlightened, and one's consciousness trans/formed (from ego toward self), via the patterns of such dreams? Could the dream state show, for instance, that death can be a peaceful doorway into another existence rather than fear-provoking? And further, more than pictures of an afterlife, what do death dreams tell us about our life right now?

Just like explorers in countless ages have been led into the uncertain mysteries of the underworld, in this study we will be led into the vast unknowns of our unconsciousness. The journey is vital because we have forgotten our mythic ancestors who have explored death's underworld before us. We have forgotten the Babylonian king Gilgamesh, who (at the death of his friend, Enkidu) set forth across the sea of Death through utter blackness to reach the Lord of the Underworld, Utnapishtim (the Far-Away One). We have forgotten about the young Nachiketas who, at the bidding of his angered father, traveled to the underworld kingdom of Yama (the Lord of Death who presided over the world of the dead) who taught Nachiketas of the birthless, deathless *atman* (or true self). We have forgotten about Psyche who, in order to appease Aphrodite, journeyed into Hades to receive a cask of beauty ointment from Persephone. And we have forgotten about Dante's journey in *The Divine Comedy* guided by the ancient Roman poet, Virgil, along the river Lethe to the other side of the earth at the shores of Mount Purgatory.

Why have we, as a culture, become so disconnected from these and other such passageways to the underworld? Why do we not—as the ancient Egyptian and Etruscan, Greek and Roman, Tibetan, Chinese and Vietnamese cultures did, and do—honor the underworld region? James Hillman, in his provocative book *The Dream and the Underworld,* suggests that this denial is provoked by our association of the underworld with death. "The underworld," writes Hillman, "has gone into the unconscious: even become the unconscious."[4] The underworld is in need of resurrection from where it has been buried in each of us. The underworld needs to be brought back from exile so that we can again become familiar with our innermost territory. As Joseph Campbell has written in his *The Hero with a Thousand Faces,* "the hero would be no hero if death held for him (or her) any terror; the first condition is reconciliation with the grave."[5]

POINT OF VIEW

Before commencing this study, the reader should be clear about our point of view. There are many ways to approach dreams and as many ways, if not more, to attempt to understand death. How a philosopher interprets death dreams, for example, may bear little resemblance to the way a sociologist or an anthropologist interprets them. Each discipline understands data as a function of its presuppositions which, by definition, exclude interpretations considered to be outside its methodology. Here, we will take a *comparative* and *interdisciplinary* approach to the subject, one which draws upon the methodological strengths of various fields in the humanities and social sciences. By "comparative," we do not mean merely the juxtaposition of symbols, rituals, myths, codes, or spiritual practices (though it includes these), but rather a method which is at once historical, textual, phenomenological, philosophical, psychological and socio-cultural. We will engage the data (in this case death dreams) with a comprehensive attitude, from east to west, from ancient and classical to modern, by utilizing methodological insights from each of these fields.[6]

When looking this way at the teachings, teachers and texts from various cultures, one can distinguish three types or faces of death—physical, psychological and spiritual.[7] Physical death (the irreversible loss of brain waves, central nervous system, heart and breath) signals the termination of biological life and directly raises the question of life's meaning. While it takes many forms—accidental, homicidal, illness-related, suicidal— the *process* of dying becomes *final* at death. Because of this seem-ing finality, death challenges any seriously self-reflective person to formulate a response, be it religious or not, to its apparent cessation of life. Religious conversion, for example, is a well-known and oft-reported consequence of near-death experiences, even when these occur as a last-moment attempt to rectify one's life before dying.

Less physically threatening, but potentially as lethal, psy-chological death (the reversible termination of one's personal aliveness) can be characterized by the interactive numbness of habitual, or addictive, behaviors. Unstoppable, obsessively ad-dictive behaviors (even one's addiction to so-called addiction-breaking techniques) illustrate this death-in-life-to-life state— the ceasing, or diminishing, of one's life-vitality. Psychological death, or an emotional deadening, occurs when normal psychic and volitional responses are suppressed, or shut down. To some extent this psychic numbing is at times a necessity for all of us living under the nuclear shadow, in which fear of, and anxiety about, death is omnipresent. Such a state, when one becomes aware of it, provokes a crisis and, in some, a search for ultimate meaning and value.

As a paralyzing bifurcation of the self, psychological death for many is a necessary pre-condition to achieving a more authentic lifestyle, or what in this study will be called the expe-rience of human trans/formation. We will spell the word "trans/

formation" throughout this text (except when quoting another author) with a slash, to indicate its most fundamental meaning—to alter the formation or structure of, to reconfigure, from within, the characteristics which identify something or someone. While there are many ways to characterize human trans/formation, here we will be primarily concerned with the way it has been defined by the world's classic religious traditions. This intention leads us to the third face of death, what can be called a spiritual death experience.

Spiritual death (the trans/formational realization of authentic humanness) is a death-rebirth process in life. Directly put, it is neither a subjective activity nor an objective forgetfulness. Rather, the habitual attachment to one's isolated, self-seeking ego (or psychological death) begins to dissolve, spontaneously, as one's ordinary responses, thoughts and feelings are dehabituated. In a special sense, when a person is able to surrender attempts to control or influence his or her life, a new aliveness is born. Another way to put this is to say, as have the various religious traditions of east and west, that a life-generating, life-renewing trans/formation is a function of dying, spiritually, before dying physically. Expressed in a Buddhist metaphor, self-negation is true self-affirmation. Expressed in a Christian metaphor, dying with Christ is also rising with him. As a consequence, one is then fully able to face death fearlessly.

Obviously, death in all its forms has provided significant data, as well as profound questions, for students and scholars. Research into funeral rites, ancestor veneration, the underworld, the last judgment, reincarnation, heaven and hell and immortality, spans a wide range of cultural history. Yet in this plethora of scholarship, a vital component is often neglected—that of dreams and, more specifically, death dreams. It is as if researchers have, whether of necessity or predilection, restricted themselves to dayworld data, to conscious formulations about the role and significance of death. But what about unconscious manifestations? What does the unconscious teach about death and dying?

Certainly since Freud, if not long before, it has been evident that human consciousness cannot be studied, let alone understood, apart from the unconscious. Psychological studies

indicate, though with no fixed agreement about structural de-
lineation, that consciousness and the unconscious are neuro-
chemically as well as psychically connected. More than a mere
interface, many would agree that adequate models of the human
psyche must in some way picture interfused, and overlapping,
spheres of influence operating in both directions. Whether
containing repressed desires (Freud) and/or collective symbols
(Jung), the human psyche represents its larger-than-conscious
self in and through dreams recalled by the dreamer upon waking. To fully address the subject of death then, we will investigate
the way death is expressed in and by the unconscious. We will
focus exclusively upon death dreams and, in the process, link
two of the most rapidly expanding fields of study in America—
death and dreams.

To the question "What is the purpose of studying death
dreams?" our answer is twofold: first, to identify and exemplify a
wide variety of such dreams in their cross-cultural context, and,
second, to point toward, and focus on, their potential trans/
formational nature. While the first point is obvious, the second
point may need further clarification. By human trans/formation
we do not mean merely a linear change (e.g. from being unliber-
ated to being liberated), but a structural reorientation of one's
viewpoints, that is, a core-reformation of one's attitudes, values
and practices. Trans/formation, in this context, does not just
mean a change of beliefs, or a substitution of one viewpoint for
another, but a fundamental shift in one's perspective, or attitude,
toward life as a whole, as well as toward death. This inner-
subjective experience can be characterized as (1) a *de-formation*
of the dreamer's pre-death identity, and (2) a *re-formation* of a
post-death identity in life. Mutually interdependent, this twofold
dynamic results in a singular aliveness, a perception of reality as
really real, a sense of simplicity and effortlessness, an overcoming of the fear of death, and a self-authenticating rightness to life.

By focusing on this way of interpreting death dreams, we do
not intend to, nor could we, prove an afterlife. Neither do we
imply, as some have, that all death dreams produce radical alterations of the dreamer's personality. Rather, by highlighting
dreams in which the dreamer's consciousness continues beyond
death, we have selected not only the most interesting death

dreams, but also those which provide a deepened perspective on what we have called spiritual death. To the extent that dreams are underworld configurations which mirror dayworld actions—not as shadows or phantoms, but as "twins"—to that extent dreams in which the dreamer outlives death mirror what we have called spiritual death experiences.[8] Rather than ways in which death dreams image an afterlife (though some provide graphic images of a beyond death existence), their primary significance to us is how they image the need for, ways to, and the effects of dying without dying.

In what follows, we will discuss and present examples of various types of death dreams (Chapter 1); survey more than 700 death dreams according to who die, how they die, their emotive state, and whether the dreamer lives on in the dream after death (Chapter 2); research various ways in which death dreams have been understood in and by various disciplines (e.g. anthropology, eastern and western religious traditions, literature, philosophy and psychology) in order to provide cross-cultural interpretations for our study (Chapters 3–8); and then investigate various experiences analogous to death dreams, such as near-death experiences, altered states of consciousness and lucid dreaming (Chapter 9). By highlighting death dreams in which the dream-soul does not die, but continues either as a passive observer or as an active participant in the dream, our conclusion underscores the possible trans/formative significance of the dreamer's confrontation with death.

NOTES

[1]Vladimir's half-awake realization appears toward the end of Samuel Beckett's *Waiting for Godot* (New York: Grove Press, 1954), 58–58a.

[2]Freud (and many followers of Freudian psychoanalysis) had long maintained that all dreams are the products of unconscious, wish-fulfilling desires. But after examining the night-

mares of several traumatized soldiers and civilians, Freud admitted that some dreams could instead represent failed wish-fulfillments. In this case, it was the nightmare which represented an attempted fulfillment. See Robert Van de Castle's *The Psychology of Dreaming* (New York: General Learning Press, 1971), 17.

[3]Dr. Alan Rechtschaffen, University of Chicago. Quoted in the documentary film "Journey into Sleep," a KCSM (College of San Mateo) broadcast [Channel 60, 1/29/90]. Produced by Vision Associates/Health Science Media, 1989

[4]James Hillman, *The Dream and the Underworld* (New York: Harper & Row, 1975), 65. Psychotherapy, he writes, rescues death and the underworld through attention to dream images and symbols and thereby treats the soul as the patient. Hillman further distinguishes between "underground" and "underworld" at one point, stating bluntly: "underworld is psyche" (46).

[5]Joseph Campbell, *The Hero with a Thousand Faces* (Princeton: Princeton University Press, 1949), 356.

[6]Death, and the presence of dreams, have long been two central issues with which religious traditions have dealt. In fact, it can be argued (1) that the religious impulse arises in response to problems posed by death, and (2) that pointers toward solutions to death issues have arisen in dreams. The variety of answers to the threat of death (e.g. immortality of the soul [Greek], resurrection of the body [Hebrew, Christian, Islamic], reincarnation of the soul [Hindu] and birth into the Pure Land [Buddhist]), has become *a,* if not *the,* major subject in the religious studies data bank.

[7]See my *Sacred Art of Dying* (New Jersey: Paulist Press, 1988), especially Chapter One.

[8]James Hillman writes: "Admittedly, the dream-ego and the waking-ego have a special 'twin' relationship; they are shadows of each other, as *Hades is the brother of Zeus*" (102).

Chapter 1 DEATH DREAM PATTERNS

> I was in bed and realized that suddenly I could not move any part of my body that I could see. It was as if I were paralyzed. I tried to sit up. As I did so I noticed that I (my soul) did sit up. My soul which I saw as a ghostly, translucent copy of my body did indeed sit up. When I did, I looked down at my body and it was unmoved. I stared at my arm which just lay there, whereas my ghostly arm, light as a feather, moved in and out of my bodily arm. I became terribly frightened because I assumed this meant that I had died. I did not want to die! I screamed and shook myself violently, shaking my head as if to clear it and to get out of this predicament. Then I woke up and I was back.[1]

In her treatment of the way in which dreams prepare us for our own death, Jungian psychotherapist Marie-Louise von Franz writes: "All of the dreams of people who are facing death indicate that the unconscious, that is, our instinct world, prepares consciousness not for a definite end but for a profound transformation and for a kind of continuation of the life process which, however, is unimaginable to everyday consciousness."[2] Likewise, philosopher Michel Foucault states that "the dream of death appears as what existence can learn that is most fundamental about itself," and that "in every case death is the absolute meaning of the dream."[3] Worthy of deep consideration, these two unusual quotations are pivotal for our study, for they reverse the ordinary view according to which death dreams are rejected as a curse or as the expression of repressed anxieties. Following these leads, which suggest that dreaming of death may offer the dreamer (as well as others) significant clues about dying (as well as living), we will explore the images, symbols and interpretations of over 700 death dreams. First however, in this chapter, we will briefly describe the way in which dreams are formed, and then we will compare several death dream classifications.

DREAM FORMATION

Everyone dreams. Even though some of us do not recall our dreams, most of us can remember childhood nightmares. For some, it was a dream in which we were running from danger but our feet would only move in slow motion. For others, it was the sudden appearance of monsters, or "bad people," who were coming to capture us. Whether we recall them or not, our dreams provide a graphic connection between conscious awareness and what has been termed the "unconscious." But what are dreams?

From earliest recorded history it has been evident that human beings, aside from being *doers* and *thinkers,* have been *dreamers.* The world of sleep has always produced images, visions and situations, at times seemingly more real than waking life. Psychologist Charles Tart suggests that sleep is not a state of behavioral inertness since sleepers are "capable of incorporating some external stimuli into the content of (one's) dreams," and since "at least some sleepers are capable of sometimes altering their state of consciousness from sleeping (or dreaming) to waking."[4] A question which arises at this point is whether dreaming is a function of any physiological laws which can be observed and charted.

The breakthrough which guides today's dream studies occurred in 1953 when Eugene Aserinsky and Nathaniel Kleitman attached electrodes to sleeping infants' eyelids to study their sleep states. Noticing that their eyelids moved rapidly in specific periods of the night, it was theorized that these movements might be dream-related. In 1955 they followed their hunch by waking adult sleepers during rapid eye movement periods. Their subjects reported dreams 74% of the time, whereas only 7% of the sleepers reported dreams when awakened in the non-rapid eye

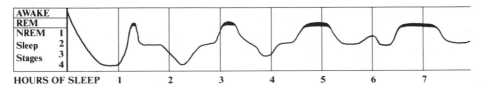

Changes in stages of sleep during the night.

movement periods. During this dream-intensive period, known as REM (Rapid Eye Movement), the blood pressure alters (more so with disturbing dreams), respiratory irregularity occurs (more so with vivid dreams), and variations in heart rate are detected. Normally, there are three to five REM (or "dream") periods which punctuate one's sleep. This is not to suggest that dreams only occur during the REM state, for it has been shown that vivid dreams can also occur in NREM (Non-Rapid Eye Movement) sleep.[5]

But what about those who claim they do not dream? Although one's "dream recall" may be almost non-existent, we know that periods of rapid eye movement continue through the night, and that dreams are very definitely taking place. In fact, when so-called "non-dreamers" were awakened in REM periods, they too reported dreams. One explanation for this may be as follows. "Non-dreamers" seem to have greater difficulty waking up, needing a stronger waking stimulus, and they often claim, upon waking, to be "thinking" instead of "dreaming." This has led one dream researcher to speculate that non-dreamers have a surplus of visual material and may in the *hypnagogic* state (drowsiness before sleep) have elaborate visual images.[6] Others have attributed poor dream recall to everything from waking up to the sound of an alarm clock (which shatters the dream scene) to a lack of conscious focus, upon falling asleep, on remembering one's dreams. Here, however, our interest will be to peer into the cartography of dreaming in order to characterize its landscape.

Since no definition sufficiently captures the multivalent nature of dreaming, we will draw upon several characterizations. Rejecting mechanistic theories, psychologist Calvin S. Hall writes: "A dream is a succession of images, predominantly visual in quality, which are experienced during sleep."[7] He suggests that dreams resemble a motion picture inasmuch as the succession of mental pictures seem just as real to the dreamer as waking life. For Hall, dream images are projections of the mind and as such embody what is in the mind (e.g. settings, characters, actions and emotions). Of the two kinds of projections—the distortion of objective reality (or delusion), and the perception of objects without external causes (or hallucinations)—most dreams, for Hall, are the latter. For example, if one dreams of fighting and then killing another person, this event has not actually occurred.

Psychologist and sociologist Erich Fromm locates his discussion of dreams alongside his understanding of myth and fairy tale. Each portrays inner experiences in symbolic language. In each, the categories of space and time are neglected. And in each, the impossible occurs in vividly real situations. The dead live; humans fly; scenes change in an instant. In order not to distort, or narrow down, the phenomenon, Fromm writes: "Dreaming is a meaningful and significant expression of any kind of mental activity under the condition of sleep."[8] Like myths, dreams are expressed in a logic which can signify both the most irrational, as well as the most elevated, functions of the mind. If for Sigmund Freud dreams are expressions of the asocial, irrational human nature, and for Carl Jung they are revelations of an archetypal wisdom which transcends the individual, for Fromm each can be true. The trick is to recognize whether a dream is the expression of an irrational wish, or of a transrational wisdom.

More recently, psychologists have begun to explore the biology of dreaming. The discovery that REM incidents are initiated in the brain stem (an area devoid of rational thought) led psychologists J. Allan Hobson and Robert W. McCarley of the Harvard Medical School to suggest that dreams have little relation to the unconscious. Instead, they write:

> A dream may be defined as a mental experience, occurring in sleep, which is characterized by hallucinoid imagery, predominantly visual and often vivid; by bizarre elements due to such spatiotemporal distortions as condensation, discontinuity, and acceleration; and by a delusional acceptance of these phenomena as "real" at the time that they occur.[9]

According to them, dreams are disconnected and random images incorporated into detailed stories by the sleeping mind. Dreams, therefore, are scenarios produced spontaneously by the brain.

These definitions indicate that there are as many ways to characterize dreams as there are dream therapists, dream analysts and dream theoreticians. For our purposes, it is not necessary to select one over the others. Rather, for us a dream is a lifelike projection of moving images onto an unconscious screen which expands our conscious understanding of who we are, what we are about, where we are, and what possibilities are available to us. Dreams open up the dreamer's past and future life, and as well may picture other life forms. Dreams also allow the dreamer to play various roles with insight, sensitivity, and empathy. One could say therefore that dreaming is a very special kind of theater in which actors act in unpredictable ways, and in which scenes change faster than the blinking of an eye.

DREAM TYPES

Anyone who reads hundreds of dreams would begin to notice that certain types of dreams are repeated. Some dreams, like dreams of falling or of being chased, are more typical than others. Here we will briefly review four dream typologies which provide a context for our study.

Van Eeden

To begin with, the Dutch physician and pioneer dream researcher Frederik Van Eeden, who wrote early in the twentieth century, listed nine types of dreams.

- *Initial dreams:* these occur "only in the very beginning of sleep."

- *Pathological dreams:* these occur when one experiences a "full recollection of day-life."

- *Ordinary dreams:* these dreams "leave very faint traces after waking up."

- *Vivid dreams:* these dreams are "generally extremely absurd, or untrue, though explicit and well remembered."

- *Symbolic or mocking dreams:* these dreams produce "the impression of being invented or arranged by intelligent beings of a very low moral order."

- *General dream-sensations:* these are dreams in which "there is no vision, no image, no event, not even a word or a name."

- *Lucid dreams:* in these dreams, "the sleeper remembers day-life and his own condition, reaches a state of perfect awareness, and is able to direct his attention, and to attempt different acts of free volition."

- *Demon dreams:* in these dreams, one *sees* demons and fights them.

- *Wrong waking up dreams:* in these dreams one has the sensation of waking up while still being asleep.[10]

While not to be accepted uncritically, Van Eeden's types allow the reader to begin to reflect upon his or her own dreams, and to realize their variations. Of note is the fact that Van Eeden was one of the first western thinkers (though it had been known for centuries in Tibet) to write about lucid dreaming. In 1913, he suggested that one could awaken in dreams while continuing the dream (see Chapter 9). But more specifically, what about death dreams?

Herzog

A student of Carl Jung, Edgar Herzog in *Psyche and Death* examines death images in myths and dreams. His purpose is to locate "the way (*humankind*) *as a whole, in the center of (its) being, feels touched by the inevitability of death.*"[11] The material of the first part of his book is comparative, ethnological and mythological, and includes rites, stories and surviving folk customs. In the second part of the book, Herzog draws upon contemporary dreams and attempts to trace correspondences between them and ancient myths. Herzog suggests that an "inner crisis of transformation is often foreshadowed by dreams in which the patient is confronted by death, either directly or in the form of an archaic image," and that "such an experience of dying is potentially an expression of the full reality of life in that it symbolizes transformation."[12]

Herzog analyzes five death dream sequences, or types:

- Repression of Death (Flight and Initial Acceptance);
- Killing;
- Archaic Forms of the Death-Demon;
- The Kingdom of the Dead (Procreation and Rebirth);
- Dreams of Death as an Expression of the Process of Development.

Herzog's death dream types do not deal so much with the one who dies, or how he or she dies, as with psychological interpretations of the dream after waking. His first category, for instance, "repression of death," focuses on the dreamer's refusal to face the death situation. Instead of facing the threatening situation or person, the dreamer runs away.

The second category involves dreams of killing. There are several scenarios in these dreams; being killed oneself, killing someone else, or watching someone else being killed. Remembering Aristotle's suggestion to look for resemblances, Herzog interprets this kind of killing as a sacrifice. He notes that killing is a ritual in which the killer comes to terms with death through being a killer. No matter how horrible, the killing must be accomplished for the dreamer to come to terms with death.

The third dream type is the image of death as an archaic figure, a Death-Demon made up of mythological components. Herzog suggests that the dreamer sees or makes up ghoulish figures which represent someone else. The meanings that these demons represent may not even be conscious, but are a sort of stand-in for dreamers who are not able to confront the ogres and monsters in their subconscious. The dreamer usually does not die, but observes and comments on the actions taken by the

Death Demon

Death-Demon which are, in essence, specially ordered for each
dream. For example, consider the following dream:

> I was standing at the side of the freeway, with many cars
> speeding by. I was trying to figure out how to get to the other
> side when the Devil walked up to me. He was complete with
> all the horrorish trappings of hooves, horns and the color of
> red. His sight terrified me. He started to talk to me, I tried not

to listen. I wanted to get to the other side. He told me he would walk me around the freeway to safety, but I kept telling him that I was a child of God, and God would take care of me. He decided to take me by force. At that split second, I decided to either leap out in front of cars or be seized; it seemed like a lifetime. I saw my family, my childhood, my son and then I stepped out with all faith I would be rescued. I watched my body being hit as from an outsider's viewpoint, and I watched it lay there oozing with blood as the image got smaller and smaller. I was sucked into a tunnel backwards, and I woke up in a sweat.[13]

Dreaming of the land of the dead is Herzog's fourth type. Here he reiterates that motifs suggested in archaic myths and legends have found their way into modern dreams. These he associates with love, procreation, birth and rebirth. He broadens this category even further by including the presence of animals, which likewise share similar traits of rebirth.

Herzog's final type includes those dreams in which there is an encounter with death which reflects or aids the development or maturation of the dreamer's personality. Consider the following dream:

I was in a car with friends and we drove over the edge of a cliff. Half of the car was over and it was swaying. I was screaming and trying to get out of the window of the side of the car that was on the ground. All of a sudden I stopped screaming, sat back in the car and thought to myself, "No, don't try to get out. If it is your time to die you will—and if it's not then you will be saved. Besides, it is not scary to die; it will be the peace you are waiting for." At that moment a tow truck came and pulled us back on the road. I woke up and could not believe my dream. I felt calm and satisfied.[14]

Although this is technically a near-death dream, it illustrates Herzog's final death dream type. Note that the dreamer awoke feeling "calm and satisfied" in the face of death.

Most significantly, Herzog suggests that the experience of dying in a dream can symbolize a life-transformation. But this occurs only if the dreamer (1) can transcend the negative reaction to death's image, and (2) be touched "by the dream's deep resonance with the experience of death as transformation and also by the elemental power of enthusiastic joy in life."[15] This "transformation" occurs if one's waking activity is affected such that the dreamer comes to terms with the vicissitudes of life, as well as the reality of death.

Vande Kemp

Still another way of depicting death-related dream types is presented by Hendrika Vande Kemp (former president of Psychologists Interested in Religious Studies, a division of the American Psychological Association). Focusing on pre-Freudian periodical dream literature of 1860–1910, Vande Kemp delineates the following death dream types:

- *telepathic* (in which the dying person appears in the dreams of friends or relatives);
- *premonitory* (in which the dying appear in the dream with those who are already dead to announce their impending death);
- *hypermnesic* (in which the dead convey information which has been forgotten by the dreamer's waking memory);
- *predictive* (in which the dreamer predicts the time of his or her own death);
- *archetypal* (in which death appears in a symbolic form);
- *revelatory* (in which the dead reappears to convey a religious or philosophical truth which the dream subject had promised to announce to the living).[16]

What Vande Kemp discovered was that death dreams, among these various types, formed a major category within the dreams of this period. She reports that at least seventy such dreams were described. It is especially interesting that death so often appears in telepathic, clairvoyant, and premonitory dreams, and that many dreamers predicted their dying with astounding accuracy. In one dream, for example, a woman dreamt that she drowned in a boating accident. She described to a friend exactly where her body was found. A month or two later, while crossing the Truro river, her boat was upset and she drowned. When her friend went to the spot foretold in her dream, there the woman's body was found. Such dreams, it should be pointed out, do not always result in the dreamer's death. A post-Freudian, post-Jungian approach to dreams in which the dreamer dies may suggest that the dream indicates the death of an aspect of the dreamer's ego. Such would be the interpretation of Ann Faraday.

Faraday

Quoting Goethe: "As long as you do not know how to die and come to life again, you are a sorry traveler on this dark earth," Ann Faraday begins her discussion of death dreams by challenging the age-old belief that dreaming of death foreshadows one's impending death. If this were so, she suggests, the world would have been depopulated long ago. Normally, she writes, death dreams serve as metaphors which express that someone's feeling for us, or our feeling for someone, has died, or that a limiting factor in our life needs to die. Such dreams, especially dreams of our own death, may indeed point to a dimension of vitality which helps overcome the fear of physical death.

Faraday mentions in *The Dream Game,* that the dreaming mind poses at least three relationships to death:

- as a metaphor to express, through the *death of others,* that our feeling for someone, something, or an aspect of ourselves is dead;
- as a reminder, when those *already dead appear* in dreams, of something in need of resolution;
- as a symbol, when *we die,* which indicates the need for an old self image to be transcended. "The most interesting dream (of) death is our own," she writes, "for this indicates the death of some obsolete self-image, from which comes rebirth into a higher state of consciousness and authentic self-being."[17]

Let us briefly consider her three death dream types. The first type, the death of others, Faraday divides between death in the family (or of close friends), and death of a stranger (or those with whom one is not emotionally involved). In either case, not all dreams of this kind are negative or predictive, but may often indicate a "happy release." Faraday posits that such was the case with one of her close friends who, after dreaming that her husband had died, decided to stop attempting to turn him into the man she thought he should be. As a result of the dream, she left the family home to begin a new life on her own.

The second type of death dream involves those dreams in which someone whom we know in waking consciousness to be dead returns to visit the dreamer. The most frequently asked question about such dreams, she reports, is whether the dream is about that person's "surviving spirit," or merely a fulfillment of the dreamer's wish for the ongoing existence of that person. Faraday suggests that if the latter is the case, then only several such visitations would presumably be necessary. Beyond that, in the case where one repeatedly dreams of such visitations, it is probably for the purpose of transmitting a message to the dreamer about which the dreamer must make a decision.

Consider, for example, the case of a high school student (Carol G.) who lost her father to cancer in her freshman year. She subsequently had a series of dreams about him, what she termed "fatal dreams":

Dream #1

> I was standing in a hallway of a school building and I was remembering a phone call that my dad had made and he said he would be coming home that weekend. Then I heard his voice tell me he couldn't make it and that he wouldn't be coming back.

Dream #2

> We were in a room and I was watching him closely, hoping that he would get better, and finally, all of a sudden, his hair started growing back in. He gained his weight back and gave me a huge hug and kiss.

Dream #3

> (This was a dream I had right after he died.) I was upstairs with my dad and he needed to go to the bathroom, but was too weak to get up. He was trying so hard to get up and was hitting and pushing me. Finally he tried to stand up and run to the bathroom. I tried to catch him, but he fell and immediately died. I had killed him. His own daughter killed him.

Dream #4

> I was in a dark room and I couldn't see anything except people. A lot of men were attacking my dad and yelling at me, saying, "We're taking your dad; you'll never see him again; say goodbye now!" He was struggling to stay with us, hitting, pushing everyone to get away. They wouldn't let me touch him and I was crying. People were taking my dad away from me. Right before I woke up, I heard them say, "You'll never see him again."[18]

From Faraday's point of view, beyond needing to be reassured of her father's continued existence, Carol needed to be released from her attachment to his memory, an attachment which impeded her own development.

Months later, after having no further dreams in which her father appeared to her, she again dreamed about him.

Dream #5

> I am in my room looking at a picture of my dad. Someone comes to the door. They don't knock but I know they are there. They give me a piece of paper and say nothing. It has a phone number written on it along with the initials of my dad—B.F.G. Then there is a dream switch and I am at the beach where my dad and I used to go. I see a phone and dial the number. There is no answer. Ten minutes later I dial again. No answer. An hour later, I call again and get a male voice. I am excited that it is my father. Even though it didn't sound like my dad, he knew what my dad knew, and so I thought he was my dad. "I love you, daddy!" I said to him. "This is not your dad!" he said.

Shortly thereafter, Carol had the following dream which, though not about her father on the surface, troubled her, and puzzled her as well.

Dream #6

> I am in a barn area with Yvonne and another friend. We are about to leave and Yvonne says, "I forgot my sweat shirt." And so she wants to go back to the barn. But we are late, and so I hesitate. When we go to the barn windows and peek inside, I see a lot of men with guns holding all the high school kids hostage. I shut the door. "Let's go!" I say.
>
> As we begin to leave, a man comes and stops us. "You're here with your friends," he says and we are taken inside with the rest of our friends. They want to punish us, but I don't know why. I lose track of Yvonne. The men were poking kids' eyes out one-by-one. When my turn is next, I beg: "How can I get out of here?" A woman says: "Make yourself cry and put ketchup on your face so that it will look like you're hurt!"
>
> I go to another room to do this, and I see a phone. I call my mom to come get me. She says: "NO! You must do this by yourself!" I say "Please, mom, help me!" And she says, "You can't depend on me." I tried to get away, but a man hears me and I am caught. They are ready to poke my eyes out when I wake up.

Briefly, a few comments are worth noting about Carol's dreams. In three of them (#1, #5 and #6), the phone is her primary means of communication. At the same time, the messages received are either negative vis-à-vis her dad (#5) and her own situation (#6), or they are immediately contradicted (#1). In two of the dreams, men are attacking either her father (#4), or herself (#6), and in the latter dream her mother will not come to rescue her (as her father surely would have). In these dreams she seems divided in her feelings toward her father: *hoping* that he will get better (#2); *guilty* at having been responsible for his death (#3); *anxious* and *sad* that she will not see him again (#4);

excited to speak with him and *loving* him (#5); *frightened* about being threatened by the men (#6).

When viewed together, these dreams provide the dreamer (and anyone who identifies his or her experience with Carol's) a rich field of death-related images and symbols. Not only is the complex mixture of her emotional responses to her father's death made clear; made equally clear are her attitudes toward afterlife. While her father's spirit—indeed her father—survives death, initially at least, his voice remains unavailable to her. Even more importantly, however, what is true of many death dreams is true of these—they are primarily life-significant. These dreams indicate potentially trans/formational elements in the structure of the dreamer's relationship with both her father and her mother, elements which may be overlooked by the non-dreaming consciousness.

The third type of death dream, the dream of one's own death, according to Faraday, almost always reflects the dreamer's need to relinquish outmoded self-images and to receive powers beneficial to a reborn self-image. Faraday speaks of a dream experiment in which (before falling asleep) she asked her dreams for enlightenment about death. In a dream that this question occasioned, she found herself on the floor of her childhood home where she was about to be killed by two young men (Mafia types) because she had accidentally disobeyed an order they had given her. When she awoke, she immediately associated the Mafia men with her family and realized that her view of death was flavored by her childhood experience of punishment. Such a dream, it is suggested, may in fact reveal unconscious views of death which shadow one's attitudes and behavior.

While not to dispute Faraday's threefold ordering, based upon more than 700 dreams collected from students at San Jose State University, we have noticed three additional types: a fourth type, *mass death,* in which everything dies; a fifth type, *death personified,* in which the archetypal figure of Death appears in the dream; and a sixth type in which animals die.

The fourth type that we have found is the apocalyptic dream. By far the least frequent death dream, it is one in which the entire world is destroyed. Everything dies. Such dreams hardly need comment, and can be appreciated in their utter finality. The following is a perfect example of such a dream:

> The boy walks slowly through a large empty house. He approaches a door; he knows (somehow) that the "central" or "important" room lies beyond. He enters. The room is empty (windows are high and amber opaque) except for a stand holding a massive book, handsomely bound. The boy recognizes it (somehow) as being strategic, important, containing secrets. He opens it and as he does so—the moment his eyes fall on the surface of the pages—he, the book, the room, the walls, the building, the UNIVERSE all "blisters" instantaneously in a flash fire of nuclear-fission-like white light explosion.[19]

In the fifth type, Death appears bearing a scythe or an axe, at times wearing a large, black cloak, at times appearing as a

Death Personified

skeleton free of skin. One dreamer provides an extremely graphic image:

> I saw a male figure entering the church very quickly as though in a great hurry. When my eyes recovered from the sudden ray of light which had made the surrounding gloom seem all the deeper, I perceived that this was the figure of Death, in the horrid semblance of a skeleton, though I could see only the upper part of the body on account of the screens and curtains that came between. The head, a "peelit skull," was surmounted by a kind of postillion's hat, set jauntily upon one side.[20]

And in the sixth type, the dreamer witnesses the death of an animal, usually the dreamer's pet or a threatening wild beast.

BEFORE AND AFTER DEATH

Studying death dreams, it becomes apparent that they often occur during times of great stress, whether caused by relationships, or school, or vocational changes, or by death itself. While a terminal illness may generate such dreams in the dying person, as we saw in Merle's case (see Introduction), often before and after a loved one dies a member of the family will receive "visitations" from the deceased. The following dreams are reported by Annie C. who was born in southern India to native Christian missionary parents and who, after her father's death, moved to California with her mother. When her mother was diagnosed with cancer, it became very important for Annie that her mother attend her graduation. Before her mother died, Annie reported:

> I am dreaming that it is my graduation. My mom is busily running around arranging things as she always does. But the funny thing is that no one is able to see her. It is time for me to go to the graduation and I am crying because my mom is not there—but she is there. I can see her in my dream and I can also see myself in the dream. When the graduation time comes, I know she is there, but I can't see her there, so I am crying.

Annie's mother died (on September 15, 1990) before Annie graduated. One result of her mother's death, Annie said, was that she dreamt of her every night, even though she could not remember all of the dreams. She said: "When I wake up, I am crying so hard. I am thankful to see that she is happy. But when I saw her cancer bleeding, and that no one cared, I feel so hurt." When she retold the dreams she has dreamed, it is as if they are happening again in the present moment.

> I enter the hospital to visit my mom and everyone says that she is dead. They are all making arrangements to move her body to the funeral home. At this point I am alone with her by her bed. And then, suddenly, I call her and she opens her eyes, and she smiles. All her disease goes away, no I.V., no oxygen, no tubes. There is nothing there. She is well and alive, and I can't hold my happiness. I start screaming and run out to get my brother. I yell, "She's alive, she's alive. You are making a mistake for moving her body to the funeral home because she's alive!" They think I am crazy. They don't believe me. They come into the room and they are telling me that she is gone and is with God. But I am still seeing her smiling and talking to me. But they do not listen to me. Then I wake up.

Reflecting on her dreams, Annie reported that when she was in the hospital she would pray in the chapel to ask God to give her mother a few more days, "so that she could see my only sister who was still in India. This was my mother's last wish. But my sister arrived three days after she died. And I didn't want to pray after that." Then she said: "When people tell me this was God's will, I get angry at them, because her last wish did not come true. I want to know what God's purpose was for not granting that wish. The nurse told me later that my mom said that it was her time to go." Shortly thereafter, Annie had another dream.

> I am with my mother at a gathering. Many of my mother's close friends are there. There is this lady who was like a daughter to my mother because she had no mother. I know that my mother is going to die because of her cancer. And so the time comes that my mother is dying, but my mom is say-

ing that she is all right and that she will be fine. I am running around in circles saying that it is time for my mother to die, so come on and get ready. But no one is paying attention. They are all so busy. I know that something is going to come up and take her, but they do not pay attention. Then her cancer starts bleeding. My mom is smiling and saying, "I am OK; there is nothing to worry about." Then all these people come and say goodbye because they are leaving. I am saying that they should realize that she is dying, but it is like I am invisible because they are not realizing what I am saying. Then my mom slowly collapses and as she does, she continues to say, "I am OK." Finally she says, "I have to go. I am being called." Then I wake up.

When asked how this dream made her feel, Annie noted that sometimes after seeing this she wished she didn't see it, because the more she dreams about her mother, the more it hurts. "It hurts so much that I wish I got a chance to make up for all the lost times we had. Seeing her in dreams makes me feel so guilty. She gave so much and what did I return?"

And then she recounted another dream:

My sister-in-law and myself are in the kitchen talking about several things, laughing and having a good time. Then my mom appears from the blue. She is behind us watching us, and she is happy. Two minutes later my sister-in-law goes into her room and my mom and I are alone in the kitchen. I tell my mom, "Don't worry about anything. I am very happy. Things are working out fine. I will be all right." She smiles and then disappears. Her expression told me that she was so happy and content that everything is working out in her absence.

Most recently, she had this dream:

I see my dad who died seven years ago. We are at our house back in Kerala, India, where my parents did mission work. My mom is in the kitchen and there is a birthday party for my mom and my dad. It (their birthday) is not really the same day, but still I am seeing it that way. We hired a photographer and they place me and my father together to take pictures. All

of a sudden the scene changes from back home to America in
my living room. Then I see my mom's face. She is so happy
because she is with my father and she is saying in our language that she is the most happy woman in the world when
she is around my father.

When I asked Annie to reflect on all of these dreams, her
words came easily: "In real life my mother was always waiting up
for me if I was late. She always came and prayed with me every
day in the morning, and sent me to school. I don't know if I told
her in words how much I appreciated those prayers and how
thankful I am for her (even though at her deathbed, I told her
that she was the person I admire more than anyone in this
world). She said, 'Dear, you don't have to tell me that. I already
know it.' But I wanted to say it over and over again."[21]

There are many features in Annie's dreams which are commonly dreamed by surviving family members and friends. The
loved one (who has died) appears alive, healthy, and happy, but
no one, besides the dreamer, can see them. Often the person who
has died assures the family member that he or she is fine and
that it was his or her time to die. Appearing suddenly, and disap-
pearing as suddenly, seems to be no problem for the one who has
died. Many times the dead person returns to the place of their
origin (in this case India) and joins other loved ones who have
died (in this case the dreamer's father). The question which most
naturally arises—indeed it arose for Annie—is whether these
dreams are mere projections of the dreamer's deepest wishes for
the loved one, and/or whether it is possible that the dreams are
the loved one's way of communicating with the living. While it
would be premature to address this question here, it will be considered later in several contexts.

COMMENTARY

As we have seen, there are numerous ways to classify death
dreams. We have isolated, in reverse order, Faraday, Vande
Kemp, Herzog, and Van Eeden—but there are many others
whom we could have recognized. As it stands, the theorists

whom we have mentioned thus far are downright contradictory when set side-by-side. Who is right?

One way to respond is to suggest that each is correct, to an extent, for one can see a great deal of overlapping and cross-mixing of their categories. Van Eeden is a prime example. He lists dream types (lucid dreams, hypnogogic) alongside dream causes (pathological abnormalities) and dream contents (demons, vivid visual qualities). Conversely, Vande Kemp maintains a consistent division. She concentrates only on dream types (telepathic, hypermnesic, etc.) without mixing in dream causes. There are many other ways to classify dreams. We could, for instance, take heed of the dreamer's actions, motivations, emotions, and immediate or post-sleep effects.

Since there are as many dream typologies as there are dream therapists, why did we select the four we did? One of the earliest, modern dream classifications was outlined by Frederik Van Eeden (in 1913) who carefully recorded and studied his own dreams. We were interested in Van Eeden because he was a chronic death dreamer and, as well, was experienced with lucid dreaming. Although he did not distinguish death dreams as a type, many of his dreams (and dream types) contain elements of death in them.

Edgar Herzog, especially in his *Psyche and Death* (1966), focused on death from the point of view of Carl Jung's psychology. Starting with the view that myths are dream-originated, Herzog interested us because he provided a series of mythically personified figures of death. Less interested in the dreams of persons who are near death, Herzog pointed to the "die and become" process (i.e. the process of trans/formation) as it occurred in death dreams. Most importantly, Herzog's work has influenced the recent writers in the field like Marie-Louise von Franz who discusses death dreams in terms of the death and resurrection symbolism of the western alchemical tradition.

Even more than Herzog, Hendrika Vande Kemp's focus is primarily on death dreams. However, rather than focusing on mythic archetypes, she trained her attention specifically on nineteenth century dream literature. In other words, instead of beginning with a methodology and applying it to death dreams (as Herzog does), she limited herself to a specific grouping of

dreams, and then developed her types from the dreams themselves. In a similar fashion, we will focus primarily on the death
dreams of San Jose State University students (of varying nation-
alities and ranging in age from 18 to 56), and allow our types to
emerge from the dreams we collected.

Ann Faraday's work, exemplified in *The Dream Game,* was
selected for several reasons. First, she is one of many popular
writers on the subject of dreams whose books, like those of Patricia Garfield and John Sanford, are readily available. Second,
like Herzog and von Franz, Faraday is particularly attentive to
trans/formational symbols in dreams. Such a symbol—a pre-
cious stone, a magical animal or object—bestows strength and
power upon the dreamer in dangerous situations. Third, and the
most important reason, Faraday distinguished three basic types
of death dreams (i.e. of others, where the dead return, and of the
dreamer). Faraday's categories, though they fail to include three
other death dream types (i.e. total annihilation, death personified, and the death of animals), will serve as a springboard for
our study. In the next chapter, we will develop and sophisticate
these types based on our collection and statistical arrangement
of some 700 death dreams.

NOTES

[1]Anonymous student in "Death, Dying, & Religions" class at
San Jose State University, 1989.

[2]Marie-Louise von Franz, *On Dreams and Death* (Boston:
Shambhala, 1987), 156. She continues that symbols which appear in death dreams "present a thematic or structural harmony
with the teachings of the various religions about life after death."

[3]See Michel Foucault's "Dream, Imagination, and Existence,"
trans. by Forrest Williams, in *Dream & Existence,* a special issue
from the *Review of Existential Psychology & Psychiatry* (xix, 1,
1986) 55.

[4]See "Toward the Experimental Control of Dreaming: A Review of the Literature," in Charles T. Tart's *Altered States of Consciousness* (New York: John Wiley & Sons, Inc., 1969), 133–134. This is accomplished, he suggests, "either by means of a discriminative response to external stimuli or by using the occurrence of dreaming itself or a given time of night as a stimulus."

[5]See Robert Van de Castle, *The Psychology of Dreaming* (New York: General Learning Press, 1971), 29 ff. There are five stages which are repeated in sleep—four stages of non-rapid-eye-movement (NREM) sleep (measured by low-frequency, low-amplitude Theta brain waves, and low-frequency, high-amplitude Delta waves), and one stage of rapid-eye-movement (REM) sleep. During REM sleep, brain activity is of a low-amplitude (or Theta waves, six to eight cycles per second). As these stages occur in cycles, we tend to pass through as many as five periods in each of the five stages during a normal eight hours of sleep.

[6]See Norman Mackenzie's *Dreams and Dreaming* (New York: Vanguard Press, 1965), 271–272.

[7]Calvin S. Hall, *The Meaning of Dreams* (New York: McGraw-Hill, 1953), 2–3.

[8]Erich Fromm, *The Forgotten Language* (New York: Grove Press, 1951), 25.

[9]J. Allan Hobson and Robert W. McCarley, "The Brain as a Dream State Generator: An Activation-Synthesis Hypothesis of the Dream Process," in *The American Journal of Psychiatry,* 134:12 (December 1977), 1336. According to Hobson and McCarley, dreams reflect physiological and biological, not psychological, activity and are generated by the stimulation of the brain stem by "the perceptual, conceptual, and emotional structures of the forebrain" (1347).

[10]Frederik Van Eeden, "A Study of Dreams," in Charles T. Tart's *Altered States of Consciousness,* 145–158.

[11]Edgar Herzog, *Psyche and Death* (New York: G.P. Putnam's Sons, 1966), 16–17.

[12]*Ibid.,* 136. "What this means," Herzog writes, "is that when the *reality of life* forces transformation upon a (person s/he) encounters the *reality of death,* so that (s/he) has to come to terms with both together."

[13]An anonymous student at San Jose State University.

[14]An anonymous student at San Jose State University.

[15]Herzog, 209. "Here we see once more how," he includes, "light shines out of Death upon Life, and that only the (one) who is prepared in (his/her) soul to pass through the Gate of Death 'becomes a living human being.'"

[16]Hendrika Vande Kemp, unpublished dissertation, 326. See Hendrika Vande Kemp, "The Dream in Periodical Literature: 1860–1910," *Journal of the History of Behavioral Sciences,* 17 (1981), 88 and footnote 105 on page 109.

[17]Ann Faraday, *The Dream Game* (New York: Perennial Library, 1974), 267.

[18]These, and the following two dreams, were reported by Carol Gardner, Santa Cruz, California, 1991.

[19]William Martin Benedict McKinley (born during the detonation of the first atomic device, July 16, 1945).

[20]Mary M. Currie, "The Way of Dreams," in *The Nineteenth Century,* 53 (1903), 964–966. Quoted in Vande Kemp, 354.

[21]These are the dreams of Annie Chandy, a student in "Death, Dying, & Religions" class at San Jose State University, 1990.

Chapter 2 700 DEATH DREAMS

> I was on an airplane, flying to India. I had no idea why I was supposed to visit India, but the trip had a sense of urgency about it.
>
> All at once the door of the airplane flew open and I was sucked out, slowly swirling in a free fall. I panicked. Then I realized that this was only a dream, so I relaxed and began to enjoy it.
>
> Suddenly my fears returned as I remembered that I can feel pain in my dreams. I remained terrified until the moment of impact. I was aware of my bones crushing, but it wasn't a painful experience. The body itself remained whole, though I knew it was dead. It was as if my consciousness was separate from my body. The last thing I remember before awakening is looking down from a distance at my lifeless body.[1]

Like a sun to surrounding moons, this chapter will be different from all the others because in a sense it generates the light which each of them will reflect. As in no other chapter, here we will be concerned with statistical comparisons of 700 death dreams, as well as 793 death dreamer surveys collected over two and a half years in "Death, Dying & Religions" classes at San Jose State University (1987–1990). While we have collected dreams from various other sources as well (e.g. from literature, and from philosophical and psychological studies), it is dreams like the ones represented in this chapter with which we will be primarily concerned.

For the sake of comprehension and clarity, we will consolidate our findings according to four questions:

I. Who dies in death dreams?

II. How do people die in dreams (especially when compared to *de facto* death statistics, and to ways people imagine dying)?

III. What is the dreamer's emotional response to death, both at the moment of death and afterward?

IV. How often, and in what ways, do dreamers survive death?

To close the gap between the reader and the text, and to provide the clearest results of our information-gathering, we will statistically crystalize our findings to each of the above questions in a chart. Our purpose is both to introduce the reader to the amazing variety of death-in-dream experiences on the one hand, and to provide hard data for the purposes of discussion throughout the remainder of the text on the other. Interpreting dreams is a practice which requires professional training, counseling experience and knowledge of the dreamer's life situation and circumstances. Rather than interpretation, we will provide informed commentary which underscores, compares, questions and raises possibilities for the reader to explore among, and within, the dreams themselves. We do not begin, in other words, with interpretations or with an agenda to prove. We begin merely with a question into which this chapter is an inquiry: How do human beings dream of their own death and of the death of others? Only after we have collected our data will we ask the second question: What does it all mean?

I. WHO DIES?

The question "Who Dies?" might at first appear to generate a self-evident answer—the dreamer dies. But is that really always the case? When the dreamer appears to die in his or her dream, is that in fact what is really occurring? Another way to ask the question is this: Can a dreamer *actually* die in the death dream? While this question opens out into fascinating possible avenues of thought, for the time being we will restrict ourselves to the data collected when we asked university students to respond to the following questions:

- Have you ever dreamed of death in any form?
- Have you ever had a dream in which either you died or someone else died?

• If so, recreate your dream in as much detail as you can remember.

In addition, toward the end of each semester, to supplement the dream data, we asked students to complete a death dream survey in which we structured questions so as to provide the widest range of data. Responses to the survey questions indicated that students from each semester experienced more death-related dreams prior to the semester than during the semester. Their death dreams, therefore, were not simply the result of highly evocative images and symbols discussed in class, but were largely present independently of the course of study. In a culture that has developed endless euphemisms for death (e.g. "passed away," "expired," "wasted," and "laid to rest"), and which continues to deny its presence, these responses suggest that death is alive and well (so to speak) in the unconscious.

Who then dies in death dreams? As we mentioned in the previous chapter, one can find at least six different "dyings" in death dreams—(a) the dreamer himself or herself, (b) others who die in the dream, (c) others who have already died and who return in the dream, (d) all living beings at once, (e) the personification of death itself, and, last, (f) animals and monsters. Our research has indicated the following statistics:

Table 2.1		
Death Type	**Total /**	**Percentage**
Dreamer	363	43%
Other Dies	253	30%
Dead Returns	143	17%
Mass Death	44	5%
Death Personified	30	4%
Animal/Monster	12	1%
	845	

Death Dreams

Table 2.1

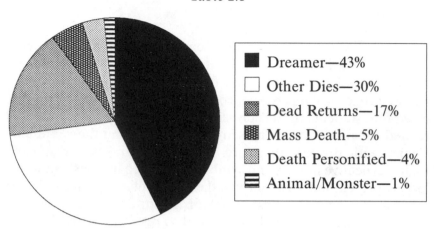

Table 2.1

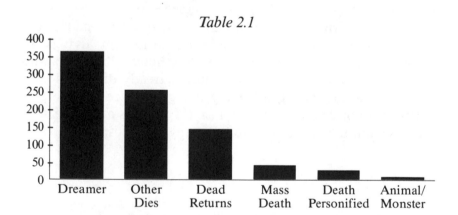

Of the dreams collected, those in which the dreamer dies (43%) nearly equal those in which *all* others die (57%). And of the "others," 31% were family members, the rest were strangers and 12% were friends. The figures can be charted on pages 41 and 42.

It should be noted that in these last charts, the totals (of 845 and 482 dreams respectively) represent the total number of occurrences of that particular phenomena among the 700 death dreams. Similarly, items in the columns represent occurrences within the 700 dreams, and *not* total death dreams. To understand the significance of these statistics, one must be able to

Table 2.2: **Who Dies?**
DREAMER vs. OTHERS

Who Dies?	Total /	Percentage
Dreamer	363	43%
Others:		
Family	259	31%
Friends	96	11%
Strangers	41	5%
All/Many Lives	44	5%
Demon/Angel	30	4%
Animal/Monster	12	1%
	845	

Table 2.2: **Who Dies?**

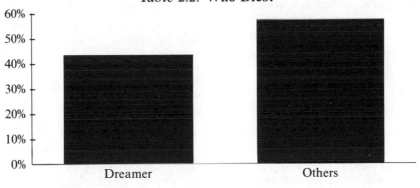

Table 2.2a

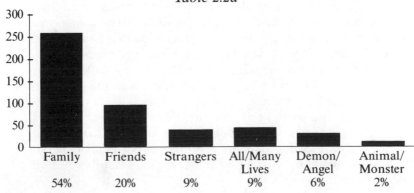

Table 2.2a

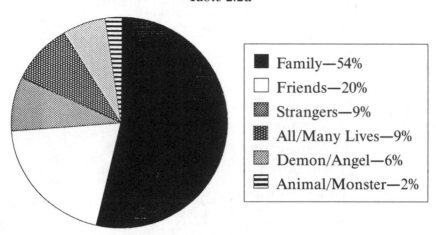

Legend:
- ■ Family—54%
- □ Friends—20%
- ▨ Strangers—9%
- ▦ All/Many Lives—9%
- ▩ Demon/Angel—6%
- ≣ Animal/Monster—2%

associate them with dreams. The following are representative of the two most common death dreams, first where the dreamer dies, and second and third where someone other than the dreamer dies.

I

It all happened in a foreign country. I remember that my family (mom, dad, and sister) was vacationing in an old village that had a lot of street vendors. My sister and I were walking along and all of a sudden a troop of guerillas were marching down the street toward us. I knew right away that we were going to die. I made a frantic search through my mind for a certain word—the word that Professor Kramer told the class to say right before you died. I kept saying over and over to my sister, "What was that word that Kramer told me to say??!!" Well, you know how dreams happen. They either jump from one thing to another or are recalled in bits and pieces. I'm not sure what did happen to me, but I do know I died in my dream. How do I know? After the guerillas came and went, I was with my mom looking at shawls a street vendor was selling. Soon she began talking to me about the things I *used* to like and then began reminiscing about me. Suddenly I realized that she saw me as another person (or I was another person). June was dead. I realized that I was killed and I felt pain for my family, trying to imagine how it felt to experience the death of a close family member.[2]

II

My girlfriend, our two best friends, and I were standing on the Golden Gate Bridge on a beautiful, sunny, summer day. We were admiring the beauty of the sea, the clear blue sky, and the boats sailing on San Francisco Bay. I was telling them that I was happy to be there because I loved this place and that we should move to Marin County and stay there forever. "Forever?" they asked. "Yes, forever," I answered. I felt very happy because we were sharing the experience of such a wonderful view, the wind in our faces, the warm sunshine, and because we were good friends and were lucky to be there together. The bridge was full of people; we were leaning on the railing looking out at the bay, smiling, when suddenly I felt a painful electric shock in my back. I turned and I saw an old woman, a witch; her finger was what had touched my back. She was pointing at me; she was laughing, and saying over and over again that there was nothing I could do to free myself from the spell she had cast upon me. I was feeling weak, my body was ill with increasing pain and I fell to the floor. People gathered around me. I could see myself on the floor because I was outside my own body, I was there lying still, not moving, like dead. How? Why? I asked myself. Then I saw that my girlfriend was leaning over my body; she and our two friends were crying, and then one of them said in a calm voice: "Let's go; we have to leave him here, behind." I tried to tell them with all my being "Don't leave me here, please!" but the lips of the body on the floor could not move and my friends did not hear me. They were leaving, and I saw in amazement how my girlfriend and my two friends elevated into the air. At that moment, I was again inside my body, on the ground, and I could see how they were elevating high into the beautiful big blue heavens until I lost sight of them. Then I realized that I was able to move and speak again. I was feeling weak but I stood up. I looked around and everything seemed normal, the same beautiful place, the same people, but my friends were no longer there so I began to ask the peo-

ple on the bridge what had happened. The tourists put down
their cameras, the people walking, jogging, or riding bicycles
stopped, even the cars stopped; then all of them turned looking at me, all at once, some with grim faces, others laughing,
and all their voices said: "It is they who have died; they are
free, but you—you are still trapped in this world." A feeling of
desperation came to my being; I remembered what I had said
about staying in this beautiful earthly place forever; I looked
up to the big blue sky which this time seemed to me so beautiful, peaceful, infinite; and then looking at the people around
me I said, "I am trapped in this world, but for how long?"
And they answered, "You do not have any right to know." I
woke up.[3]

III

I am in the Philippines, and an old lady has died, and she is
to be embalmed. There was a big coffin box in which the lady
lay. The embalmer got in the box too and they shut the lid on
him. He was dressed in grey slacks and white shirt. He was a
Filipino. I knew it was hot in the box—like a smoke box—to
which heat was added. I lifted the lid and I said: "No, it's not
like that. There's always something that's alive."

Her body was shriveled like a mummy but her head was
moving. Her mouth and jaw were moving. She was alive *and*
mummified. I was surprised and then it became clear that
this was the message—that death is not the way we think of it.
There is like a continuum between death and life and each
co-exist. You could stretch it out and look at each of them at
each stage.[4]

At first reading, these dreams may seem unrelated save for
the fact that, in each, someone dies. In the first dream, June is
killed in a foreign country by a troop of guerrillas but, at first, she
is unaware of her death. It is not until she realizes that her
mother is speaking to her (as if she were another person) that she
is aware that she had been killed. In the second dream, an old
woman (a witch) interrupts the dreamer's heightened experience
of Marin County by casting a spell upon him which causes him

to fall to the floor, as if dead. Then Luis' girlfriend and two other friends elevate into the air and disappear. When he regains the use of his body, tourists, pedestrians and drivers all stop and tell him with one voice: "It is they who have died; they are free, but you—you are still trapped in this world." In the third dream, Geoff is in the Philippines where he sees an old lady dead in a coffin, but he refuses to accept it. When he lifts the coffin lid, he sees that her mouth is moving, that she is both dead *and* alive.

Without any attempt to interpret these dreams, it is worth noting several similarities which lead us to several questions. Each dream took place in a foreign country, or a new place, or included people from foreign countries. In each dream, the dreamer does not accept, or challenges, the death event. None of the dreams ends with death, for in each dream scene, the one who has died continues, in some form, to live (whether in the original location or another). These observations lead us to a fundamental question which has several sub-questions embedded in it: Can one actually die in a dream? That is, can the dreamer, or someone else in the dream, completely and finally cease to exist, with no remaining trace of life? Subordinate to this is another question: Is there a difference between the dream-body and what might be called the dream-soul? Put another way, is there a difference between the dream-body, which dies in the dream, and dream-observer, which continues to watch and/or interact with the dead dream-body and its surrounding environment? It may be, as we will consider in this book, that the "Who dies?" question is far more profound than the mere statistics would indicate.

We will return to these questions at the end of the chapter, but for the moment we turn to a particularly important point— the distinction between kinds of "others" who die in dreams. We can delineate two categories: first, dreams in which the "other" *dies,* (which total 29.9%), and, second, those in which the "other" *has already died* and, in the dream, returns from the dead (which account for 16.9% of the dreams). As this distinction will become crucial in the following chapter, if not throughout our study, we present here one example of each kind of non-dreamer death dream.

I. Other Dies

After seeing Pink Floyd's "The Wall" (a movie) several times, there was one particular scene that seemed to change me and never let me truly enjoy the movie again. A child's father gets killed in WW II, and the child goes into his father's bedroom, into his drawers, and finds his father's uniform, and bullets, and the medal that he received for his death in the war. The scene closes.

My dream was that I went under our house, where we keep storage, and found a memorial set-up of my father. There was his picture, and some bullets (for he was a policeman) and other memorabilia. I picked up the picture and then I woke up crying, for my dad was dead. When I realized that it had been just a dream, I ran into my parents' bedroom and was so happy that my dad was alive; I never really watched the movie again.

Since then, my dad has passed away, but that will be the bulk of the subject area in future writings.[5]

II. The Dead Returns

I once dreamed that my grandfather who's dead came back to life while we were at the mortuary, and the funeral procession of limo's turned into a caravan to a bar where we had a huge party. When I woke up I was happy until I realized it was only a dream and that my grandfather was still dead.[6]

What is the difference, if any, between these dreams and dreams in which the dreamer himself or herself dies? Does the fact that one can return from the dead lend extra credence or weight to the messages that person communicates to the dreamer? In what way, if any, do such dreams suggest the possibility of rebirth or of a life after death? And can a deeper significance be attributed to a dream if the one returning from the dead brings a message specifically meant to address an element of the dreamer's life? Rather than seeking to answer these questions at this point in our study, it is more important to ruminate upon them, and then to notice which questions the reader considers most significant, and why.

II. HOW THE DEAD DIE

Our next concern is the variety of ways, and statistical frequencies, with which death occurs in dreams. As might be suspected, there seem to be as many ways of dying in dreams as there are in real life: from violent to natural causes, from accidental to self-induced occurrences, from illness and disease to electrocution and freezing. The following list provides a breakdown of the ways in which people died in the dreams we collected.

While we have collected 700 death dreams, 573 of them specifically describe a cause of death. In the rest of the dreams, the way in which death happens is not indicated. For example:

> When I was about 15, I dreamed of my own death. In this dream, I died, and all my family went to the mountain to bury me. After they buried my body, they all left me. I was horrified and wanting to go back home. When I finally went

Table 2.3
HOW DREAM TOTALS

Group	Total /	Percentage
Accident, Misc.	109	19%
Natural Disaster	32	6%
Natural Causes	53	9%
Violent Causes	91	16%
Murder	171	30%
Warfare	18	3%
Demonic Encounters	32	6%
Suicide	25	4%
Astral Falling	42	7%
	573	

Table 2.3

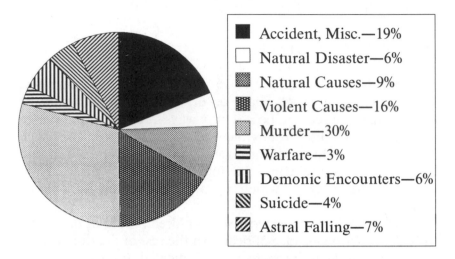

■	Accident, Misc.—19%
□	Natural Disaster—6%
▨	Natural Causes—9%
▦	Violent Causes—16%
▨	Murder—30%
☰	Warfare—3%
�III	Demonic Encounters—6%
▨	Suicide—4%
▨	Astral Falling—7%

home, they were eating noodle soup, talking and laughing. Also even though I could see and hear them, they didn't notice me. So I went back to my grove without fear or grief and ate some food and that was the end.[7]

Reflecting on the dreams which specify the manner of death, one notices that a significant number of deaths involve falling, whether from a vehicle, from a high building or cliff, or what might be described as an astral falling. Of the 573 death dreams, 15.3% involve a falling of some kind. Statistically speaking, almost half were accidental (airplane, automobile, building, cliff, ladder, pitfall, roller coaster and tree). Others included suicides, sensations of floating and astral falling.

Along with the death dreams, we also collected 594 responses to the following survey question: "Imagine your own death; how do you think you will die?" At first our purpose in collecting responses to this question was to provide an alternative for students who claimed not to remember any death-related dreams. Then we became interested in the comparative possibilities between the dreaming-mind and the imagining-mind, between sleeping imagery and awake imagery, between seemingly involuntary, unconscious material and creatively voluntary

Table 2.4 CAUSE OF DEATH	Death Dreams	Imagined Deaths
Natural Causes	**9%**	**61%**
Illness/Health Problems	(NA)	238
Old Age/Sleep	(NA)	125
Violent External Forces	**91%**	**36%**
Accidents	109	105
Astral Death	42	10
Demonic Encounter	32	25
Murder/War	189	11
Natural Disaster	32	22
Suicide	25	37
Violent Causes	91	0
Does Not Know/Will Not Die	0	18
TOTAL	520	591

Table 2.4a: **Death Dreams**

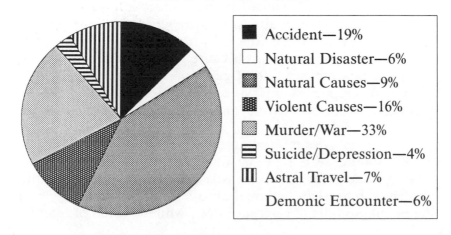

- Accident—19%
- Natural Disaster—6%
- Natural Causes—9%
- Violent Causes—16%
- Murder/War—33%
- Suicide/Depression—4%
- Astral Travel—7%
- Demonic Encounter—6%

Table 2.4b: **Imagined Deaths**

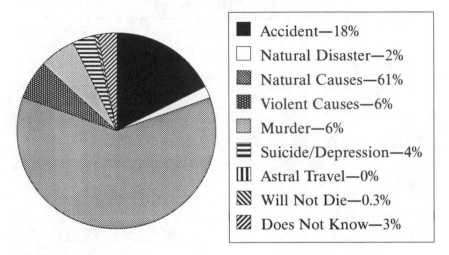

- ■ Accident—18%
- □ Natural Disaster—2%
- ▨ Natural Causes—61%
- ▦ Violent Causes—6%
- ▨ Murder—6%
- ≡ Suicide/Depression—4%
- Ⅲ Astral Travel—0%
- ▧ Will Not Die—0.3%
- ▨ Does Not Know—3%

material. When juxtaposed with the death dream statistics, the results listed above raise several perplexing questions.

The largest category by far—almost 40%—are those who imagined themselves dying of old age or in their sleep. Slightly more than half as many (or 21%) imagined a death by illness or miscellaneous health problems. Almost as many (18%) imagined death by accident, whether in a moving vehicle, or as a result of a recreational mishap. In fact, if we further refine our categories, roughly 36% of the respondents imagined a death by what we have termed "violent external forces" (accidents, homicide, suicide), whereas almost 61% imagined a natural death caused by age or various illness—what we have termed "internal" causes. We mention this because when compared to death-related dream statistics, the figures are almost reversed; 91% of dreamers report external forces, as opposed to only 9% who report deaths due to internal, natural causes. How can this disparity be explained?

These statistics take on an even greater significance when we add another set of figures, namely death rates taken from the National Center for Health Statistics, U.S. Department of Health and Human Services. National statistics indicate that only 7% of the population die of external forces, while 93% die of internal

Table 2.5
DEATHS & DEATH RATES

Cause	Death Dreams	Imagined Deaths	National Statistics (1978)	(1988)
Natural Causes	**9%**	**61%**	**92%**	**93%**
Old Age/Sleep	(NA)	40%	(NA)	(NA)
Illness/Health Problems	(NA)	21%	77%	65%
Other	0%	0%	15%	28%
Violent External Forces	**91%**	**36%**	**8%**	**7%**
Doesn't Know/ Will Not Die	0%	3%	0%	0%

or natural causes. In the dreams we collected, it is almost the reverse—91% die of external causes while only 9% die of internal causes.[8]

What would explain this total disparity? Why would the dreaming mind (along with the imagining mind to a slightly lesser degree) envision death in numbers which are radically out of proportion with the way in which people in fact die? Why do dreamers more consistently dream of a violent external death when in fact the odds of such an occurrence are overwhelmingly counter-indicative? We ask these questions—not that unequivocal answers exist—because we are interested in pondering various avenues of thought which arise as we reflect upon them.

III. EMOTIONAL RESPONSE

Having looked at *who* dies in dreams, and *how* they die, our next concern was to chart the dreamer's emotional responses to the death event, both in reaction to the moment of death itself and, where indicated, to post-death existence. We detected five types of responses: negative, positive, neutral, and then negative to positive and positive to negative.

Table 2.6a
EMOTIONAL QUALITY OF DREAMS

	Death Dreams		Imagined Deaths	
Negative	467	(67%)	103	(25%)
Positive	57	(8%)	184	(45%)
Neutral	116	(16%)	74	(18%)
− to +	43	(6%)	38	(9%)
+ to --	17	(2%)	9	(2%)
TOTAL	700		408	

These can be condensed into three types:

Table 2.6b

	Death Dreams		Imagined Deaths	
Neg. & + to −	484	(70%)	112	(27%)
Pos. & − to +	100	(14%)	222	(55%)
Neutral	116	(16%)	74	(18%)
TOTAL	700		408	

When we analyzed the dreams themselves, the ratio of negative and initially positive attitudes which shifted to negative responses climbed to 69.5%, while those which shifted to positive responses were 14.4%. For example, the following is the dream of a sixteen year old female student.

I am on a private yacht. My mother and stepdad are staying in a separate cabin. It was a party, but no one knew who this one 12 year old was. She had totally psycho eyes, raggy hair, and was running around with a knife. She was acting psycho around a rack of clothes for sale. I was scared of her. I thought she wanted to kill me.

Finally I took a basket that had her baby in it, only it was a giant egg with a small egg face on it. I cracked its head with my fist to prevent another evil person from growing up. It cracked open. There was nothing in it. Then I threw the shell overboard. The girl ran after me for killing her baby. Then mom tried to help me kill this girl. I was totally scared.[9]

While negative emotional responses clearly outnumbered positive ones, as one would expect, what interested us was the fact that there were positive responses at all in the face of death. When we looked more closely at them, we discovered two types— positive dreams (in which the dreamer faces death in an emotionally comfortable fashion), and what might be called positive trans/formation dreams (in which the dreamer shifts from a negative to a positive response to the death event.) The following are examples of each of these types:

I am involved in a story of intrigue where I am being chased by robbers who want me dead because of what I am wearing. My clothing has the contraband they are seeking sewn into its lining. The "goods" which might have something to do with drugs are/were actually stolen twice. They were taken originally and then taken a second time from the crooks who stole it the first time. They were therefore doubly sought after. How I came to possess it, I do not know, but I did know that they had to find me and that it was no use fleeing. When they see me, I say: "YOU MIGHT AS WELL KILL ME!" One of them immediately pulls a gold pistol, points it high at my head, at the midpoint of my forehead just beneath my hairline. My head is slightly bowed. It feels too high at first. The gun reflects a splash of sunlight and for an instant is golden. He shoots me once. I barely (if at all) hear a sound. I know he has pulled the trigger, however. I do not feel anything. I fall forward. Before I hit the ground everything goes black. When I awaken, I am aware that seconds have passed during which I was completely dead. No "I" at all.[10]

While the first dreamer is afraid of death and the second dreamer is not, in the next dream, a variety of emotions occur.

I am a middle-aged, rather large man at some type of business place. (There are buildings with a parking lot.) Also there are at least two men (probably more) with semi-automatic guns, the kind we always see terrorists wielding on TV shows. I am trying to escape the situation. In the parking lot, I've almost succeeded. The gunman hasn't noticed my absence when suddenly he turns, sees me, and shoots me once in the leg. The pain is almost unendurable. I scream and writhe. I am very angry at him for hurting me. Thinking I am no longer a threat, he turns away again. I seize my chance and, despite the pain, get up to go. The movement attracts his attention again and he shoots at me several times. I hold my bag out in front of me, realizing it won't offer much protection. Miraculously, none of the bullets hit me, but I moan and groan, feigning wounds. He walks closer to me, doesn't buy my phony pain and shoots me once in the torso. Pain washes through me like I've never felt and suddenly I begin to feel detached from it. I realize I am dying.

Dream Skip—Time has passed, minutes or hours, I can't tell. Two men bend over me, assess my condition, and throw me in the back of a large truck. I land on top of a large pile of garbage. I sense that they aren't malicious; they just believe me to be dead. I manage to mumble: "Please don't put me here. I'm a dying man." They are surprised to hear a voice out of me, and immediately come over to make me more comfortable. In a burst of time I realize I am now dead. An incredible sensation of freedom, understanding and contentedness fills me and I see that all that previously was is only illusion. The feeling is wonderful. I see my body laying very still about ten feet beneath me and realize I am one—even more so—without my body.

Dream Skip—I am Lesley H. again, playing "light as a feather, stiff as a board" with some friends of mine. I am laying in the center, trying to convince them that anything is possible since this is all illusion anyway. Why wouldn't they be able to pick me up with two fingers? I relax my body and let myself drift away into the utterly blissful state I felt before. Drifting in between, I feel myself being shaken. In a split second, all my thoughts, emotions, realizations and consciousness hit me as if I dove into a swimming pool. I am awake in bed during an earthquake.[11]

A series of questions arise. What does the giant egg mean in the first dream? Do you find it strange that the second dreamer who was being chased by the crooks would, when confronted, say "You might as well kill me"? What sense do you make of the reflection of a splash of sunlight off the golden revolver, or that the gun was golden for that matter? What about the third dreamer (a female student) who dreams she is a middle-aged man who is shot? What sense do you make of the dreamer's post-death realizations: the sensation of freedom, the realization that life was an illusion, the out-of-body experience? And then, what about her trans/formation back into her living identity to play "light as a feather, stiff as a board"? If you had any of these dreams, how might they affect your waking reality?

Of the 8.2% of positive responses to death, and the 6.2% of the positive trans/formation dreams, when we analyzed them on the basis of *what* happens to the dead persons, we arrived at the following figures.

Looking at these figures, what is immediately noticeable is the fact that it was easier for the other person to face death in a positive way than for the dreamer to do the same. Then too, only 100 dreamers (out of 700 dreams) reported a positive death experience. It should be remembered, however, that while almost half of those who dreamed of dying could recall nothing more of

Table 2.7 POSITIVE & POSITIVE TRANS/FORMATION DREAMS		
Heaven/Utopia	8	8.000%
Dead Returns	49	49.000%
Resurrection/Trans/formation	4	4.000%
Positive Dying Process	39	39.000%
	100 Total	

Table 2.7
POSITIVE & POSITIVE TRANS/FORMATION DREAMS

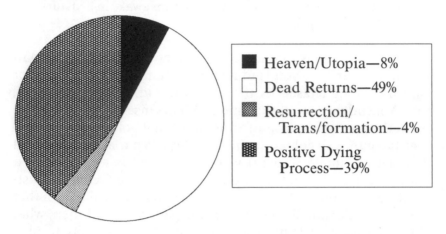

■ Heaven/Utopia—8%

□ Dead Returns—49%

▨ Resurrection/
   Trans/formation—4%

▥ Positive Dying
   Process—39%

the dream, for many their anxiety may have prevented further recall. It is also interesting to note that the positive and positive trans/formation dreams covered the gamut of ways in which one dreams of death, with figures not unlike the ratios discussed earlier in the "How the Dead Die" section of this chapter.

We noticed surprising discontinuities when we compared the emotional quality of the "imagined deaths" to those of the death dreams. While 25% of the imagined death scenarios expressed negative emotions, 45% were positive, and while 2% shifted from positive to negative, 9% shifted from negative to positive. The following chart exemplifies this:

Table 2.8			
	Imagined	**Dreamed**	**Surveyed**
Positive & − to +	54.8%	14.4%	12.0%
Negative & + to −	26.6%	69.5%	68.5%
Neutral	18.6%	16.1%	20.0%
Total Number	429	700	709

What might explain the surprising reversal of emotional responses from negative to preponderantly positive in the *imagined* situations? Why do fears, anxiety and dread dominate the *dream* deaths while hope, peace and confidence dominate the *imagined* deaths? Does the negativity of the *dream* responses call into question a kind of wish or projection of the imagined death's positivity? Could it be that one needs to distinguish between manifest and religious consciousness in dreams, such that the moment of death evokes only the later or shadow side of the former? Might it be that the fearful anxious response in dreams is a survival-oriented mechanism manifesting itself in the unconscious?

IV. SURVIVING DEATH

What turned out to be most fascinating were those dreams in which the dreamer, or others, survived death, dreams in which the dreamer's consciousness did not die with the dreamer's body, and dreams in which someone who was dead returned from the dead as though alive. The following is a fairly typical, if more detailed, example of the latter:

> Our family was returning to a vacation home at the beach. When we arrived we found the porch covered with dry octopus type animals. I had collected them on past vacations because I loved them, but I didn't return them to the sea and they lay dead upon the porch.
>
> I felt my family was upset with me because they didn't understand how I couldn't let them go, yet I didn't want them to die; so I just left them on the porch so fate could take them.
>
> At some point in the vacation I decided to clean up the porch. It felt good because I knew inside I was doing the right thing and the animals belonged back in the ocean. It was a beautiful, clear day; the sky was exceptionally blue and the air was fresh because it had rained the night before. Everyone else had gone off somewhere and I was going to surprise them with a clean porch. I gathered the animals in four buckets

and started carrying them across a hill of dark, green grass. I remember feeling the glorious day and the beauty around me. I crossed the grass and walked on the sand trying to keep my white tennis shoes clean. (There was a lot of mud from the rain.) As I reached the water's edge, I picked out a perfect spot to say goodbye to my friends. I poured the contents of the first bucket into the water as it swept the shore at high tide. An amazing thing happened. As the animals touched the water they came alive again. They swam away as if I had never disturbed their serenity. As I finished with the second bucket and started to leave, I realized I wasn't alone.

A man in a scrubby dark coat was digging a grave in the sand, which was submerged in water. The grave was a perfect rectangle and floated above the grave on the surface of the water. In the water was the body of a man. He was facing down and his eyes were open. I knew that he knew what I knew, namely that he was really alive. The man told me he had accidentally killed this person but no one would even believe him so he had to destroy the body. I remember thinking that what he doesn't know is that the man is not really dead, and as soon as he puts him in the grave the body will come alive again.

I left to get my other two buckets of animals and I felt such a joy and freedom. I passed a woman and man and told them there was someone disposing of a body. They knew who the man was and they were trying to decide which authorities should be called. They were the caretakers of the beach but not police authorities. I left the problem to them because I had more important things to do. My animals were waiting for me so they could be reborn. I knew that it didn't matter who took care of the man with the body or, for that matter, how. He would be judged by the world law and the body is in God's hands.

I returned to find my family there and pleased that the porch was now clean. I felt so good because I had found a secret. We don't die when we die, we are born again or returned to another life after and before death. There is no death, only temporary existence in life as we know it.[12]

Of the death dreams we collected, in 49% of them the dream ended with the death of the dreamer. Of the remaining 51% of the dreams, four types emerged in which there was a continued consciousness:

1. *Passive* (14%) in which the dreamer's consciousness continues to observe ongoing dream events without physically interacting with any of the other characters or ongoing dream events.
2. *Active* (14%) in which the dreamer's consciousness continues to observe and to move from place to place, or into another dimension, but without interacting with anyone.
3. *Interactive* (19%) in which the dreamer's consciousness continues to observe, to be active, and to attempt to be involved with persons in ongoing dream events.
4. *Special* (3.7%) in which there is death but no one dies, for example those in which death is mentioned as a concept only.

Because readers may be especially interested in dreams of consciousness continuing after death, the following are examples of the three major types—passive, active and interactive:

Passive

I am lying dead in my bedroom. I realize that I'm dead and I marvel at the fact that I've retained my consciousness. I lie perfectly still, yet my attention is directed to the next room. I can see all of what's going on in there. My daughter is reading a book about whales and there is a song called "Will I Live Tomorrow?" playing on the stereo.

I look up through the skylight and see the trees and the blue sky. Then I wake up.[13]

Active

My first encounter with a death dream was when I was attending Frostburg State University in the hills of Maryland. I went to bed at 2 a.m. just like normal for my 10:30 class the next day. I started to dream. Then it was interrupted by a feeling of weightlessness. I felt scared. Then after the initial fear, I tried to control it. Amazingly I was able to direct myself left and right, up and down. I was also able to see all around me, but I could not see myself in my bed. That did not seem to bother me. In fact, I thought nothing of it. As I was gliding over mountains, trees, etc., I felt compelled to go in a certain direction. Then I came to a clearing. It seemed to me like it was an overhead view of a cemetery. The way I ended up interpreting this in my dream was I was buried down in the cemetery along with my closest friends. I do not remember any more of the dream or any others that night. Surprisingly, I did not wake up nor was I scared. I felt at peace. The next morning when I did wake up, I was scared shitless (excuse the language). Also I would like to say that even though I was not studying until 2 a.m., I also was not drinking or doing drugs, just having fun.[14]

Interactive

This was when I was 25–26. In my dream I was *dead but didn't realize* it until the end of my dream.

I was *planning* a funeral, making all the arrangements, *cooking for the "mourners"*—everything one does when a death occurs. When the time for the service arrived, I realized I was the one that died and I had to get into a coffin (*one of my biggest fears*). I *woke, shaking* and *crying* and I woke my husband in the process and, sobbing, told him the dream.[15]

We have seen that roughly half of all dreamers who die in their dreams continue, after death, in some form of consciousness. Does this, in any way, confirm one's views of an afterlife? Or does the fact that roughly half of the dreamers experience no after-death consciousness challenge one's after-life beliefs? What is the connection, if any, between surviving death in one's dreams and the possibility that one may in fact survive death in reality? To explore these and similar questions in a fuller context, we will now initiate a multicultural, interdisciplinary investigation into what the unconscious teaches about death.

COMMENTARY

For purposes of comprehension and clarity, we have statistically arranged the 700 death dreams (collected largely from
students at San Jose State University) according to four categories: Who Dies?; How the Dead Die?; Emotional Responses
to Death; Surviving Death. While our study is limited to university students, it includes a wide range of ages (17–65), nation-
alities (Vietnamese, Japanese, Chinese, Indian, Israeli, African,
Iranian, American), vocations (computer technology, secretarial,
sales and food services along with full-time students), and family-
experiences (married, divorced, engaged, separated, adopted,
orphaned and, of course, unmarried). By collecting as many
dreams as we did over a two and a half year period, we hoped
that the sheer number of examples would compensate for the
institutional similarity of the dreamers surveyed.

First, we noticed that aside from the 9% of dreams (in which
everyone dies or the personification of death enters the dream),
the majority of the death dreams were almost evenly divided between the dreamer's own death (43%) and the death of another,
whether family, friend or stranger (48%).

Second, when we compared national statistics with imagined deaths and death dreams, we noticed some interesting dis-
parities with regard to how one dies. While national statistics
indicate that 7% of the population die of "external forces," and
93% die of "internalized" causes, it was almost the reverse in the
dreams collected—91% die of external forces while only 9% die of
internal causes.

Third, when we compared the quality of one's emotional
response to death, again we noticed a disparity between imagined deaths and death dreams. Whereas, in the imagined deaths,
54.5% were positive or positive trans/formations, only 14.4%
of dreamers exhibited this shift. And whereas 27.5% of imagined deaths were negative or negative trans/formations, 69.5% of
dreamers made this shift.

Fourth, what may be the most interesting category is that of
surviving death. Of the dreams we collected, almost half (49%)
ended with the death of the dreamer. Of the remaining dreams,
four types emerged in which there was a continued conscious-

ness: passive consciousness (14%), active consciousness (14%), interactive consciousness (19%) and other (3.7%).

In the following chapters we will examine death dreams in a variety of contexts and through the methodologies of several disciplines—ethnographic, religious, philosophical, psychological and literary—in order to provide a context for our investigations, and to suggest possible interpretative points of view. Each of these chapters will point the reader in two directions—beyond issues raised in this chapter (so as to expand our understanding and appreciation of them), and to specific themes raised here (so as to deepen our interpretation of them).

Our purpose will be to expose death dreams to a variety of interpretative contexts as well as to discover how death dreams are said to affect human consciousness. While we will not pretend to be comprehensive or extremely technical, we will strive to penetrate to the heart of the matter for each discipline, so that the reader can make appropriate connections. Throughout, our focus will be upon the trans/formational nature of some death dreams, and what they may offer even to those who have not dreamed them.

NOTES

[1]Anonymous student at SJSU.
[2]June Oka, student in "Death, Dying & Religions" at SJSU.
[3]Luis A. Molina, student in "Death, Dying & Religions" at SJSU. About his dream Luis wrote:

> Over the years I think about this dream.
>
> I am a foreign student. The first time I saw the Golden Gate was when I was twelve. I was very much impressed of how beautiful Marin County and the San Francisco Bay are during the summer.

When I had the dream I was a teenager. For three years, my girlfriend, my two friends and I had always done everything together, went everywhere together; we saw each other at least six days a week. We even took trips abroad together.

Four days after I had the dream my girlfriend and I broke up. Three weeks after I had the dream my sister and I were sent to our surprise to the U.S. to study. We came to the San Francisco Bay Area. My ex-girlfriend is now married and lives on the U.S. East Coast; one of my best friends lives in Germany, the other one in Latin America, and I have not seen them since the time when I came here, after my dream.

Sometimes I feel like making comments like "I think life is an illusion of which one day we will wake up to true reality," and when I do my friends look at me with wide open mouths, change the conversation, make fun of it, or say that I do not make any sense.

[4]Geoff Norman, artist and craftsperson.

[5]Anonymous student at SJSU.

[6]Jim W., a student in the "Death, Dying & Religions" class at SJSU.

[7]Sook O., a student in the "Death, Dying & Religions" class at SJSU.

[8]It should be noted that the distinction between violent, external causes and not necessarily violent causes is made problematic by another distinction—that between instant versus prolonged.

[9]Leila Kramer, a high school student.

[10]This was my first death dream and it occurred on Christmas morning, 1989.

[11]Lesley H., a student in the "Death, Dying & Religions" class at SJSU.

[12]Karen S., a student in the "Death, Dying & Religions" class at SJSU.

[13]Kelly S., a student in the "Death, Dying & Religions" class at SJSU.

[14]Adam D., a student in the "Death, Dying & Religions" class at SJSU.

[15]Anonymous student at SJSU.

Chapter 3 ETHNOGRAPHIC TRADITIONS

In this world, the Goddess is seen in the moon, the light that shines in darkness, the rain bringer, mover of the tides, Mistress of mysteries. And as the moon waxes and wanes, and walks three nights of its cycle in darkness, so, it is said, the Goddess once spent three nights in the Kingdom of Death.

For in love She ever seeks her other Self, and once, in the winter of the year, when He had disappeared from the green earth, She followed Him and came at last to the gates beyond which the living do not go.

The Guardian of the Gate challenged Her, and She stripped Herself of her clothing and jewels, for nothing may be brought before Death Himself.

He loved Her, and knelt at her feet, laying before Her his sword and crown, and gave Her the fivefold kiss, and said, "Do not return to the living world, but stay here with Me, and have peace and rest and comfort."

But She answered, "Why do you cause all things I love and delight in to die and wither away?"

"Lady," He said, "it is the fate of all that lives to die. Everything passes; all fades away. I bring comfort and consolation to those who pass the gates that they may grow young again. But You are my heart's desire—return not, but stay here with Me."

And She remained with him three days and three nights, and at the end of the third night She took up his crown, and it became a circlet that She placed around her neck, saying:

"Here is the circle of rebirth. Through You all passes out of life, but through Me all may be born again. Everything passes; everything changes. Even death is not eternal. Mine

is the mystery of the womb, that is the cauldron of rebirth.
Enter into Me and know Me, and You will be free of all fear.
For as life is but a journey into death, so death is but a pas-
sage back to life, and in Me the circle is ever turning."

In love, He entered into Her, and so was reborn into life. Yet
is He known as Lord of Shadows, the comforter and consoler,
opener of the gates, King of the Land of Youth, the giver of
peace and rest. But She is the gracious mother of all life; from
Her all things proceed and to Her they return again. In Her
are the mysteries of death and birth; in Her is the fulfillment
of all love.[1]

From as far back as *extant* written accounts can take us, and
no doubt much further, dreams about the presence of the dead
have been a common human experience. Anthropologists who
have studied pre-technological societies have discovered that
dreams about dead ancestors function as an important source of
a culture's beliefs and practices. It has been theorized that fune-
rary rituals, animistic beliefs, role transmission and the nature of
tribal identity result from the possible influence of these dreams.
Some even venture to theorize that so-called "primitive" cultures
were terror-struck by beholding, in dreams, figures of those
known to be dead. Such a dream-generated fear, it is theorized,
caused pre-literate peoples to bury corpses (along with victuals
and goods as an appeasement) to prevent the dead's return.[2]
Such dreams of the dead convinced ancient peoples that every
living thing had a soul, or a secret life force, which in sleep or
death could become separated from the body of the dreamer or
of the corpse.

According to Sir Edward B. Taylor, a pioneer in the field of
anthropology, the religious impulse originated as a belief in *im-
material souls* which not only occupied objects (like trees, stones,
animals or humans), but also which were experienced in dreams
wherein the dead continued to exist independently of their
physical bodies. Taylor noted that certain Greenlanders, the New
Zealanders and certain Amerindians "consider that the soul
quits the body in the night and goes out hunting, dancing and
visiting," and at the same time some Amerindians suppose "a
dream to be a visit from the soul of the person or object dreamt

of, or a sight seen by the rational soul, gone out for an excursion while the sensitive soul remains in the body."[3] And according to Bronislaw Malinowski, while studying the dreams of the Melonesians of the Trobriand Islands (who seem to show little interest in dreams), he discovered that these natives "reverse the Freudian Theory of dreams; for them the dream is the cause of the wish."[4] For example, as the direct result of a ceremonial spell, an amorous dream is induced which then makes the dreamer wish for the partner in the dream.

What do these accounts, and accounts like them, tell us about the view of dreams in ethnographic cultures? More specifically, how does death appear to such dreamers? In what follows we will examine, first, the shamanic experience of death dreams, then briefly focus on two specific ethnographic cultures (the Australian Aborigine, and the Senoi), then explore the teachings of a Yaqui Indian, Don Juan Matus, and, finally, present fragments from a recorded conversation with a contemporary shaman.

THE SHAMANIC EXPERIENCE

As with other so-called "primitive" peoples, North American tribal cultures lack a term to designate what literate cultures in the west call "religion." There are, however, no lack of sacred elements (e.g. the totem), sacred spirits (e.g. the high god), sacred ceremonies (e.g. the ghost dance), and sacred persons (e.g. the shaman). Shamans, it has been suggested, were perhaps the earliest representatives of, or authorities on, religious experience because they verbalized (through trances, visions, dreams and ecstatic chants) a transition from disassociated spiritual behaviors to a disciplined search for the *real* (or deep) self. In tribal cultures, shamans were men or women who possessed a form of supernatural power and who had access to helping spirits, psychic resources, visionary insight and ecstatic dispositions. In a general sense, the term shaman included those who were called medicine men. Indeed, the term shaman is derived from the Siberian equivalent of a medicine man (though not all medicine men were shamans).[5]

How does one become a shaman? Commonly, one becomes a shaman by acquiring the above mentioned powers which come through visions or dreams (e.g. of bears, eagles, owls, antelope, or snakes) which teach the dreamer songs or rituals necessary to receive power and attain authority. In the following account, a woman received shamanistic power by dreaming of her dead father:

> When Rosie's father had been dead about eighteen years she started to dream about him. She dreamed that he came to her and told her to be a shaman. Then a rattlesnake came to her in dreams and told her to get eagle feathers, white paint, wild tobacco. The snake gave her the songs that she sings when she is curing. The snake appeared three or four times before she believed that she would be a shaman. Now she dreams about the rattlesnake quite frequently and she learns new songs and is told how to cure sick people in this way.[6]

Often taking journeys into the land of the dead in order to return with messages and special powers bestowed by the beings of the beyond, shamans have always had an intimate relationship with death and life after death. According to Nalungiag, a Netsilik Eskimo, the world is "enormous and also has room for people when they die and no more walk about down here on earth." He continues:

> This is not simply what the shamans tell us, those who understand the hidden things; ordinary people who know how to dream have many times seen that the dead appeared to them, just as they were in life. Therefore we believe that life does not end here on earth.[7]

In tribal cultures shamans became "technicians" of the Beyond by exploring the routes of travel to and within the Beyond, by ascending or descending to the realm of the dead, supported by protectors and helpers. Arriving in the realm of the afterlife, the shaman contacted people who had died, and met demons and spiritual beings who provided advice on ways to contend with daily life on earth.

After years of training, a shaman was able to intentionally

induce a death state and to allow the soul to leave the body and
journey to the land of the dead, where it learned how to handle
the dangers and trials of the afterlife. The shaman became, in
this way, a messenger between the material, earthly world and
non-material existence inhabited by the dead. (This ethereal
world was only accessible to ordinary tribal members in death,
or as a result of a serious illness, accident, shock, violent emotion or in dreams.) As a shaman explored the inner world (which
has the outer appearance of a death realm) he or she appeared
"dead" while the soul was off exploring the realm of the dead.
In the Beyond, soul communication was a telepathic and feeling-
oriented exchange from person to person, rather than language-
based; and the actual experiences of the shaman were presented
in pictures and sensory images which led the uninitiated to believe that material experiences were being related[8]

   While the ability to perceive souls who were separated from

Shaman

their bodies was usually restricted to shamans, ordinary tribal members also could see souls in dreams, or in near-death experiences. In fact, a collection of eighty-six verbatim reports of dreams collected from tribal cultures (like the Kwakiutl Indians of British Columbia, and the Navajo) classify thirty-eight as dreams of death and spirits of the dead. The next nearest category, totaling twenty dreams, represents incidents of everyday life.[9] A member of a Samoyed tribe stated, for example, that he had been prematurely pronounced dead during a severe illness. While his funeral ceremony was in progress, he journeyed to the underworld and eventually returned to his body.

> I had been sick in bed for a long time, and the heat (fever) had plagued me badly. Finally my spirit left its body and flew away. I came to regions where I had never been before, and the further I went, the duskier it became. I crossed a large ocean through wondrous forests and high mountains. Finally I reached a ridge of high hills from which I could see a black river. There were many people in the black river all trying to escape from it. Some of them sank ever deeper into the stream and they tried in vain to work themselves out. Others climbed the smooth mountain slopes until their bloody hands were no longer able to continue and they would fall down again. In the river there was a tremendously high pole which many climbed. . . .
>
> In the forests above the river, people were hunting and living just like on earth. A few of them were there with their entire families; others waited for their wives and children. After I had looked around, I walked on for a while and then went to sleep. When I awakened I found myself back on earth and the sun was just rising. Its rays awakened me and I felt completely healthy. Only when arising did I notice that I had been dead, for my mother had dressed me beautifully, brought me outside and covered my corpse with a bark mat, as one is accustomed to do with the dead. My mother told me later that I had died toward evening but that the rays of the sun had given me new life.[10]

It was from death and near death dreams and visions such as this, that the shaman received a trans/formational power.

AUSTRALIAN ABORIGINES

In Australia more than 500 distinct tribes have developed over a span of 50,000 years. Though these tribes were very diverse—the two basic groups were inland, desert communities (concerned mostly with fertility), and the woodland, coastal communities (concerned mostly with death)—they shared much in common concerning their beliefs about death. The one feature which united them more than any other was the so-called Dreamtime, or the Dreaming, in which their dead ancestors returned to share both mythic and practical information. The dreams themselves included at least four dimensions: the time of beginnings, the power of the ancestors, the ways of life and death, and the source of new life, or the spirit child.[11]

As the fundamental reservoir of power and knowledge, the Dreaming tells how, in the beginning, the ancestors shaped the flat, featureless and lifeless land into a place for humans to live. The ancestors did this by roaming the land, and living with all of the human characteristics and foibles that people have shown throughout history. Groups of ancestors wandered around within a small geographical area (each group forming a clan), giving life to the landscape by forming rocks, caves, hills, trees, rivers, waterholes, plants and animals. When the ancestors disappeared, the remaining landscape contained the sacred essences of those ancestors who had shaped the environment. At these sacred spots, the spiritual power of the ancestors was embodied in the landscape, in sacred totems (the objects left behind by the ancestors), and in certain animals and plants. By reliving the Dreamtime experiences of their ancestors, the Aborigines were connected to the time of their creation and also to the power of their ancestors, which is still present in the world.

Most significantly, the Dreamtime contained not only the ways of life, but also the ways of death for the Aborigines. In their dreams, the ancestors established the annual nomadic path that the tribe followed, and received the ritual ceremonies and relics to connect the tribe with the heroic adventures of the ancestors' annual migration. During these ceremonies, which occurred at specific sacred spots, the Aborigines did not just imitate their ancestors; they became their ancestors.

The Australian Aborigines believed that at death they returned to the clan's sacred totem located in Dreamtime. Life and death formed a cycle beginning and ending in Dreamtime and sustained by totems, ancestral sacred spots and rituals that kept the tribe connected to the ancestors. Death was an integral part of the life cycle, not a final end, but part of the nomadic lifestyle animated by the Dreamtime.

Among the early Australian people, there were several explanations of the origin of human death, each of which was understood to have begun in the original Dreamtime. In one, the moon wanted humans to drink his urine so that when they died, they would return to life as the moon did. Instead, however, humans chose the urine of the Wallaby and thereby chose mortality. In another, there was a certain tree in Dreamtime near which women were forbidden to go. One day a woman, wishing to obtain honey from a beehive in the tree's hollow, began to chop at it with an ax. Immediately a large black bat ("The spirit of death") flew out of the tree and brought death into the world.[12] These myths of death's origin were not merely imaginative attempts to explain death, but were generated by the dreams of a tribal people.

THE SENOI

The Senoi of Malaysia (a culture largely destroyed during World War II by the Japanese Allied forces), whose remnants live in mountainous jungles, have been well known for their dream control techniques. Partly Indonesian, and related to the Highlanders of Indo-China and Burma, the Senoi are a tall, thin, light-brown people who live in family units of long, communal houses. One of their most striking features is an extraordinary lack of psychosis, neuroses and violent crime common to western civilizations. One reason for this, according to anthropologist Kilton Stewart, is because the Senoi were practiced at attaining a kind of dream lucidity (being aware, while dreaming, that one is dreaming) and dream control, which allowed them to deal "directly with potential conflicts on the unconscious level as they arose, thus efficiently dealing with them before they reached the stage of overt problems in everyday life."[13]

According to Stewart, many social and psychological processes are involved in the dream interpretations of the Senoi, which are a mainstay of the education of children and are "common knowledge" to many Senoi adults. Part of the daily social intercourse revolving around dream interpretation begins at the breakfast table when the father and older brothers hear and analyze the dreams of the other children. After breakfast, the men of the tribe gather to discuss the dreams reported to them that morning. The Senoi believe that everything in a dream has a purpose beyond one's understanding when asleep.

To become an accomplished dreamer one must relax and enjoy falling into a dream. In fact, "falling is the quickest way to get in contact with the powers of the spirit world, the powers laid open to you through your dreams."[14] But what exactly are the elements of the Senoi dream process?

- First, children receive social recognition and esteem for discovering and relating what might be called an anxiety-motivated psychic reaction to dreams.

- Second, to the Senoi the working of the child's mind is rational, even when asleep, and it is just as reasonable for the child to adjust his or her inner tension states as it is for a western child to submit homework for the teacher.

- Third, the Senoi interpretation characterizes the force which the child feels in the dream as a power which can be controlled through a process of relaxation and can be reclaimed and directed.

- Fourth, the Senoi teach that anxiety is not only important in itself, but that it blocks the free play of imaginative thinking and creative activity to which dreams could otherwise give rise.

- Fifth, the Senoi establish the principle that the child should make decisions and arrive at resolutions in his or her night-time thinking as well as in that of the day, and should assume a responsible attitude toward all psychic forces.

- Sixth, the Senoi encourage their children to better control psychic reactions by expressing them and thinking upon them, rather than by concealing and repressing them.

- Seventh, the Senoi initiate children into a way of thinking which will be strengthened and developed throughout the rest of their life, and which assumes that a human being who retains good will and communicates psychic reactions to others for approval and criticism is the supreme ruler of all the individual forces of the spirit-world.[15]

Most significantly, the Senoi believe that when one is dying in a dream, he or she is in fact receiving the powers of the other world (i.e. one's own spiritual power which wishes to be reunited with the dreamer). Therefore, the Senoi teach that the dreamer should always face danger head-on in dreams. Though the dream images of friends can be called on, if needed, the dreamer should fight alone until friends arrive. The Senoi believe that true friends will never attack the dreamer or refuse to help in a dream. Moreover, when the dreamer kills a hostile dream character, the spirit of that character will then become the dreamer's servant or ally. Thus one should attack dream enemies, even if it means fighting to the death. As Patricia L. Garfield writes in her *Creative Dreaming:* "The death of a dream enemy releases a positive force from the part of you that has formed the antagonistic dream image."[16]

The Senoi believe that with aid any human being "can outface, master, and actually utilize all beings and forces in the dream universe."[17] One should call on other dream figures to assist and even ask the life-threatening enemy for a gift, whether something beautiful (e.g. a song, a story, a painting) or something useful (e.g. a solution to a problem). This experience leads to the belief that if one cooperates with one's neighbors, or opposes them with good will in the daytime, their images will help in dreams. Every person, therefore, should be the master of his or her own dream universe, and should be able to demand and receive the help and cooperation of all its forces.

THE YAQUI WAY

By now, many people are familiar with the series of works by Carlos Castaneda, a cultural anthropologist who in 1960 traveled to northern Mexico to research medicinal plants. Instead he met, and fell under the influence of, a Yaqui Indian named Don Juan Matus who later introduced him to Don Genaro Flores, a Mazatec Indian from central Mexico. Each of them were practitioners of an ancient belief system commonly known among anthropologists as sorcery. In the first of a series of books—*The Teachings of Don Juan: A Yaqui Way of Knowledge,* and in subsequent works—Castaneda depicts himself as an apprentice to Don Juan's belief system (e.g. states of "non-ordinary reality") and to some of his techniques (e.g. "seeing," "stopping the world" and "dreaming"). In what follows we will focus on Don Juan's teaching about death and dreams.[18]

As a trained "warrior," Don Juan practiced the sacred art of dying. He spoke about death as if it were a constant companion. In *The Teachings of Don Juan* and *A Separate Reality,* Don Juan teaches Castaneda how to become a man of knowledge, to explore non-ordinary realities, to contact the power of an ally, and to experience the crack between the worlds. In the third book, *Journey to Ixtlan,* he teaches Carlos that death is waiting for each person, and that one must focus on the link between life and death without remorse or anxiety. "Our death is waiting, and this very act we're performing now may well be our last battle on earth," Don Juan instructs. "I call it a battle because it is a struggle. Most people move from act to act without any struggle or thought." On the other hand, he continues, a hunter "has an intimate knowledge of his death; he proceeds judiciously, as if every act were his last battle."[19]

Early in 1961, Carlos reports visiting Don Juan to ask him about the ritualistic use of peyote. "He looked at me," Carlos says, "as if I were crazy, and then, as we walked, warned me repeatedly about the uselessness of my self-importance and personal history." His words put Carlos in a turmoil, as they usually did, and Carlos became depressed and dejected. At that point, Don Juan told Carlos to turn to his left. When he did, he experienced the sensation of a flickering shadow. "Death just gave you a warning," Don Juan said. "Death is our eternal companion. It is always to our left, at arm's length."[20] With insights gained from dreaming, Don Juan tells Carlos:

> "The thing to do when you're impatient," he proceeded, "is to turn to your left and ask advice from your death. An immense amount of pettiness is dropped if your death makes a gesture to you, or if you catch a glimpse of it, or if you just have the feeling that your companion is there watching you."[21]

Often Don Juan would put Carlos under the instruction of one of his female apprentices for guidance and supervision. Zuleica was such a supervisor who taught Carlos the intricacies of dreaming. By dreaming here is not meant ordinary dreaming as we shall see momentarily, but dreaming with intent, "second attention" and luminous realization. Zuleica taught Castaneda "that if dreaming is going to be done indoors, it is best to do it in total darkness, while lying down or sitting up on a narrow bed, or better yet, while sitting inside a coffin-like crib."[22] The appropriateness of this image—"coffin-like crib"—becomes apparent when we understand what Don Juan means by dreaming.

To understand "dreaming," it is necessary to make a distinction between the dreamer and the dreamed. In dreaming, as opposed to ordinary dreaming, the self of the dreamer moves away from the body of the dreamer and cultivates a "feeling of indifference" toward the sleeping body, almost as if it were dead and of no further use. This process, according to Don Juan, occurs in the space and the time of "the double," that is, when one watches oneself sleep. In one sentence Don Juan says that "the double is the self," in the next that "the self dreams the double," and a few sentences later that "it is the double who dreams the self."[23] Another sorcerer and a friend of Don Juan, Don Genaro, explains this seeming contradiction to Castaneda by speaking of his first experience with dreaming.

The Double

"When it first happened to me, I didn't know it had happened," he explained. "One day I had been picking plants in the mountains. I had gone into a place that was worked by other herb collectors. I had two huge sacks of plants. I was ready to go home, but before I did I decided to take a moment's rest. I lay down on the side of the trail in the shade of a tree and I feel asleep. I heard then the sound of people coming down the hill and woke up. I hurriedly ran for cover and hid behind some bushes a short distance across the road from where I had fallen asleep. While I hid there I had the nagging impression I had forgotten something. I looked to see if I had my two sacks of plants. I didn't have them. I looked across the road to the place where I had been sleeping and I nearly dropped my pants with fright. I was still there asleep! It was me! I touched my body. I was myself! By that time the people that were coming down the hill were upon the me that was asleep, while the me that was fully awake looked helplessly from my hiding place. Damn it to hell! They were going to find me there and take my sacks away. But they went by me as if I were not there at all.[24]

In his description, Don Genaro wakes up in the dream (what we will later discuss as "lucid dreaming" in Chapter 9) and leaves his body behind. His body becomes as if dead, and he becomes its double, with the ability to look back at his body as if it were not there at all, as if he no longer existed in that form. Don Juan interprets this dream to Castaneda by suggesting that "you yourself are a dream, that your double is dreaming you in the same fashion that you dreamed him."[25] (This theme will emerge again in the next chapter when we discuss the dream of Chuang Tzu.) The point is that to Don Juan, more important than dreaming of one's own death is the process of controlling one's dreams in order to realize that one is not controlled by them. In this trans/formational process, the dreamer dies, as it were, to the ordinary dream, dies to the images of the dreaming ego, and wakes up to the double which operates independently of the dreamer's body. In this way, one can witness the ordinary dreamer's body being killed without fear or, if desired, alter the outcome of the dream. Such is the testimony, as well, of the following interview with a contemporary shaman.

AN URBAN SHAMAN

We conclude this chapter, appropriately enough, with fragments of an interview with Henry M., a young, urban shaman who lives in the frontier of awareness where unconscious imagery emerges into conscious thought. It was through a student at San Jose State University, who heard of our research, that we were led to Henry, a native American and student of comparative mythology and literature. As the interview began, in an outdoor cafe in downtown San Jose, Henry remarked: "That's what dreams are all about—making supra-swift, supra-creative connections into the unconscious." The following are fragments of that interview.

Henry: In my meditation, I go into dreams, but it's not sleep, I don't sleep. A lot of times my eyes don't close at all. It's not the same. It's not a repose. I don't have any deep sleep, you know. Once the journey is ended, I will come back.

Q: When you die like that, even in your latest dreams, are you ever . . . ?

A: I haven't died for a while.

Q: You haven't? How long?

A: February, the beginning of February. But that was—see, the beginning of February, I was in and out of, awake and not moving. A lot of the time during it, I was moving. You know, what happened in February was almost entirely different from anything that had happened before. It was not a meditation. I've been able to fragment myself. I stop the fragmentation at a certain point. So as far as I can tell, I was resisting, you know, in many different selves at the same time. I was seeing myself physically doing many different things. And when I go back, I can remember myself. I was on a beach. I was literally on a beach. I was sitting on a beach, at a fire. I was with a friend, you know; I was at a fire, and I started just wandering around the beach. After wandering around the beach, I started doing things. I started climbing cliffs, jumping off cliffs, watching myself down on the beach, watching different me's all over the place. I went out onto the road, looked at cars, saw myself get hit by cars, saw myself get hit by trains. You know, I fragmented my being out and then watched a lot of them die, a lot of them live, and just watched myself do this. Because I was experimenting. I took it to be nothing, the fragmentation, but I'd never stopped a fragment.

If my body fragments out into all these different selves, can I have all these selves? Do I know those selves, or are they just reflections of what was going on? I do not know. But I know when I got hit by a car, I saw myself hit the car and then I felt myself hitting the car. When I saw the train come by, I felt myself hit the train.

Q: Did you feel pain?

A: Yeah, I felt pain. Actually it was almost like there was me, except that I left it. But I don't think that—if it was me, I wasn't entirely successful, because I didn't create an equal balance between my selves. I had one self that kind of had all the rest tied to that one and was just watching them out there.

Q: You say you created this fragmentation of yourself?

A: Yes.

Q: How do you set this up initially? I mean, in your consciousness? Before you meditate/dream, as you are right now, do you say to yourself, "All right, now I am going to set this up as an experiment, or now I'm going to do this?" What is the "this" that you do?

A: Well, there's something outside of me. At least as far as I can tell, there is something outside of me. I don't—there is not a name for it that I can give. There is something outside of me that I can catch, it's almost like a wave, it's like a flow that you can catch, you know, that I can catch. You kind of wander with it for a little while and then you make a certain decision on it, a decision which you—to go with it, to let it go. And my decision was that I decided to go out in the ocean, and I climbed up on this rock, this cliff, and the quality of things, the quality changed in terms of I felt almost like a mythical person, like—the way I jumped out on the rock, the way I climbed the rock, got to the top of the rock, looked around, had this vision of dolphins. I had this vision of wanting to be a dolphin. I jumped off this rock and I didn't hit the ocean; I don't remember hitting the ocean. The next thing I remember, I was up on the road. I was going down the road, and when I did that, that's when the fragmentation—when

I got to the top of the cliff and made the decision to go off the cliff, it's that decision that allowed me to fragment. It was almost like hitting a barrier. When you make that decision, you are able to fragment your body kind of—not your body, your self. It kind of fragments, and I looked down and I could see myself crawling back up the beach, see myself in the water at the same time. It was not that many, but when I got to the road, there was a lot. I noticed a lot of me's I was seeing.

Later in the interview, Henry said: I had a dream while I was meditating; I don't know if I fell asleep or anything, but either way I had an adventure I guess you'd call it. Everything in the dream was red and black, no in between, just red or black, except me, I couldn't see myself. For some reason I didn't think that I was red or black. I was running across this desert, a dune desert.

Q: You were running across the desert and you couldn't see yourself?

A: No, I was running. When I first started running I was almost like a centaur, a horse. I pictured myself on a horse but there was no difference between me and the horse. We were one. We were running across the desert. It wasn't a desert like here in America, it was a dune desert, sand dunes, and the dunes were red and black, sometimes black shadows overlapping black shadows.

And I came across, first, a man who was—well, I was looking for something. It was something that I had lost, I remember that, I was looking for something else, searching for it. Because in the beginning of the dream—where I had set myself in the meditations wasn't where I realized I was—where I set myself was in a sweat lodge, an Indian sweat lodge, and I took all of my clothes, everything off, and put it aside. And when I came out of the sweat lodge, my *wasichus* (symbol) that I had been searching for was gone, and I got a horse and went, and that's what I was searching for.

And my *wasichus,* the way I pictured it is a panther, a black panther. And before that I had some experiences where I myself had transformed into a panther, just in meditation, transformed myself into the panther. While it was gone I ran after it into this desert. An old man told me—was singing almost, it was like a folk song, "It shall be or not shall be, it shall be or not shall be," he kept repeating. It was a song, a folk song. And I looked at him, and I think he was an older man, and he really reminded me of an old man. It was like you hear stories of certain beings that are among the human class that are acting really crazy—that's what it reminded me of.

So I kept going, and I came across a younger man who said—he told me I was going to die tonight, and that's all he said. I disregarded him and kept going.

Q: You didn't believe him, or you didn't want to believe him?

A: It didn't matter. It had no bearing on what I was doing. So I kept going. Suddenly I saw this woman, this beautiful silhouette. She wasn't dressed in anything, but her hair was as long as her body, just flowing in the wind. Her hair was going in one direction and she was pointing to another direction. Where she was pointing I looked and saw a panther, the panther leaping from the red and black. When it jumped into the black, I couldn't see it; when it jumped out into the red, I could see it. So I chased it for a long time, chased this panther across the dunes.

Finally I came across this mesa. I went toward the panther and it had the *wasichus* in its mouth. I went toward it and it was a female panther. I went to grab it, and the panther leaped at me and ate me. I was changing—perceiver and perceived—between me and the panther while I was being eaten or eating. And so I was dead and I sank into the sand, and the panther also sank into the sand. Well, I just got eaten and was eating.

Q: And the dream ended there?

A: No.

Q: Because you said you were eaten, and then you said, "and I sank into the sand." What "I"?

A: Both the panther and the body that was left, what was left of my body.

Q: But the panther was still alive?

A: Yeah. The panther was eating.

Q: As the panther/you are eating you, you the eaten are dead . . .

A: I wasn't really dead, because I'd gone into the panther, and the first slash gave me a dual image of things. Two things happened at once.

Q: So as soon as the panther first bit into you, then you became both?

A: Yes, I was both.

Q. Any feeling or emotions attached to this—like fear, anxiety?

A: I wouldn't say—it was eating.

Q: Was your picture of you seeing the panther and the body, after you were sinking into the sand—was it you from a detached standpoint watching the body and the panther sink, or were you actually switching back and forth watching each other sink?

A: Well, I was getting—until I saw—until at the end of that part I had one image of both sinking into the sand from a detached point of view. But before that, before that there was a duality. I couldn't really tell you which one I was seeing more or less.

And then I remember the panther. I don't remember the panther going into the sand, but the panther didn't run off, it was just gone, and then I remember coming out of the sand, rising out, and then at the same time seeing myself rise out of the sand, and I rose out of the sand. That's where I saw the sun. I don't think I remember seeing the sun at all before that. But I saw the sun.

Q: And did you have what you were looking for?

A: It didn't matter.

Q: Beautiful. Where was the sun then? Because I'm thinking, maybe you sank and came up in a different place and then you saw the sun.

A: No. It was the same hill, the exact same dune.

Q: I'm suggesting that after you sank, you came up in a different consciousness or trans/formed nature.

A: Yes, there was no doubt.

Q: What you were looking for in the first place was now no longer essential; in other words, you had found what you weren't looking for. You found something greater than what you thought you were looking for.

COMMENTARY

The human concern with dreams, and especially death dreams, is not new but, as ethnographic reports illustrate, is as ancient as human culture. This does not mean that there is agreement about the meaning and source of dreams among pre-literate peoples. In fact, the reverse is true. For the Australian Aborigines, life and death was believed to have originated in Dreamtime, in which the dreamer was united with the ancestors and connected to the correct nomadic path as well as the sacred meaning of death. For the Senoi, dreaming was an opportunity for the dreamer to confront adversaries, including death, with the help of allies, and to secure from the dream enemy a trans/formative gift. For the Yaqui Don Juan, the dreamer is also being dreamed, and it is therefore important to control one's dreams in order not to be controlled by them.

In tribal cultures, it was said that the shaman was the person (male or female) who possessed supernatural powers and who had access to helping spirits, psychic resources, visionary insights and ecstatic dispositions. Commonly, a shaman came into his or her powers through a dream or a series of dreams. Often the shaman would journey in dreams to the land of the dead in order to return with messages and special powers bestowed by the beings of the Beyond. The appearance of the dead in dreams convinced the shaman, and those who were empowered by the shaman's activities, that life does not end here on earth. Clearly, for the shaman and the Aborigine, if not as well for the Senoi, the landscape and the characters of dreams were not projections but realities reflected, as it were, from the other side of consciousness. Dreams thus were viewed as the region where those who have died return with messages from the dead which, because of the post-life perspective that they represent, bring with them a certain authority and illumination.

The ethnographic data which we have examined indicates that the interpretation of dreams was as important as dreaming itself. In fact, usually dreams were understood and acted upon in a manner consonant with their interpretation. We are met here by a question which appears throughout the book: What is the relationship between dreams and the interpretation of dreams? The ethnographic literature suggests that the "culture pattern dreams" were induced, sought after and interpreted trans/ formationally—especially death dreams. That is: for the Australian Aborigine, the myth of the origin of death and destiny of life arises in dreaming; for the Senoi, death in dreams releases a positive force within the dreamer; and for the Yaqui, the dreaming ego dies in lucid dreams and trans/forms into "the double" who is dreamed by the Self.

From the comparativist's point of view, a fundamental question which arises while studying ethnographic traditions is where to locate the origin of, or earliest evidence for, religious life. While there is no final agreement among scholars about the earliest source—some pointing to *mana* (a force or power), some to *totem* (an object of awe), some to *animism* (the presence of spirits), some to a High Being—we have highlighted here Edward Taylor's view that the religious impulse arose in early peoples' reflection on dreams and death. For Taylor, the fact that the dead appeared in dreams and visions, and often brought messages vital to the living, leads to two significant insights: (1) that souls transmigrate from this life to the next, and (2) that powerful spirits, of nobler and baser origin, became important sources of guidance. Shamans were among the earliest practitioners to develop techniques for traveling between the two worlds. To them, dreams (especially dreams of the dead) were not unreal fantasies, but revelations of the spirit-filled nature of reality. Death dream experiences then can be said to be one of the earliest components of pre-historic religion. They both reminded the dreamer of life's finitude, and pointed to the possibility of human trans/formation from dissociative actions and emotions to disciplined, focused responses, especially in the face of death.

In the next chapter we shift from pre-literate cultures to literate ones, from oral traditions to written ones, from anthropological materials to sacred texts. More specifically, in the next two chapters we will explore how the so-called eastern religious traditions (Chapter 4) and the so-called western religious traditions (Chapter 5) view death in dreams. Our purpose, as it was in this chapter, will be to expand the context in which we examine death dreams by viewing ways in which the world's sacred traditions reflect on the human unconscious in general, and upon death dreams in particular. Are death dreams to be feared, avoided, or interpreted negatively as the result of repressed anxieties, the dread of one's own mortality, or even the influence of demonic forces? Or is there anything positive, liberating, or even revelatory about the nature of human destiny involved in such dreams?

NOTES

[1]A traditional craft myth quoted in Starhawk's *The Spiral Dance: A Rebirth of the Ancient Religion of the Great Goddess* (San Francisco: Harper & Row, 1979), 159–160.

[2]The distinction between "primitive" and "civilized" or "literate" cultures is one based in part on a different understanding and interpretation of such processes as dreams and death, and in the ensuing myths, legends and supernatural beliefs that these produced. For instance, some anthropologists argue that pre-literate cultures do not distinguish between dream and reality

(e.g. Taylor), while others suggest that the dream experience is given a greater value than ordinary events. Jackson S. Lincoln in *The Dream in Primitive Cultures* (London: Cresset Press, 1935) writes that numerous religious beliefs have been generated "largely on dreams of the dead" such as "beliefs in immortality, in spirits, and in the soul's arising" as well as in "ancestor worship and the idea of transmigration of souls" (49).

[3]Sir Edward B. Taylor, "A Primitive View of Dreams," contained in *The New World of Dreams,* edited by Ralph L. Woods and Herbert B. Greenhouse (New York: Macmillan, 1974), 111–112.

[4]Bronislaw Malinowski, "The Dream Is the Cause of the Wish," *ibid.,* 119.

[5]To avoid delving into the etymological and etiological nuances of these terms, we will follow the practice of some American anthropologists and refer to the "shamanic complex" which includes the activities of both. Of the functions or powers which characterize the shamanic, two main types emerge: the ecstatic (one who, in deep trance, departs from his or her own body, and at times is possessed by guardian spirits), and the visionary (one whose trance, if any, is light and who exhibits a clairvoyance) or perception of non-present objects.

[6]Quoted in *The Dream in Primitive Cultures, op. cit.,* 71.

[7]Quoted in Holger Kalweit, *Dreamtime and Inner Space: The World of the Shaman* (Boulder: Shambhala Publications, Inc., 1984), 8.

[8]The Canadian Tlingit Eskimos call the soul Quatuwu, "That which feels." Therefore, when a person loses all feeling, he is considered dead, because he is seen as having lost his soul. So when the shaman separates his soul from his body in his travels to the Beyond, his body had "died."

[9]Quoted in *The Dream in Primitive Cultures, op. cit.,* 42. Other leading categories were sexual (18), food and eating (14), fighting (12), animals (12), journeying (10), and falling (9).

[10]Quoted in *Dreamtime and Inner Space, op. cit.,* 46.

[11]David Chidester, *Patterns of Transcendence: Religion, Death and Dying* (Belmont: Wadsworth Publishing Co., 1990), 50–51.

[12]See Kenneth Maddock, *The Australian Aborigines: A Portrait of Their Society* (London: Allen Lane/Penguin Press, 1972), and

K.L. Parker, *The Euahlayi Tribe: A Study of Aboriginal Life in Australia* (London: A. Costable, 1905).

[13]Charles Tart, "From Spontaneous Event to Lucidity: A Review of Attempts to Consciously Control Nocturnal Dreaming," in *Conscious Mind, Sleeping Brain: Perspectives on Lucid Dreaming,* edited by Jayne Gackenbach and Stephen LaBerge (New York: Plenum Press, 1988), 98.

[14]Kilton Stewart's "Dream Theory in Malaya," in Charles T. Tart's *Altered States of Consciousness* (New York: John Wiley & Sons, Inc., 1969), 162. According to anthropologist Robert Dentan, who traveled to Malaysia to corroborate Stewart's findings, Stewart's claim that the Senoi had evolved an elaborate understanding and reliance on dreams is not fully true. Dentan, however, did say that dreams do play an important role in Senoi life, but not to the extent that Stewart contended. G. William Donhoff, psychology and sociology professor at UC Santa Cruz, suggested in "The Mystique of Dreams" that it was Stewart, not the Senoi, who first proposed dream control. Yet, Stewart's findings appear to be congruent with other ethnographic traditions, especially with the Hawaiian Kahuna beliefs that one can change one's life and even one's destiny, by creating what one wants in dreams.

[15]*Ibid.,* 164.

[16]Patricia L. Garfield, *Creative Dreaming* (New York: Simon and Schuster, 1974), 137.

[17]Tart, *op. cit.,* 162.

[18]Among the critical responses to Castaneda, some have contended that his work is not of an anthropological nature but is, rather, more creative and should be read as a fictional narrative. R.E. DeMille, an ethnobotanist, in *Castaneda's Journey: The Power and the Allegory* (Santa Barbara: Capra Press, 1976), claims that the flora and fauna Castaneda describes in the Sonoran desert are suspiciously inaccurate. Stephen LaBerge in *Lucid Dreaming* (New York: Ballantine Books, 1985) questions Castaneda's account of the world of dreaming. He suggests that it is impossible to discern whether Castaneda's works are "fictional nonfiction" or "nonfiction fiction" (58). While one can arguably challenge Castaneda's data, it should be kept in mind that the material he presents stretches anthropological categories toward

allegory, even mysticism, and therefore should not be dismissed simply on the basis of its unusual conceptualizations. We choose here to examine his writing as if it is a true reporting of data gathered by a researcher who, no matter how far he wanders beyond academically sanctioned categories, at least began his search (in his mind) as a cultural anthropologist.

[19]Castaneda, *Journey to Ixtlan* (New York: Simon and Schuster, 1972), 160.

[20]*Ibid.*, 54.

[21]*Ibid.*, 55.

[22]Carlos Castaneda, *The Eagle's Gift* (New York: Washington Square Press, 1987), 249.

[23]Carlos Castaneda, *Tales of Power* (New York: Simon and Schuster, 1974), 81. Earlier Don Juan has specified that all "luminous beings" have a double, that "the double is oneself" (61), that "the double can perform acts" (63), and that "the double begins in dreaming" (67). For further details see Castaneda's *The Second Ring of Power* (New York: Simon and Schuster, 1977), especially Chapter Five.

[24]*Ibid.*, 68.

[25]*Ibid.*, 82.

Chapter 4 EASTERN RELIGIOUS TRADITIONS

> Takkan was dying. His disciples asked that he write a death poem. He refused, but when they insisted, he wrote the character YUME (Dream), and died.[1]

To place this chapter in its most profound context, let us begin by paraphrasing a remark made by Stephen LaBerge of the Stanford University Sleep Research Center on an audiotape called "Controlling Your Dreams": Our ordinary dreams stand in relation to lucid dreams (dreams in which the dreamer is aware of dreaming) as our ordinary consciousness stands in relation to lucid consciousness. Provocative in its own right, the implications of this statement underlie much of the data of this chapter which briefly explores eastern religious attitudes toward death dreams. The first two sections introduce the early Hindu tradition, while the third and fourth depict the later developments of Zen Buddhist and Tibetan dream analysis. In the last section, we will consider in some detail a well-known Chinese example of dreaming in which the identity of the dreamer dies.

VISHNU'S DREAM

Ancient India developed at least three approaches to, or expressions about, dreaming—the mythic, the philosophic, and the yogic—which inform a richly varied constellation of theory and practice. In fact, to the extent that India is the origin of subsequent Eurasian cultures, one can compare her to a deep, mysterious region (not unlike the unconscious), from which the religio-philosophic and mytho-poetic scriptures of the east arise.

The earliest Indic references to death and dreams are found in the myths of the beginnings of the universe—myths found in the *Rig Veda* (written around 1200 BCE). Early Hindu sages (the rishis) produced a plethora of tales which attempted to pierce through the mysterious unknown at "The Beginning."[2] For our purposes, the most notable of all the Indic creation myths is that of the lord of sleep, Vishnu. Vishnu (the preserver), the second of the triune Vedic godhead—besides Brahma (the creator), and Shiva (the destroyer)—is depicted in the *Vedas* as the universal dreamer. Described as floating on a cosmic milky ocean, Vishnu is crouched upon the coils of Amanta, the abyssal serpent whose name means "Unending." Vishnu is said to dream the universe into being.

Also pictured are the five Pandava brothers (including Arjuna, the hero of *The Bhagavad Gita*), along with their mutual wife, Draupadi. With their eyes open, and ready to fight, one could say that they are being dreamed into being by Vishnu, that they are the content of Vishnu's dream. Or can we? Joseph Campbell writes, "Are these youths, we might ask, a dream of that luminous god, or is the god a dream of these youths?"[3] Campbell's question is not one of idle speculation or whimsical curiosity. It is a question, as we shall see by the end of the chapter, which has haunted eastern dream attitudes from the beginning. Is the entire world dreamed into being by a god, or is that very god who dreams the world the result of a sleeper's dream?

When one shifts from a mythic to a philosophical approach, this question is deepened by another which appears in ancient Indian texts. Are dreams merely the projection of the dreamer's unconscious thoughts and ideas? In *Dreams, Illusions and Other Realities,* Wendy Doniger O'Flaherty suggests that projection in the Hindu context literally means to "emit," the way for example a spider emits a web. She quotes from an Upanishadic text which, she suggests, passes no judgment on projection other than to understand the relationship between the two worlds as equally real and unreal.

> A man has two conditions: in this world and in the world beyond. But there is also a twilight juncture: the condition of sleep [or dream, 'svapna']. In this twilight juncture one sees both of the other conditions, this world and the other world. ... When someone falls asleep, he takes the stuff of the entire world, and he himself takes it apart, and he himself builds it up, and by his own bright light he dreams. ... There are no chariots there, no harnessings, no roads; but he emits char-

iots, harnessings, and roads. There are no joys, happinesses, or delights there; but he emits joys, happinesses, and delights. There are no ponds, lotus pools, or flowing streams there, but he emits ponds, lotus pools, and flowing streams. For he is the Maker ['Kartr'].[4]

In this passage, the key phrase is by "his own bright light." It is by that light that a person disassembles the images of this world and rearranges them into images of the other world.

A-U-M

When we reach the era of the *Upanishads* (c. 700 BCE), the place of dreams is presented in a more precise way. In the *Mandukya Upanishad,* the primal *mantra* (or sacred sound) of "AUM" (or "OM") is presented as an acronym for the four states of consciousness. Each of the letters—"A", "U" and "M"—along with the resonance of their totality (represented by three dots) stands for one of the four stages of consciousness, or four quarters of Brahman.

AUM

For all this [world] is Brahman. The Self is Brahman. This
Self has four quarters. . . .

The waking state, conscious . . . of what is without, seven-
limbed, with nineteen mouths, experiencing what is gross,
common to all men . . . is the first quarter. . . .

The state of dream, conscious of what is within, seven-
limbed, with nineteen mouths, experiencing what is subtle,
composed of light . . . is the second quarter. . . .

When a man is asleep and desires nothing whatever,
dreams no dream, that is deep sleep.

The state of deep sleep, unified, a very mass of wisdom
. . . composed of bliss, experiencing bliss, with thought as its
mouth, wise . . . is the third quarter. . . .

Consciousness . . . of neither within nor without, nor of
both together, not a mass of wisdom . . . neither wise nor
unwise, unseen, one with whom there is no commerce, im-
palpable, devoid of distinguishing mark, unthinkable, inde-
scribable, its essence the firm conviction of the oneness of
itself, bringing all development . . . to an end, tranquil and
mild, devoid of duality, such do they seem this fourth to be.
That is the Self: that is what should be known.[5]

In the first state (the waking state), one knows cognitively
what is outside and what is common to everyone's perception—
so-called *maya*. In Hindu thought, the term *maya* (the so-called
stuff of reality, or all that is) is often translated as "illusion," in
the sense of a measured out, documented reality. One is subject
to a false attachment to *maya* because of *avidya* (beginningless
ignorance of the true identity, both of self and world), and therefore suffers within what might be called a *maya*-induced habit
of mind.

To illustrate this, the story is told of a man who, in a dream,
is being chased by a tiger. Seeing a nearby tree, he climbs it to
avoid sure death—or to at least postpone it, for the tiger merely
lies down beneath the tree and waits for the man to fall from its
branches. The sage's question is, "What is the way out of this predicament?" And the answer is, "Only one—*wake up!*" Just as
waking from nightmares displaces fears of dying in the dream,
by consciously awakening to one's true self one is liberated from
fearing death in life.

In the second (the dreaming state), one knows privately what is inside the unconscious imagination, and may, as well, be given a glimpse of the god who dreams existence into being. More likely, in the dreaming state the mind is filled with desires and wishes (including the possible desire to thwart desires), regrets and fear and various objects of sensory perception. But how does dreaming occur?

Indic psychology is based on a distinction between the gross body (physical, exterior, surface consciousness), and the subtle body (ethereal, interior, sub-surface consciousness). While the gross body is materially oriented, the subtle body is an extremely sensitive, interior double which is comprised of breath or energy (*prana*). When we dream, only the gross body is asleep. Awareness, in dreams, withdraws from the gross body and consolidates in the subtle domain. Dreaming, from this point of view, is the activation of subtle body consciousness which is covered over (or asleep, so to speak) when we are awake. Analogously, liberation is achieved when one is detached from the gross body in waking consciousness.

In the third stage (of deep, dreamless sleep), there is neither desire nor dream, but rather a glimpse of the truth of undifferentiated consciousness. The sleeper, in this state, knows nothing—neither within nor without, neither of dreams nor of conscious perceptions. The mind is wholly quiet. Normal ego-functions are temporarily suspended. As the *Upanishads* indicate, in dreamless sleep there is neither king nor pauper, neither male nor female, neither wise nor foolish.

The fourth state (neither outward nor inward, neither cognitive nor imaginative), is called the Self (*atman*). At the heart of the *Upanishads*, the *jiva* (individual soul), and the *atman/Brahman* (cosmic soul), are said to be one, and through the stages of hearing the truth, thinking about the truth, and meditating on the truth, one is able to realize truth about one's existence and the reality of one's death. This realization of true self is beyond waking consciousness and beyond sleep and dreams, for it is a *non-dualistic* actualization (which includes everything by excluding nothing). This is the Self which the *Upanishads* calls beginningless and endless, which does not come into being at birth nor die at death, and which is the goal of yogic practice.

The whole point of this four-fold analysis, of course, is to pass through the first three (or preliminary) states of consciousness—waking, dreaming, and dreamless sleep—in order to reach Absolute Reality. At the same time, "since all four stages are regarded as progressive approaches toward what is most real (the Godhead), some Indic philosophers assume that dreaming is more 'real' than waking." This is because "in dreams one sees both the real ('*sat*') and the unreal ('*asat*')."[6] As we have seen, in the *Brihadarnyaka Upanishad,* when asked by Vaideha—"Who is that Self?"—Yagnavalkya replied: it is "The person of light" who is "within the heart," the person who is "self-illuminated."[7]

In the final analysis, however, the dream must be transcended. To realize the truth of the universe, and in the process of oneself, one must journey beyond dreams. Therefore, to dream of one's own death, or the death of another, might be viewed as an illusion equal in its deception to one's conscious fear of death. Death is finally, according to a Hindu worldview, a kind of collective hallucination with no reality behind its mask.

THERAVADAN BUDDHISTS

According to a Buddhist legend, Queen Maya conceived her son, Siddhartha Gautama, in a dream. While on a spiritual retreat in the Himalayan Mountains, she dreamed one evening that a white elephant with four tusks (the Hindu god, Ganesha), descended from the heavens. Upon reaching the earth, he circled her bed three times and then struck her right side with his trunk. At that moment, the Buddha entered her womb. (It was likewise in a dream that Mary was told by an angel that she would bear a son by the power of the Holy Spirit.)

While dreams play a significant role in Buddha's own story—in fact, Gautama experienced several significant dreams just prior to his enlightenment—it is more interesting to note the radical non-distinction between waking and dreaming developed in the Buddhist tradition. Dreaming "per se" for Buddhists was deemphasized since dreams were thought to be the result of worldly attachments, past lives and bodily sensations. Even

Maya's Dream

dreams of the Buddha were not given any special religious significance, as they were viewed as a product of the thinking mind.

Most ancient of all Buddhist schools is the Theravadan
(tradition of the elders) which is said to transmit the original
teachings of the Buddha. To a large degree, Theravadan monks
were unimpressed with dreams, because they included images
and sensations which, as in waking consciousness, had no self-
existence. Dreams were said to be of two varieties: *inauspicious*
(delusioned dreams occurring during various periods of sleep),
and *auspicious* (prophetic dreams occurring in the early morning).

Inauspicious dreams were said to be composed of attachments to greed, anger, and ignorance. "Defilements" of this sort
are apparently produced by the delusioned mind from negative

karmic tendencies which come to surface in the unmindful consciousness. Further bodily sensations (e.g. hunger or illness) are also possible causes. From the Theravadan standpoint, dreams are generally ignored because the attachments which they express hinder one's spiritual condition. In fact, human experience is often characterized by Theravadans and other Buddhist schools as a dream from which one must awaken.

When interpreting the more auspicious dreams (those which can either instruct or inspire one's spiritual condition), the Theravadans maintained that they were not actually distinct from "ordinary" (inauspicious) dreams, other than what the dreamer made of them. The same dream in a dozen other individuals, for instance, might not arouse the same meaningfulness. Similarly, dreams of the Buddha were generally given no collective religious meaning other than what the dreamer envisioned it to be. Insights, when they do occur, can be seen as originating from the same internal source as meditative insights, though on rare occasions such visions may be deliberately imbedded into a dreamer's mind by the conscious influence of a spiritual master.

ZEN'S WAKING-DREAMING

We are now ready to consider two Buddhist developments in Indic dream theory—Zen and Tibetan Buddhism—each of which elicits the phenomenon of death.

More important than dream theory or interpretation (in the Zen Buddhist tradition) is the significance of the relationship between waking and dreaming. Questions—e.g. Who dreams when I dream? Is dreaming a function of sleep, or can sleep be a function of dreaming? Do enlightened people dream? And what is the distinction, if any, between waking reality and dreaming reality?—are answered by the following Zen stories.

Emperor Taishu of the Sung dynasty dreamed one night of a god who appeared and advised him to arouse his yearning for enlightenment. In the morning the Emperor summoned the official priest and asked, "How can I arouse yearning for enlightenment?" The priest made no reply.[8]

The priest made no reply because the desire for enlightenment was already aroused by the dream experience, itself not different from waking experience. In the Zen tradition, this would be considered as a type of death dream for at least two reasons. First, it indicates the necessity of a death to the dreamer's old self-identity, and, second, it points to the necessity of the enlightenment experience which, as we will see, involves passing through death while alive.

In the second story:

> There was once a monk who was met by a well-known teacher in a cemetery, weeping at the edge of a tomb because he had been kicked out of his house, and driven from his village. When asked why, he replied: "Because I like to sleep! I sleep all the time. I wake up to eat, and then I go back to sleep. I really love to sleep!"
>
> "Well you're a lucky man," said the master. "Don't you know that sleeping can be the pathway to Buddhahood?"
>
> So the teacher initiated him in a sleep yoga. He told him to mix his sleep with the *dharma-kaya* [suchness or "being-body"] and death. He taught him to study the transition from waking to sleeping consciousness as the transition from *nirma-kaya* [transformation body] to *dharma-kaya,* and to withdrawing the emanation of consciousness into *dharma-kaya,* into the clear light of *dharma-kaya* emptiness. He taught him to move from sleeping through compassion into dream, and to accomplish the aims of living beings through the subtle body of the dream. Then he taught him to withdraw those emanations back into the *dharma-kaya* of sleep and then to re-arise in a waking body. The master encouraged him therefore to spend as much time as possible asleep.
>
> So the monk slept for twelve years, after which by the practice of this yoga, he achieved perfect enlightenment.[9]

Clearly this is an unorthodox, and highly creative, approach to enlightenment. Through sleep and disciplined dreaming, the monk was able to die to that which kept him from waking to his true self.

Simply put, the Zen tradition speaks not of one, but of two deaths—ordinary death at the termination of this life, and extraordinary death, or *Great Death* in the midst of this life. Zen is one of the few traditions whose major practice is to live as though thoroughly dead. This experience is termed the Great Death. It is the Great Death that Siddhartha actualized under the Bodhi Tree, and to which the entire history of Buddhist spiritual practice has pointed ever since. In Zen, the Great Death means dying to ordinary, dualistically conditioned consciousness in which: I am I, I am not you, and I am not not-I. Dying to all ideas of self, to all dualistic clingings, to all dependency on the patriarchs, is the expression of Zen's awakening.

When the Great Death (which is the Great Birth) is achieved, the dualistic self (i.e. the internal division between self as subject and self as object) has been annihilated. One becomes not-self, or selfless self. Now, in Zen's illogical logic: I am I, and I am you, and I am not-I. In this mode of awareness, there is no struggle between life and death, for one is both fully alive (I am I, and I

Enso

am you), and fully dead (I am not-I) at the same time. The Great Death uncovers what Zen calls the "Original Face"—the nature of self before God said: "Let there be Light!" In Zen, therefore, it is said that a person who dies (spiritually) before dying (physically) never dies again.

The most significant aspect of this Great Death, for our study, is that it points to *a fully-living, fully-dying, eternal moment.* As Zen Buddhist philosopher Masao Abe has indicated: "One should not speak of 'life and death' but 'living-dying' which is a process without beginning and without end."[10] Abe further states that to achieve "transformation" in Buddhism (i.e. from *samsara* to *nirvana*), one must clearly realize:

(1) the non-duality of life and death;
(2) the beginninglessness and endlessness of our living-dying;
(3) the total living-dying at this moment of the absolute present.

By analogy, therefore, one may be able to view death dreams (or all dreams) as not different from enlightenment:

(1) the non-duality of waking and dreaming;
(2) the beginninglessness and endlessness of our waking and dreaming states;
(3) the total waking-dreaming presence at this absolute present.[11]

In this sense it is sometimes said: "A Zen master does not dream." Perhaps this is because the master has already died to his or her attachments, to worldly concerns and to dualistic thinking which separates waking from dreaming. Thus, dreaming is waking as waking is dreaming.

In the Rinzai Zen school, a favorite spiritual practice (often mistaken as a method) is called the *koan* (a totally illogical puzzle/riddle or challenge to ordinary dualistic consciousness). For example: "Without speaking and without not speaking— speak!" A *koan* is given to a student with the intention of driving the dualistically calculating mind temporarily out of commis-

sion. *Koans* force the human proclivity toward intellectualization
to exhaust itself, once and for all.

A monk once asked Joshu: "Has a dog Buddha-nature, or
not?" Said Joshu, "Mu!" (No or Nothingness). D.T. Suzuki was
given this *mu* by his master as a *koan,* and he was instructed to
think of it regardless of what else he was doing or where he was.
Suzuki reports that when he finally ceased being conscious of
mu, he became one with Mu, so that there was no longer any
separation between himself and his no-self. The solution to the
Zen koan, in other words, does not pertain to the language of
one's answer, but to the *realization* beneath (or prior to) language.

This is an extremely significant point, for it refers to the
deepest level in Buddhist psychology—absolute *alaya* consciousness. As the chart illustrates, there are at least four levels of mind:
empirical thought (ignorance-bound), consciousness, the unconscious (both personal and collective), and pure, formless
self-consciousness (absolute *alaya*). The mind, like the ocean,
contains many unconscious undercurrents. Suzuki's realization
of *mu* is not a rising up of unconscious emptiness, but rather the

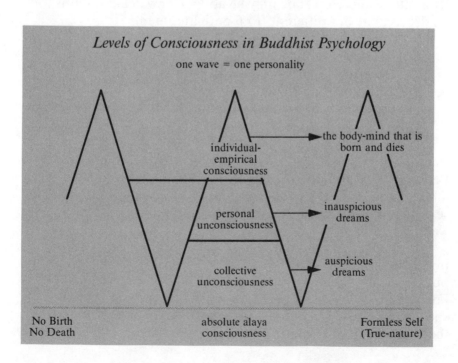

Levels of Consciousness in Buddhist Psychology

one wave = one personality

individual-
empirical
consciousness

the body-mind that is
born and dies

personal
unconsciousness

inauspicious
dreams

collective
unconsciousness

auspicious
dreams

No Birth
No Death

absolute alaya
consciousness

Formless Self
(True-nature)

actualization of the still-point source of both consciousness and the unconscious. Zen Buddhist philosopher Nishida described *alaya* consciousness this way:

> There's something bottomless
> Within me I feel.
> However disturbing are the waves
> Of joy and sorrow,
> They fail to reach it.[12]

The use of koans is aimed at plunging one's mind down through layers of consciousness to the bottomless, formless storehouse from which all forms arise.

In his book *Clinical Use of Dreams,* James Hall writes that he has noted occasional dreams in his studies which he calls "koan dreams." For example, one man who had practiced Zen meditation in Japan dreamed:

> I was in Philadelphia, in the train station, desperately trying to find someone who could tell me what train to take to get to Philadelphia.[13]

What is this dream saying? At first it appears to be a flat contradiction. It seems to pose an illogical situation. But in Zen terms, this is not the case. Like the well-known koan "What is the sound of one hand clapping?" this has no logical answer. Rather its answer is contained in its question. How am I to be fully "present" when I am not that I am! In Zen, the way is to pass through the door of (spiritual) death in order to be reborn, truly, where one always, already is—empty and meaning-less—whether dreaming or awake.

TIBETAN DREAM-LIKE FORMS

For Tibetan Buddhists, the analysis of recurring dreams or visions (by use of *analytical* meditation) helps one come to understand personal attachments in order to destroy them. Tibetans perceive the anger and fear of death dreams as general falsities, just as the self is false, and the cycle of life and death is also inevitably a hallucination. Since liberation involves a recognition of impermanence incorporated into one's lifestyle, an insightful spiritual master would be in control of his dream state, and would no longer need review of the law of impermanence. Similarly, a monk would hope to refrain from dreaming of death, since such dreams reveal non-virtuous defilements of weaknesses (i.e. anger and fear) which the monk would be obliged to purge.

If early Hindu texts approached dreams mythically, and later Hindu and Buddhist texts approached dreams more philosophically, Tibetan texts shift their faces to a yogic approach. No living tradition has paid more undivided attention to death and its dream connection than Tibetan Buddhism—so much so, in fact, that Tibetan Buddhists have developed a manual of instruction—for the dead, the dying, and the living—in order to help prepare one for the "bardo" state (the state between death and rebirth). *The Tibetan Book of the Dead* presents details of three "bardos" or interim states through which consciousness passes: the "Chikai Bardo" which depicts the psychic events at the moment of death, the "Chonyi Bardo" which details dreamlike forms and apparitions, and the "Sipai Bardo" which concerns the rebirth instinct and how the new womb is chosen at rebirth. We will return to *The Tibetan Book of the Dead* in a moment, but first we must place our discussion of this venerable text in a larger context, that of human trans/formation.

Death, for Tibetans, instead of an event to be resisted, feared, and denied, is rather an opportunity for self-liberation. Therefore, one of the most important spiritual techniques taught by Tibetan masters is that of Death meditation (*Ge-she Nga-wang Dar-gye*). In *The Sutra of Buddha's Entering into Parinirvana,* it is written:

> Of all footprints,
> That of the elephant is supreme. Similarly,
> Of all mindfulness meditations,
> That on death is supreme.[14]

But how does one meditate on death? Tibetan culture developed a number of responses to that question, of which we will mention three: one that is practiced while in good health, one practiced in both good health and at death, and, lastly, a technique practiced as one is dying. The point of each method is the same—to achieve liberation.

The first technique is known as "the death simulation process." In it, the practitioner visualizes himself or herself lying in bed, surrounded by friends and relatives, awaiting imminent death. You imagine yourself as a dying person with a faded countenance, dry lips, a shrunken body, and a foul taste in your mouth. You become colder, more numb. Your breathing becomes more difficult. Negative thoughts and fears arise in your mind. Then you recall a prayer, a *mantra,* or a verse of scripture, which speaks of the path to enlightenment.

The second technique which is practiced both during life, as well as at the moment of death, is called the "transference (or ejection) of consciousness." In fact, *The Tibetan Book of the Dead* begins by specifying that as death approaches, one should "apply the Transference, which conferreth liberation by merely remembering [the process]."[15] Its translator, W.Y. Evans-Wentz, notes that liberation in this context is a liberation of the "life-flux" from the dying body. For the more proficient yogi, this process is employed "to prevent any break in the flow of the stream of consciousness, from the moment of conscious death to the moment of a conscious rebirth."[16]

From the Tibetan viewpoint the dying moment is filled with beauty and peace. It is the reverse of the process of birth. Everything in life is summed up in this moment. Thus *The Tibetan Book of the Dead* stresses cultivating the proper last thoughts, for one's mental condition at death is likely to be retained after death. In this last moment the True Self can most directly be revealed. By means of the ejection of consciousness, practitioners learn how to shoot awareness up the spine through the crown of the head into the visualized Buddha, and in this way to enter the Clear Light realm. Of course, it is not necessary to wait until death is near to begin such a practice. In fact, Tibetans bring death in an anticipatory way into life through this practice of transferring consciousness while yet alive. The more adept at this transference one becomes in life, the easier it becomes to accomplish just at the moment of death.

Meditator

The third technique, also practiced as one is dying, is called "observing the signs of death." As one approaches death, it is essential to watch for death's signals as a way of controlling one's thoughts and directing one's attention. Initially, one observes the outer signs of death which are associated with the four elements:

(1) the disintegration of the "earth element": the powers of sight and limbs fail;
(2) the disintegration of the "water element": the powers of feeling and perspiration fail;
(3) the disintegration of the "fire element": the powers of smell, memory, and body heat fade;
(4) the disintegration of the "air element": the powers of volitional formation and taste fails.

While this is occurring, one's inner signs are read in two ways—by observing the breath and observing one's dreams.

Ideally, the breath is to be observed at the rising of a new moon, especially on days and months of equal length. Should the breath flow solely through either a left or right nostril, one still has up to six months to live. Should the breath flow through both nostrils, or pass solely through the mouth, then an imminent death is assumed.

Dreams are an essential part of this method of preparing for death, especially if they occur between midnight and dawn. It is considered a sure sign of death if one dreams of the following:

- riding the back of a red cat or monkey;
- climbing red hills;
- being naked and having your hair cut off;
- being killed by a king;
- riding south on the back of a tiger, or a wolf, or a corpse;
- running downhill dressed in black;
- being caught and chained;
- eating excrement;
- having sex with a black demoness.[17]

Dreaming of these images alerts the dreamer that death is imminent, that it should not be resisted and that preparations must be in earnest. This emphasis on practicing death meditations and on observing the signs of one's own death has a two-fold purpose: first, to ascertain whether the signs are merely preliminary and thereby reversible; second, in the event of imminent death, to begin immediately the Yoga of Transference of Consciousness, and to begin group readings from *The Tibetan Book of the Dead*. From the Tibetan viewpoint, either one or both of the choices open the possibility of trans/forming the death experience from one that results in a lower rebirth, to one that achieves rebirth in the celestial realms (or Pure Land—if not a full liberation and *nirvana*).

Let us look more closely at the dying process. At the moment of death, empirical consciousness is lost, and in its place arises, no matter how briefly, the Clear Light of the Void. Formless, colorless, spaceless, empty of all characteristics (including emptiness itself), those who have the power to recognize it, to enter and rest in it, are reborn. At that moment, "all things are like the void and colorless sky, and the naked, spotless intellect is like unto a transparent vacuum without circumference or centre."[18] This is the state of pure enlightenment awakening to itself.

However, since most people's life-formed, "karmic" tendencies have not yet been dissolved by yogic practices, one is awakened to the "Second Bardo," where visions and hallucinations take on a dream-like quality. Depending upon one's training and spiritual practice, or lack thereof, these dream-forms will differ in content (i.e. between a Christian's Heaven, or a Muslim's Paradise, or a Buddhist's Pure Land). What does not vary, however, is their dream-like state. Multitudes of forms now appear: the so-called "Peaceful Deities" (male and female Bodhisattvas) and the so-called "Wrathful Deities" (evil and frightful forms). It is for this reason that words from *The Tibetan Book of the Dead* are read into the ear of the dead person, even for several days after his or her medical death, words like:

> May I recognize whatever appears [visions], as the reflections of mine own consciousness; May I know them to be of the nature of apparitions in the bardo.[19]

and like:

> Indeed, all these are like dreams, like hallucinations, like echoes . . . like mirages, like mirrored forms, like phantasmagora, like the moon seen in water—not real even for a moment.[20]

So it would seem from these teachings in *The Tibetan Book of the Dead* that Tibetans would be largely disinterested in the dream state. Yet this is not the case. In fact, the opposite is true. Tibetan *tantra* (esoteric yoga) points to an intimate correspondence between yoga and the enlightened body of Buddhahood. For instance, among the most highly regarded tantric practices in Tibet are the "Six Yogas of Naropa," which prepare the yogi's body for the trans/formation into the Buddha. The six yogas include: Mystic Heat Yoga, Illusory Body Yoga, Dream Yoga, Clear Light Yoga, Bardo Yoga, and Consciousness Transference Yoga.

The core of *Dream Yoga* is what Naropa calls the "recognition of dream," the achievement of which depends upon the practitioner's removal of all obstacles to Awareness, and "thinking continuously in the waking state that all he sees, hears, touches, thinks, and acts upon, are in a dream."[21] Dream yoga can be said to be a special type of death dream in which "the dreamer" dies to obstacles which keep him or her from recognizing that the dream is a dream. Naropa's practice involves holding steadily to the apparitions of existence as one falls asleep, and keeping one's attention focused on the center of the throat or "Throat Chakra" (one of the seven subtle psycho-spiritual energy centers). Of course, the yogi should avoid rich foods, overeating, and should not be exhausted by over-strenuous activities. A thin quilt and a high pillow are used to promote dream recall. If one cannot accomplish this, he or she should remove all clothing, jump and run about in the nude, and shout loudly, "This is a dream!" In the same way, when one encounters a frightening dream (or death dream), one should say to oneself, "This is a dream!"

The next step in *Dream Yoga* is called "Transformation of Dreams." In the dream state, the dreamer is encouraged to try to change his or her body into that of a bird, an animal, a Brahman ("holy person"), a noble person, or a "Buddha body" in one of various forms. Dreamers are encouraged to trans/form dream objects into people and vice versa, or to multiply the dreamer's body into millions of bodies. By now, it may be clear that "one of the main purposes of *Dream Yoga* practice is to assist one to realize the Illusory Body in the Bardo state, and in this lifetime."[22] In other words, by practicing this type of death dreaming—in which the dreamer becomes someone else—the untrue nature of the dreaming body is realized.

The more advanced one becomes, the more fun one can have by practicing the journey to Buddha's lands, as instructed in the following paragraph:

Visualize oneself as becoming the Patron Buddha, and instantaneously, like a shooting star, arrive in the Heaven of Indra, or some other Samsaric Heaven; observe the place before returning. When this is stabilized, one should then

journey to one of the Buddha's Pure Lands, such as the Pure
Land of Vairocana of Amitabha, or the like. This, too, is done
in a split second. Reaching Buddha's Pure Land, he should
make obeisance and offerings to the Buddha and listen to
His preaching.[23]

Dream Yoga, then, according to Naropa's instructions, is to
be practiced in order to complement conscious yoga—each of
which leads the practitioner to purify habitual thoughts, to realize the illusion of all forms (waking and dreaming) as manifestations of the mind, and to cleanse oneself of all attachments,
even of attachments to Nirvana. Translator Herbert Guenther
writes: "In a wider context the dream state, as in between the
events of falling asleep and awakening, is significantly compared with the intermediate state between death and rebirth." He
adds: "Falling asleep is a kind of dying, and only when the old
form breaks up can the individual be reformed into nerves and
more mature structures whose possibilities are, as it were, envis-
aged in dream and factually shaped in waking."[24]

CHUANG TZU'S BUTTERFLY

When we shift our focus from India and Tibet to ancient
China, we encounter no less of an emphasis on dreams. The
practice of dream recall and dream observation, even the incubation of dreams of which we will speak in more detail in the
next chapter, can be traced back to the earliest days in Chinese
history. Each town or village had its own local official or sage
who, after his death, was promoted to the status of a god, and
who then revealed himself to people in their dreams. These
figures would have the role of protecting the community from
outsiders, on the one hand, and also watching over the internal
affairs of the people. Wrong-doers were exposed to the local
leaders via dreams.[25]

So important were dreams to the Chinese that they, like
western cultures, developed the practice of dream incubation, in
which dreams were sought and obtained by sleeping at special
sites and by practicing prescribed rituals just prior to sleep. For
the Chinese, the induced dream was a form of divination which

was then interpreted in certain "Temples of Guidance." In the Taipei area, for example, on the mountain above the Mucha suburb, stands a well-known "Guidance Temple" where thousands of visitors at a time could be accommodated.[26]

What actually took place in dreams was a function of the Chinese attitude toward the human soul which was based on the bi-polar belief of *yin* (representing things feminine such as darkness, softness, and passivity) and *yang* (representing things masculine: brightness, hardness, and activity). According to this bi-polar pattern, each person is said to have two souls: the material soul (*p'o*) is responsible for the function of the body; the spiritual soul (*hun*) separates from the body during dreams to talk to the dead ancestors and to bring back messages from the realm of death. The dreamer, it is believed, is very vulnerable during sleep while the "*hun*" soul wanders. For this reason, dreamers should not be wakened quickly for fear of the death resulting from a "*hun*" soul's inability to return in time.

Perhaps the most famous dream narrative in all of Chinese literature is that of Chuang Tzu. A disciple of the legendary Lao Tzu, Chuang Tzu is credited with writing the *Chuang-Tzu*, a series of stories, anecdotes, and extended aphorisms in the genre of philosophical wisdom. According to Robert E. Allinson, the *Chuang-Tzu* is a book of "spiritual transformation" which can be likened to a "transforming of one's personality and one's perspective."[27] It is not, Allinson argues, a book that asks its readers to change their religious beliefs or philosophical stances, but to stand beyond all viewpoints in the freedom that ensues from so doing. At the heart of the inner chapters, the reader comes to the following story:

> Once upon a time, Chuang Chou [i.e. Chuang Tzu] dreamed that he was a butterfly, a butterfly fluttering about, enjoying itself. It did not know that it was Chuang Chou. Suddenly he awoke with a start and he was Chuang Chou again. But he did not know whether he was Chuang Chou who had dreamed that he was a butterfly, or whether he was a butterfly dreaming that he was Chuang Chou. Between Chuang Chou and the butterfly there must be some distinction. This is what is called the transformation of things.[28]

Chuang Tzu's Butterfly

There are four relevant elements to this dream: First, it takes place "once upon a time." It is a story that is being spoken for ears, more than one written for eyes only. It is an oral account, autobiographically framed, of a philosopher's dream in which he is "a butterfly fluttering about, enjoying itself." Because of the way the story is presented, the listener is drawn into the dream.

Second, while not in the ordinary sense, the dream itself is a death dream. By "not in the ordinary sense," I mean that it is not the kind of dream in which the dreamer, while in a dream-like body, manifestly dies. Rather, Chuang Tzu becomes what, in real life, he was not (i.e. a butterfly), and thereby dies temporarily to his human form. "It did not know that it was Chuang Chou."

The third movement opens arrestingly—"Suddenly he awoke"—and we are told that he did not know if he was Chuang Tzu dreaming that he was a butterfly, or vice versa. This is another type of death, for upon awakening he can no longer return to his pre-dream dichotomy of sleepfulness and wakefulness. He expresses a new mode of consciousness, that of a profound awareness of his own identity as a man and a butterfly. (And this, again, is a type of death).

The last movement is the philosopher-dreamer's twofold assertion: between Chuang Tzu and the butterfly "there must be (not that there is) some distinction," and, further, "This is what is called the transformation of things." What is the "this" that is the "transformation of things"? Is it a distinction? Or is it an "awakening" to being on each side of the distinction? One way to view the dream is to suggest that not-knowing himself liberated him from the dilemma of dualistic consciousness. As a result of the dream, the root dilemma of dualistic thinking arose, then clarified itself and disappeared into the not-knowing. To put it another way, that there must be a difference is an expression of Chuang Tzu's complete clarity for, at the same time, there is no difference. Being a butterfly and being the butterfly being Chuang Tzu is, at the same time, Chuang Tzu's not being the butterfly and the butterfly's not being Chuang Tzu. There is perfect clarity there.[29]

If we compare Chuang Tzu's butterfly dream to the dream of a student in a "Death, Dying & Religions" class at San Jose State University, the central teaching of Chuang Tzu's dream stands out all the more. In Chuang Tzu's dream, we are not sure who is dreaming whom. We cannot know. And this is what is called "the transformation of things." In the following dream, the dreamer is in a plane flying straight up. The earth is spinning below, and there is an explosion. Instantly everything turns black, followed by a bright white light. The dreamer is in a perfect meadow, with perfect light, with perfect lines, and perfect shapes. Sitting in front of him, Indian style, is a person of light.

"Where am I?" I ask.

"You are in your perfect place," he replied.

Moments pass by with nothing being said, and then Ken Kramer walks into the clearing.

"Where am I?" he asks.

"You are in my perfect place," I say, and Ken turns to face me.

"Kevin, how are you?"

"I think I'm dead."

"You can't be dead."

"Why not?"

"Because you are dreaming," Ken said.

"So why can't I be dead, dreaming?"

"You can't die in your dreams."

"Then what of you?"

"I'm dead," Ken said. The light over us was saying nothing.

"You may be dreaming."

"If I was dreaming, then you'd be dead and this would be my perfect place."

"What if we're both dreaming?"

"We can't be. One of us is dead and the other is dreaming because this is only one perfect place."

"One perfect place?"

"Yes, it's either yours or mine."

"But this is my perfect place, not yours, so I'm dreaming and you're dead."

"No—you're dreaming that you're dead, and you're dreaming that you met a dead man."

"So are you really dead?"

"Am I dead in your dream?"

"As you say I am."

"Then I die in your dream, not you."

"I don't understand."

"You will. Goodbye!" Ken says, and disappears.

The man of light laughs and says, "Dying in dreams, whether your death or another's, is all perspective."

. . . More bright light . . . darkness . . . the plane again, then I wake.[30]

If we view Kevin's dream dialogue with Chuang Tzu's dream in mind, we notice that in each dream, the dreamer enters another realm of being. For Chuang Tzu, it was flying freely as a butterfly; for Kevin, it was passing through a mid-flight explosion into a perfect meadow. When Kevin says, "I think I'm dead," he is not sure if he is Kevin dreaming himself, or whether he has actually died and is in the next life, being dreamed.

"I don't understand," Kevin says. But that Chuang Tzu did not know whether he was Chuang Tzu dreaming that he was a butterfly, or a butterfly dreaming it was Chuang Tzu, did not disturb him. Rather, the dream expressed the trans/formation of things—that he was both and, at the same time, neither. That Kevin did not know whether he was dead or alive troubled him. For the man of light in Kevin's dream, however, "Dying in dreams, whether your death or another's, is all perspective." Is this not also the teaching of Chuang Tzu?

COMMENTARY

In this chapter we have briefly examined the way death and dreams intersect in Hindu, Buddhist (Zen and Tibetan) and Chinese religious traditions. Our investigation of eastern traditions revealed a wide range of dream interpretations and theories, from dream delusion to dream yoga. Unlike western faiths, founded on theological postulations about a transcendent Being (Yahweh, Abba, Allah), these traditions spring from an immanent realization of the authentic Self or true Self Nature.

Dreams, for the Indic rishis, were said to be emitted from a twilight juncture (between this world and the other), from the subtle body or sub-surface consciousness. Dreaming was described as a metaphor for the second state of consciousness (dreamless sleep and self-actualization being the third and fourth), as well as for the creation of the world (through Vishnu's dream).

In the Zen tradition, a parallel was drawn between the non-duality of life and death, and the non-duality of waking and dreaming. In other words, from the standpoint of the Great Death there are no dreams. What in dualistic consciousness would be termed a dream is now viewed as an expression of the "total waking-dreaming presence at this absolute present."

And in the Tibetan tradition, we were struck with a curious bifocal approach to dreams and death. On the one hand, according to *The Tibetan Book of the Dead,* after death (in the Bardo), one will encounter persuasive dream-like forms which must be recognized as illusions and dismissed. On the other hand, according to *The Six Yogas of Naropa,* dreaming can be a yogic practice. By focusing attention upon life as a dream, one is then able to realize, while dreaming, that dream objects are simply that, and nothing more. Advanced practitioners are able to achieve a measure of dream control and can practice, while dreaming, acts of purification.

We concluded with Chuang Tzu's butterfly dream (and Kevin's death dream). It can be suggested that Chuang Tzu's uncertainty (whether he is Chuang Tzu or a butterfly) and Kevin's uncertainty (whether he is alive or dead) are linked to the Tibetan and Hindu suggestion that the dream appearances are, in fact, not real at all, but are rather mental projections (Tibetan), or components of Vishnu's dream (Hindu). Indeed, Chuang Tzu's question leads one to imagine that this self is an image in a dream (whether god's or a butterfly's).

In the last chapter, we saw that from a comparativist's point of view, the religious impulse arises from attempts to respond to basic existential needs and problems, most especially the problem of death. It was suggested that death dreams were a factor leading to the development of the shamanic vocation, and that their interpretation (as messages from living spirits of the dead) may have flavored the ancients' view of nature. In place of this other-worldly emphasis, in the "higher religions" of the east, a different attitude developed toward death dreams. They came to be viewed either negatively (as illusory images), or positively (as a yogic practice leading to enlightenment). In either case, the eastern focus, as illustrated especially by Zen and Tibetan Buddhist attitudes, and by Chuang Tzu's dream, is one of self-trans/formation. Death is a problem in life only if, and to the extent that, one has not yet died (spiritually) before actually dying (physically). If dreams of death arouse fear and anxiety, then they should be dismissed as illusory distractions. But if dreaming of one's death arouses a desire for enlightenment, then it may serve as a method, or practice, for human trans/formation.

When we compare our sense of waking reality to our sense of dreaming reality, a question naturally surfaces: Is there any "real" difference between the way in which I am here now represented, and the way I find myself in dreams? In the following chapter, in which we explore western religious attitudes toward death dreams, the answer to these questions (as well as the material studied) shifts radically.

NOTES

[1]Quoted in *The Wheel of Death,* Philip Kapleau, ed. (New York: Harper Torchbooks, 1971), 65.

[2]Of the variety of creation myths—from Visvakarman (the All-Maker), to Purshua (the Self-Sacrificer), and to Prajapati (the Golden Embryo)—one of the most profound is the "Hymn of Creation." It begins before the beginning ("Non-being then existed not nor being"), then moves to the specific act of creation ("By its inherent force that One breathed breathless"), and finally concludes with a questioning of the process ("Who then knows whence it [this emanation] has driven?"). *Rig Veda* 10:129, in *Hindu Scriptures,* translated by R.C. Zachner (New York: E.P. Dutton, 1966), 11–12.

[3]Joseph Campbell, *The Mythic Image* (Princeton: Princeton University Press, 1982), 7.

[4]Quoted by Wendy Doniger O'Flaherty, in *Dreams, Illusions and Other Realities* (Chicago: The University of Chicago Press, 1984), 16. O'Flaherty further suggests that the Indic texts argue "that what we call waking life is truly a kind of dream, from which we will awaken only at death" (17).

[5]*Mandukya Upanishad,* 2:7, in *Hindu Scriptures,* 201.

[6]O'Flaherty, 18.

[7]*Brihadarnyaka Upanishad,* 4:3, in *The Upanishads,* translated by Max Müller (New York: Dover Publications, 1884, 1962).

[8]Gyomay M. Kubose, *Zen Koans* (Chicago: Henry Regnery Co., 1973), 80.

⁹From a tape-recorded Dharma talk on "Vimalakirti" by Robert Thurman at the San Francisco Zen Center, 1989.

¹⁰Masao Abe, "Transformation in Buddhism," in *Buddhist-Christian Studies,* Vol. 7 (1987), 10.

¹¹In response to this suggestion, Professor Abe (in a letter dated March 28, 1989) wrote that he had no objection to this reformulation if waking and sleeping/dreaming "are taken on a more than psychological dimension," that is, on "an existential or ontological dimension."

¹²Quoted in William Johnston's *The Still Point* (New York: Harper & Row, 1970), 50.

¹³James A. Hall, *Clinical Use of Dreams* (New York: Grune & Stratton, 1977), 308.

¹⁴Quoted in Glenn Mullin, *Death and Dying: The Tibetan Tradition* (Boston: Arkana, 1986), 65.

¹⁵*The Tibetan Book of the Dead,* translated by W.Y. Evans-Wentz (London: Oxford University Press, 1960), 86. Evans-Wentz notes that liberation here does not necessarily imply the liberation of Nirvana, but rather a liberation from the dying body in such a way as to afford the smoothest transition and greatest after-death consciousness.

¹⁶*Ibid.,* 87.

¹⁷These and other dreams (such as having one's head cut off, being surrounded by ghosts, walking with the dead, and being swallowed by a fish) are mentioned in Glenn Mullin's *Death and Dying: The Tibetan Tradition,* 135–136.

¹⁸*The Tibetan Book of the Dead,* 91.

¹⁹*Ibid.,* 103.

²⁰*Ibid.,* 181. In a note, Evans-Wentz writes that "just as a dreamer in the human world lives over again in the dream state the experience of the waking state, so the inhabitant of the 'bardo' experiences hallucinations in 'karmic' accord with the content of his (or her) consciousness created by the human world"—187.

²¹*The Six Yogas of Naropa,* translated by Garma C.C. Chang (New York: Snow Lion Publications, 1963), 89.

²²*Ibid.,* 93.

²³*Ibid.*

[24]*The Life & Teaching of Naropa,* translated by Herbert V. Guenther (Oxford: Oxford University Press, 1963), 185.

[25]For further discussion of this aspect of Chinese culture see Richard Carlyon, *A Guide to the Gods* (New York: Quill/William Morrow, 1981), 78–79, 85–86, 90–91.

[26]For further information see Lawrence G. Thompson's "Dream Divination and Chinese Popular Religion," in *The Journal of Chinese Religions,* No. 16 (Fall 1988), 73–82.

[27]Robert E. Allinson, *Chuang-Tzu for Spiritual Transformation: An Analysis of the Inner Chapters* (New York: State University of New York Press, 1989), 8. While there is no systematic arrangement to the book, the title to what is called the first of the inner, or genuine, chapters (to distinguish these from the less certain outer chapters) is translated as "Happy Wandering" (by Jane English and Gia-fu Fung), or as "Going Rambling Without a Destination" (by A.C. Graham). These translators suggest a freedom of mind, a spontaneous willingness to move in any direction without pre-determined limitations.

[28]A.C. Graham, *Chuang Tzu, The Inner Chapters* (London: Unwin, 1981), 21–22.

[29]I owe this insight to Dr. Richard J. DeMartino (retired Professor of Zen Buddhist thought at Temple University, Philadelphia) which occurred in a conversation on July 17, 1991 in his home in West Hempstead, New York.

[30]Kevin Wood, a student in the "Death, Dying & Religions" class at San Jose State University.

Chapter 5 WESTERN RELIGIOUS TRADITIONS

God came to Abimelech in a dream by night, and said to
him, "Behold, thou art but a dead man for the woman which
thou hast taken; for she is a man's wife." (Genesis 20:3)

When we shift our focus from east to west, from Asian to the
European, we shift from viewing dreams as illusory mental projections to, in addition, viewing them as messages or omens from
a divine source. In fact, speaking of the ancient Mesopotamian,
Egyptian, Hebraic, and Greek cultures, we could say that dream
experiences were thought to occur on three different levels:
"dreams as revelations of the deity which may or may not require
interpretation; dreams which reflect symptomatically the state of
mind, the spiritual and bodily health of the dreamer; and thirdly,
mantic dreams in which forthcoming events are prognosticat-
ed."[1] Of these three, the second will not be of interest to us until
later in the book because it appears less frequently in the ancient
literature, and because there is little available information on
those ancient dreamers' bodily health and state of mind.

In this chapter, the bulk of the dream material will focus on
message dreams in which the dreamer receives images and signs
of a predictive nature. We will first look at the ancient Semitic
culture of Asia Minor in the Tigris and Euphrates Valley—
specifically, at one of the finest examples of Sumerian and Babylonian literature, *The Epic of Gilgamesh*. We shall then consider
the Egyptian attitude (especially as found in the *Coffin Texts* and
the *Egyptian Book of the Dead*) and then the ancient Greek practice of dream incubation. After reviewing the foundation for the
three great monotheistic faiths, we will focus our attention on an
analysis of Jewish, Christian and Islamic dream cultures.

SUMERIANS AND BABYLONIANS

In an animistic world, where spirits (especially devils and
spirits of the dead) were believed to control events in unpredict-

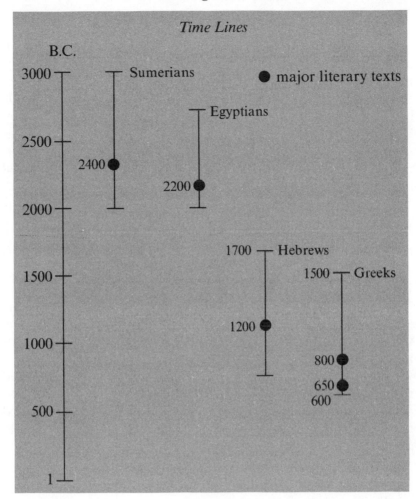

Time Lines

able ways, being in communication with the spirits was deemed essential for productive living. Of the several ways in which humans could learn the will of the spirits, the most direct was prophecy—especially through the dream. This strategy is made clear in an ancient prayer:

> Either let me see it in a dream, or let it be discovered by divination, or let a 'divinely inspired man' declare it, or let all the priests find out by incubation whatever I demand of them.[2]

Many Babylonian and Assyrian dream books, for example, were collected in a library at Nineveh, the ancient Assyrian capital. The earliest recorded instance of dream communication is that of the Sumerian ruler Eannatum (c. 2450 BCE), who related that while he was sleeping, the god Ningiesh "stood at his head" and prophesied his upcoming struggle with a neighboring kingdom. It is important to note the phrase "stood at his head" as being mythically significant. In most ancient theophanies, it was believed that the divine message of the gods or spirits entered through the head of the dreamer.[3]

A more elaborate death dream account occurred in the ancient Sumerian city of Uruk (in modern day Iraq). There, a powerfully wise though tyrannical king named Gilgamesh lived. Two-thirds god, and one-third mortal, his story is told in one of the earliest recorded texts in western civilization, *The Epic of Gilgamesh.*

So that Gilgamesh would not be alone, the story begins, the goddess Aruru created the mighty Enkidu to be his companion. After defeating the evil demon Humbaba with Enkidu, the goddess Ishtar made seductive advances which Gilgamesh spurned. Furiously, Ishtar sent the *Bull of Heaven* to kill Gilgamesh, but instead Gilgamesh and Enkidu cut out the bull's heart and offered it to Shamash (god of the sun). For this, the gods decided that Enkidu had to be put to death, a decision they revealed to him in a dream. He dreamed that he was carried off to "the House of Darkness," from which there was no return for those who entered. With graphic detail Enkidu reported his dream to Gilgamesh.

> There is the house whose people sit in darkness; dust is their food and clay their meat. They are clothed like birds with wings for covering, they see no light, they sit in darkness. I entered the house of dust and I saw the kings of the earth, their crowns put away forever; rulers and princes, all those who once wore kingly crowns and ruled the world in the days of old. And there was Ereshkigal the Queen of the Underworld; and Belit-Sheri squatted in front of her, she who is recorder of the gods and keeps the book of death. She held a tablet from which she read. She raised her head, she saw me and spoke: "Who has brought this one here?" Then I awoke

like a man drained of blood who wanders alone in a waste of rushes; like one whom the bailiff has seized and his heart pounds with terror.[4]

The dream caused Gilgamesh to weep, and he tore off his clothes in fearful anguish. Considering his utter consternation, his words are remarkable: "The dream was marvelous but the terror was great; we must treasure the dream whatever the terror; for the dream has shown that misery comes at last to the healthy man, the end of life is sorrow."[5] Thereafter, Enkidu fell into a deepening sickness and twelve days later, died.

In this remarkable predictive dream, Enkidu envisions his own end by journeying to the region of death. Rather than a god, the underworld is ruled by a goddess whose secretary is surprised to see Enkidu before his time. Even more remarkable is Gilgamesh's interpretation of the dream. In his view, the dream has revealed the fate of human beings, that life ends in sorrow. The dream therefore, even though it records Enkidu's impending death, is to be treasured as a revelatory and predictive means of understanding the environment of one's fate.

EARLY EGYPT

In early Egyptian culture, dreams were considered to be real, whether solicited or unsolicited. For instance, if a dead spouse tormented the dreamer, a statuette of the dead person, along with a list of his or her good deeds, was tied to the dreamer's wrist to ward off the dead spirit. With regard to dreams in which gods intervened, they were believed to be of three kinds:

1. Unsolicited dreams in which the Gods appeared in order to demand some act of piety towards themselves;
2. Dreams in which the Gods gave spontaneous warnings; and
3. Dreams in which the Gods granted their worshippers an answer to a question stated.[6]

Unlike other Near Eastern cultures (and some Oriental cultures), the Egyptians did not believe that the soul traveled from the body while the dreamer was sleeping. But like other cultures, they did practice dream incubation.

The exercise of dream incubation—dreams gathered as a result of the dreamer's sleeping at special, sacred sites, and by engaging in special rituals—was a practice that cut across east-west cultural distinctions. Examples of Hindu, Buddhist, Tibetan and Chinese temples, dedicated, among other things, to, dream inducement, have been found. Dream incubation in the west reached its zenith in Egypt and Greece during the second and third centuries CE. Persons desiring dream information would fast and pray before sleeping. The names of five deities would be written on a cloth which was then saturated with oil and burned.

Of the dream temples located throughout Egypt, one of the most important was at Memphis. Called *Serapeums* (temples), dedicated to the god of dreams, Serapis, they housed professional dream interpreters known as "Masters of the Secret Things," and "The Learned Men of the Magic Library."[7] Unconvinced of the demonological cause which the Babylonians ascribed to dreams, the Egyptians, on the other hand, believed that dreams were messages from the gods who appeared when demanding penance, when it was necessary to warn of a danger, and when it was important to answer the dreamer's questions.

In ancient Egypt, the incubation process usually took the following pattern: the dreamer, having fasted in preparation, entered the temple to beseech the deity's assistance. The supplicant then presented prayers and offerings on the altar before lying down to sleep. In the ensuing dream, an instruction was gleaned pertaining to a problem, question, or command. Depending on the status of the dreamer, a dream interpretation could then be sought from the Masters of the Secret Things. It is not surprising therefore, since dreams were believed to be sent by the gods so that humankind could ascertain the future, that as early as the time of the Middle Kingdom, the Egyptians had developed complex dream interpretations.

For example, an Egyptian papyrus belonging to the latter half of the second century tells the story of Setne, King Ousimores' son. One night, in a dream, he heard a voice which said that he would have a son who would be named Se-Osiris (i.e. son of Osiris). The son soon grew to know more than his tutors could teach him. After a time it came to pass that Sennacherib, King of the Assyrians, threatened the Egyptian armies. An Egyptian priest named Setnan went to the temple to pray for help. There he fell into a deep sleep and dreamed that god himself appeared and exhorted him to have courage. He was promised that the Assyrians would fail in their advance. Armed with courage from this dream, he led not only the army but the merchants and men of the street into a victorious battle.[8]

CLASSICAL GREECE

The Greeks likewise regarded dreams as worthy of investigation. To them, the dream was viewed as a real occurrence (i.e. the dream soul takes a journey). The so-called sleeping part of a person expressed itself not only in dreams but in mythic stories and divine oracles. As Hermes is pictured leading the dead souls to the underworld, for instance, he passes by the *"demios oneiron"* (the village of dreams) located on the outer reaches of the real world. For pre-Homeric Greeks, the cosmos could be seen as a series of concentric circles expanding from the center (ruled by Zeus) out past many layers of reality to the outer world, the realm of the dead. On the edge of this outer realm was the village of dreams. Here the connection between death and dreams is made immediate.

To the ancient Greek poets, the underworld was pictured as a realm surrounded by a vast marsh through which flowed the "Styx" (whose waters contained a strong poison) and "Lethe" (the river of forgetfulness). The underworld (called Hades) was marked by neither the passage of time nor change. Associated with the underworld in one way or another was the cluster of Death, Night, Sleep, and the Dreams. Night (Nyx) was the first child of Chaos; she gave birth to twin sons—Sleep (Hypnos) and Death (Thanatos). Thanatos possessed the function of the angel of death, who cut off a lock of a person's hair in order to dedicate that person to Hades before carrying him or her away. Among

Underworld

Sleep's 1,000 children, or dreams, were "Morpheus" (imitator of human beings), "Icelos" (imitator of birds, beasts, and serpents), and "Phantasos" (imitator of inanimate things).

In ancient Greece, death dreams were often embedded in myths. It is said that long ago, for example, Ceyx (after a sad farewell to his tearful wife, Halcyone) set sail into a torrential rain. A terrifying lightning shattered his mast and shortly thereafter his rudder broke. Grasping for his life, Ceyx prayed that the waves would bear his body back into Halcyone's sight. But at length, the water overwhelmed him, and he sank.

Halcyone, meanwhile, ignorant of her husband's fate, counted the days till his return. She prepared her dress and incessantly offered incense to the gods. She prayed constantly for his safety and that he might not, in her absence, find anyone who would love him more than she did. When she could bear Halcyone's plight no longer, the goddess Night sent a messenger, Iris, to ask that Sleep bring a vision to Halcyone of her dead husband.

Putting on a robe of many colors, Iris found Sleep near the Cimmerian country in a mountain cave.

> Silence reigns there; but from the bottom of the rock the River Lethe flows, and by its murmur invites to sleep. Poppies grow abundantly before the door of the cave, and other

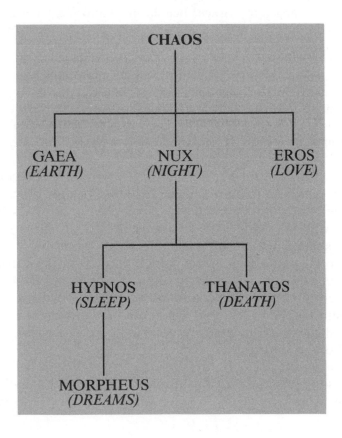

herbs, from whose juices Night collects slumbers, which she scatters over the darkened earth .... There the god reclines, his limbs relaxed with sleep. Around him lie dreams, resembling all various forms, as many as the harvest bears stalks, or the forest leaves or the seashore sand grains.[9]

In the ear of a reclining Sleep, Iris related the message to dispatch a dream to Halcyone, and then departed. To perform the task, Sleep called one of his numerous sons, Morpheus—the most expert in counterfeiting forms, countenance and characteristics. Assuming the form of Ceyx, but with beard soaked, naked and pale like a dead man, he leaned over Halcyone's bed. Then with a voice sounding like her husband, he said:

Do you recognize your Ceyx, unhappy wife, or has death too much changed my visage? Behold me, know me, your husband's shade, instead of himself. Your prayers, Halcyone, availed me nothing. I am dead. No more deceive yourself with vain hopes of my return. The stormy winds sunk my ship in the Aegean Sea, waves filled my mouth while it called aloud to you. No uncertain messenger tells you this, no vague rumor brings it to your ears. I come in person, a shipwrecked man, to tell you my fate. Arise! Give me tears, give me lamentations, let me not go down to Tartarus unwept.[10]

Reaching out for her husband, Halcyone stretched out her arms in her sleep to embrace the air. Her cries for Ceyx awakened her from the Morpheus-inspired dream. She was beside herself with wild grief. "Halcyone is no more," she cried, for "Ceyx is shipwrecked and dead." Vowing to join him in death, she leaped upon a rock barrier which was constructed from the shore into the ocean. No sooner had she done this than wings appeared on her, and she skimmed along the ocean's surface until she touched Ceyx's lifeless body. Enfolding him in her wings, she kissed him tenderly, at which point the gods changed them both into birds.

One way to speak of this dream's trans/formational significance is to recall the relationship that exists between myths and dreams. Comparative mythologist Joseph Campbell has said in many contexts (most recently in an interview with Bill Moyers just before Campbell died) that dreams are personal myths and myths are collective dreams. To Moyers' question "Why is a myth different from a dream?" Campbell answered:

> Oh, because a dream is a personal experience of that deep, dark ground that is the society's dream. The myth is the public dream and the dream is the private myth. If your private myth, your dream, happens to coincide with that of society, you are in good accord with your group. If it isn't, you've got an adventure in the dark forest ahead of you.[11]

With Campbell's remarks in mind, compare the mythic story cited above to a student's dream which occurred seven months after her husband had died of cancer. During this time, she had thought about her husband every day, and had talked to him in a journal she kept. She had been up very late studying intensely for a history exam. Since details and dates were racing through her mind, she had difficulty getting to sleep. When she did, she had the following dream:

> I'm sitting home, alone, trying to study for my last midterm the next morning. Dusk is quickly fading into darkness but I'm enchanted by the dimness of the light in the room. I'm feeling tired, frustrated, and overloaded from a particularly stressful week. My eyes close as I'm attempting to memorize a series of dates that seem insignificant in my life. My concentration comes and goes. I'm resenting the time and energy spent studying but I'm absolutely determined to excel in this course. As my mind continues to wander and the stress and frustration mounts, I'm suddenly startled by a voice calling my name, "Cinde . . . Cinde . . ."; it's Ed, I'm sure of it! Tingling with excitement, I quickly get up and follow the sound of his voice. His voice leads me into the bathroom where Ed is speaking to me, loud and clear, directly from the toilet. The bottom of the toilet bowl appears to be the back of his throat. The small amount of water in the bowl moves and gurgles with each word he speaks. I'm mesmerized and speechless over the reality of the moment. Ed's presence is all around me as I sit down next to the toilet, intent on listening. It isn't a

conversation; Ed speaks in broken phrases with passion and concern in his voice. He says, "Cinde . . . no worry . . . be sure . . . it's okay . . . Cinde . . . not important . . . doesn't matter . . . okay . . . Cinde . . . values . . . okay . . . Cinde . . ." (I could not recall exactly what he said but I remember the words and phrases quoted above. He repeated some of them several times.)

Ed (his voice and presence), disappears as quickly as he came. There are no good-byes, only his voice fading away with the last swirl of water down the throat of the toilet.[12]

As a result of this dream, her attitudes toward death, and life, had changed. Cinde wrote that (1) she did not fear death; (2) there is no death, only a trans/formation of one's being; (3) there is life after death, but of a different mode of existence; (4) the real "being" is formless and is only attached to the physical body in life as we know it; (5) it is possible to communicate with the dead; and (6) the dead are actually alive in dreams, and they appear in dreams for a reason. Her husband's aliveness in the dream, she noted, was unmistakable. It was clear that "who he was" had survived death, not in body, but in his being. "I truly felt Ed's presence as if he was in the room with me," Cinde wrote. "He was the same Ed that I knew and loved. Though out of body, Ed's identity had not changed. His voice, intonation and reflected attitudes were the same he had projected in his physical life. Who he was did not die."

DREAM INCUBATION

What characterized Greek attitudes toward death dreams more than anything else was the elaborate practice of dream incubation which had a strong popular appeal. The Greeks employed several important methods and practices whenever they sought to decipher the meaning of a dream. For the sake of clarity, we will discuss these attitudes and practices under four major rubrics: the temples of dream incubation, the gods of dreaming, the temple rituals, and the dream interpretations.

The Temples of Dream Incubation

The incubation of dreams, fascinatingly enough, may have had its origins on gravesites. In the *Iliad,* Homer mentions that the people lay on earthen beds to have dreams which they interpreted prophetically (xvi, 233). Similarly, Herodotus writes that people "slept on the graves of their ancestors in order to have

Remote Dream Site

dreams."[13] Eventually, sacred places were used for incubation—remote hillsides, caverns, gorges, streams, or ordinary temples near or within cities.

It is believed that between 300–400 C.E. temples existed in ancient Greece in honor of the god Asclepius—temples that were used until the end of the fifth century. The ground plan of some of the temples contained a labyrinthine structure into which the incubant entered to have the dream. Often the dream temple was part of a larger complex of buildings which also included public baths, a gymnasium and a stadium (for people waiting to be "seen" by the gods, in dreams). The temple's positioning with regard to nature was crucial, be it on a mountain or by a grove of trees, to allow easy access by the gods. The center of the temple, then, was located in a sacred space into which the incubant entered, as if entering a *womb to be reborn.*

The Gods of Dreaming

In all, according to the Greeks there were gods who were the cause of dreams (e.g. Hypnos), gods who were invoked for dreams (e.g. Lady Earth and the Mother of the Black-Winged Dreams), and gods which served a functional role, enabling one to invoke dreams (e.g. Asclepius and Trophonius). Sometimes the gods visited the dreamer through keyholes and stood at the head of the bed where they sought to communicate with the sleeping dreamer. Of the three types of dream gods, the snake was the most significant. In Greek art, the snake was often depicted as a guardian of home or temple because it prowled about tombs and was therefore thought to be the soul of the dead.[14] Considering the attributes of the god Trophonius, the serpent was predominant. Thus, whoever wished to consult with him would have to spend time in his cave where his serpents dwelt. The following is an account of Timarchus who, with youthful fervor, spent two nights and one day in Trophonius' cave.

> He first found himself in a great darkness; then, after a prayer, lay a long while not very clearly conscious whether he was awake or dreaming; only he fancied that his head received a blow, while a dull noise fell on his ears, and then the sutures parted and allowed his soul to issue forth. . . .

Time passed, and an unseen person said to him, "Timarchus, what do you wish to learn?" "Everything," he replied, "for all is wonderful." "We," the voice said, "have little to do with the regions above; they belong to other gods; but the province of Persephone, which we administer, being one of the four which Styx bounds, you may survey if you will." To his question, "What is Styx?" "A way to Hades," was the reply, "and it passes right opposite, parting the light at its very vertex, but reaching up, as you see, from Hades below; where it touches the light in its revolution it marks off the remotest region of all."[15]

Trophonius acts here as a messenger who instructs Timarchus, in his dream, about the geography of the underworld.

The cult of Asclepius (which had more than three hundred incubation centers), on the other hand, was more highly developed. Epidaurus was the main temple of Asclepius which attracted thousands of pilgrims to participate in the divine-human exchange (what was seen as "intercourse with the god"). Asclepius was primarily associated with healing and miracles. In fact, it was said that he not only saved people from death, but even raised them from the dead. Asclepius, in Greek mythology, unites within himself two sets of opposites: a young boy with a mature physician, and a dark, demonic figure with a Zeus-like, bearded man. Like Trophonius, the Zeus-figure was associated with the serpent. Serapis, an Alexandrian god and the most significant deity other than Asclepius, was also pictured with serpents, as a sign of his healing power.

Asclepius, like other gods of dreams—Aesculapius, Hypnos and Onciros—was thought to live near the underworld and to enter the world either through the gate of horn (the "true" dreams), or the gate of worry (the "false" dreams). As the most important god of dreaming, this deified physician (whom dreamers sought for healing) was often accompanied by feminine companions (his wife and daughters). In fact, the Asclepian sanctuaries were understood as places of *synousia* ("coitus") with the god. Barren women, for example, consulted Asclepius to become impregnated by the god in his serpentine form. How ironic, then, are the last words of Socrates: "Crito, we owe a cock to Asclepius; pay it without fail."[16] Since the cock was an offering to the god in thanksgiving for being healed, it is as if Socrates implied that death itself is the cure for life's problems.

The Temple Rituals

It is clear that the entire incubation ritual had a double aim—to communicate a divine message or command, and/or to cure bodily or psychic afflictions. These aims were facilitated by the attendants of the cult, the "therapeutes" (from which we receive the word "therapist").

Dreamers were expected to perform various pre-incubation rituals which might involve abstaining from certain foods, alcohol and sexual activities, and then bathing, practicing purification rituals and offering sacrificial gifts. Dreamers were usually shown the tablets of thanks put up by former patients regarding their cures. Shortly before sleep, the patient was taken to see a statue of the god so that it might inspire him or her with feelings of awe; then the patient prayed and sacrificed an animal—usually a ram. Finally, the patient lay down to sleep on the skin of the sacrificed animal beside the god's statue. Often the priests returned later in the night, dressed as gods, to give medical treatment. Sometimes sacrifices were expected, in other places gifts of money or food—according to one's means.

Often the incubants wore white garments which were outward signs of trans/formation, the indication of the "appearance of God."[17] This also seemed to symbolize the incubant's "rebirth" from the inner world. Doubtless the atmosphere, once in the temple, was relaxed, almost hypnotic, "though the presence of large numbers of long white snakes which would become active on the dowsing of the lights must have been disconcerting."[18]

After all of the preliminary sacrifices and ablutions had been accomplished, the person (sick or well) slept in the "abaton" (the innermost sanctuary). "Abaton" means "the place which is not to be entered uncalled." Thus, those who participated, whether the sick seeking a cure, or the healthy seeking divine direction, had to receive a dreamed invitation from the deity before going to sleep in a temple. At times, incubants were anointed and purified, then sleep was induced by drugs, herbs or potions. Sometimes the patients were put into hypnotic trances, or given suggestions by the priests to encourage or develop forms of auto-suggestion.

The Dream Interpretations

Within the temple, incubants had to wait for the "right" dream to bring about the correct cure or answer. A distinction was made between "divine" dreams, that had to be interpreted and obeyed, and "ordinary" dreams. The latter were divided into "good" dreams sent by gods and "bad" dreams sent by demons, which demanded some kind of protective or cleansing ritual. One of the functions of the priests was to tell whether a dream was good or bad. Dreamers were obliged to record their dreams and then might be invited to go to an interpreter. After the interpretation, the incubant would make a thank offering, and then would have up to one year to pay a fee.

The interpreter, after hearing the dream, might ask questions such as:

> "Was it seen, or heard—i.e., was it a vision, or an oracle?" . . .
> "Did it openly foretell the future, or was it shrouded in symbols?" If it were a symbolic dream, there would be further questioning.

> "Was it addressed to yourself, your family, your friends, your country, or the world in general? What were the circumstances in your experience that were like those in the dream?"[19]

And then the interpreter would make associations between dream images and suggested behavioral patterns. Needless to say, a great deal of charlatanism existed in the interpretations, especially when priests took over the task of dreaming for the patients and mixed various forms of magic to make the ceremonies more obscure and impressive.

In sum, we note the correspondence between the death-rebirth ritual of dreaming in Trophonius' cave, and the trans/formation arising from Asclepius' dream temple—one made more striking by the statue of Asclepius at Titane as an infant in swaddling clothes. This same theme of death and rebirth will continue, as we will see, in the scripturally based, monotheistic traditions.

BIBLICAL JUDAISM

The history of Israel, as recorded in the Hebrew Bible, is really a story about God's (Yahweh's) direct contact with the people in order to call them forth into nationhood, to instruct them in God's will—as a chosen people—and to provide them with guidance and direction. What is utterly fascinating about the divine-human encounter is how it occurred. Of the variety of ways described in the Hebrew Bible—seeing directly (as Moses did), seeing in a vision (as Elijah did), being intellectually inspired (as Isaiah and Jeremiah were), and being ecstatically shaken (as Ezekiel was)—one of the most common forms of divine communication was the dream.

> God speaks first in one way,
>   and then in another, but no one notices.
> He speaks by dreams, and visions that come in the night,
>   when slumber comes on mankind,
>   and men are all asleep in bed.
> Then it is . . . he whispers in the ear of man,
>   or may frighten him with fearful sights,
> to turn him away from evil doing,
>   and make an end of his pride;
> to save his soul from the pit
>   and his life from the pathway to Sheol. (Job 33:14–18)

Simply put, for the Jews dreams fulfilled two functions: they summoned up events from the past, and they opened channels into the future. Either way, there was in the Hebrew mind usually an element of fear and anxiety reflected in dreams, not to mention some uncertainty.

It has been claimed by certain scholars that Hebrew scriptures draw no clear distinction between "dreams" and "visions," which, more often than not, were presented as aspects of the same reality. Like the Hebrew terms for vision—*khazon* and *mar'eh*—the Hebrew word for dreams, *chalon,* comes from the root word which means "to see."[20] However, it is important to note that dreams were the lowest form of divine communication. In fact, while all other forms of divine revelation were reserved for Jews alone, Gentiles also were able to receive dreams, though they were always (as in Pharaoh's case) treated symbolically. At the same time, it is clear that there were expert practitioners of dream interpretation and divination who distinguished authentic dream practices from those of pseudo-prophets. In Jeremiah we read:

> I have heard what the prophets say who make their lying prophecies in my name. "I have had a dream," they say, "I have had a dream!" How long will they retain this notion in their hearts, these prophets prophesying lies, who announce their private delusions as prophetic? They hope, by means of the dreams that they keep telling each other, to make my people forget my name, just as their fathers forgot my name in favor of Baal. Let the prophet who has had a dream tell his dream as his own! And let him who receives a word from me deliver it accurately! (Jeremiah 23:25–28)

By far the most prolific dreamers in the Hebrew Bible are the patriarchs, especially Abraham, Jacob and Joseph. In fact, the first depiction of a biblical dream occurs in Genesis. After Yahweh had spoken to Abram (Abraham) in a vision—"Have no fear, Abram, I am your shield; your reward will be very great" (Genesis 15:1)—the storyteller informs us that Abraham, who is uncertain about what he will inherit, or how, falls into a deep sleep:

> Then Yahweh said to Abram, "Know this for certain, that your descendants will be exiles in a land not their own, where they will be slaves and oppressed for four hundred years." (Genesis 15:13–14)

This experience was so convincingly powerful that it became a covenant between God and Abraham, a divine verification of

God's calling Abraham to go forth to an unknown land and then to sacrifice his beloved son Isaac.

While it is with the name Joseph to which the title "dreamer" is affixed, and for good reason since it was Joseph who rose to prominence as both a dreamer and an interpreter of Pharaoh's dreams, in some ways the greatest biblical dreamer was his father Jacob. Consider Jacob's story. He was born into a strange house. His mother was strong-willed and mean. His father was half-blind and weakened by age. And, in order to secure the birthright from his father, he tricked him by pretending to be Esau, the eldest son. Jacob was then sent to Laban to choose a wife so that he would not have to marry a Canaanite woman. And when Jacob came to a place he called Bethel, we read:

> Jacob left Beersheba and set out for Haran. When he had reached a certain place he passed the night there, since the sun had set. Taking one of the stones to be found at that place, he made it his pillow and lay down where he was. He had a dream: a ladder was there, standing on the ground with its top reaching to heaven; and there were angels of God going up it and coming down. And Yahweh was there, standing over him, saying, "I am Yahweh, the God of Abraham your father, and the God of Isaac. I will give to you and your descendants the land on which you are lying. Your descendants shall be like the specks of dust on the ground; you shall spread to the west and the east, to the north and the south, and all the tribes of the earth shall bless themselves by you and your descendants. Be sure that I am with you; I will keep you safe wherever you go, and bring you back to this land, for I will not desert you before I have done all that I have promised you." Then Jacob awoke from his sleep and said, "Truly, Yahweh is in this place and I never knew it!" He was afraid and said, "How awe-inspiring this place is! This is nothing less than a house of God; this is the gate of heaven!" (Genesis 28:10–17)

This is not merely a dream, but a very profound religious experience which illustrates both aspects of divine revelation and prediction, of which we spoke earlier.

Let us look more closely at this dream. First of all, Jacob

selected a stone for a pillow. The Jewish sages indicate that he had gathered twelve stones (one for each of the tribes of Israel) and that the stone he selected for a pillow represented each of them. The faith of the twelve nations was hereby unified. In his dream, we are told that a ladder appeared which connected earth to heaven.[21] In one sense, the ladder stands for the functions of the dream which also connects the human reality to the experience of death.

Next we are told that there are angels climbing up and down the ladder. The Hebrew word for angel, *malak,* means "messenger" and was usually understood as God's agent of communication (see Genesis 22:11, Exodus 3:2, Numbers 22:22 and Judges 6:11), or as one who carried out God's will (see Genesis 32:26, Exodus 14:19, 23:20, 2 Samuel 24:16, 2 Kings 19:35). Here the angels do not speak, but serve as a retinue for Yahweh, transporting the dream to the sleeping Jacob.

Then we are told that Yahweh *stood above* Jacob and repeated the promise given earlier to Abraham in his vision. The key term here is the word "above," for in Hebrew it has a double meaning—"protecting" those below, and "imposing" upon those below. God's imposition is also God's protection. Yahweh's identity is also a promise. When Jacob awoke, he realized that Yahweh had been in that place, and that this had been the house of God, "the gate of heaven." No more powerful *theophany* (God's manifestation) than this appears in a biblical dream, for it completely alters Jacob's view of his own purpose and destiny. One might say that he in fact died (to his old identity) and resurrected upon waking.

We are told that Jacob remained for twenty years in his new home with Laban where he married, raised a family and accumulated wealth. Then, in a dream, he realized that he was to return to the land of his birth. Taking his two wives, his family and possessions, he set forth. The passage which follows is as remarkable as the former dream. When he arrived in a place he called "Peniel," we read:

> And there was one that wrestled with him until daybreak who, seeing that he could not master him, struck him in the socket of his hip. And Jacob's hip was dislocated as he wres-

tled with him. He said, "Let me go, for day is breaking." But
Jacob answered, "I will not let you go unless you bless me."
He then asked, "What is your name?" "Jacob," he replied. He
said, "Your name shall no longer be Jacob, but Israel; because you have been strong against God, you shall prevail
against men." Jacob then made this request, "I beg you, tell
me your name," but he replied, "Why do you ask my name?"
And he blessed him there. (Genesis 32:25–30)

Whether this is a dream or a vision, we are not told. We are
told that Jacob was left alone, in a strange place, in the night, and
that there he wrestled with an unnamed adversary. Who was this
adversary? Rabinical accounts suggest a variety of possibilities—
a sorcerer, a sage, a bandit, a shepherd—but the majority of the
commentators identify him as an angel. Elie Wiesel suggests that
Jacob was "attacked by his own guardian angel," by "the other
half of Jacob's split self."[22] In this light, we can see the attack as a
matter of life and death, as a struggle for Jacob's *raison d'être,* for
his future.

Jacob must have asked himself why he should go to this
place across the river when previously he had everything.
Wiesel writes:

> He knew that one does not kill with impunity; whosoever
> kills man, kills God in man. And so he first had to convince
> himself that it would be possible to obtain a pure victory—
> pure of death, pure of guilt—a victory that would not imply
> the opponent's defeat or humiliation. A victory over himself.
> Such, then, is the prime meaning of this episode: Israel's his-
> tory teaches us that man's true victory is the one he achieves
> over himself.[23]

At this point the Other asks him his name. This is not just
a rhetorical question, for according to the ancient Hebrews, to
know one's name was to become intimate with, just as to give a
name was to have dominion over. (For this reason, Adam was
given the responsibility of naming the animals in the garden of
Eden.) When Jacob responded, "Jacob," he was told that hence-
forth he would be called "Israel," for he had striven with the
divine and had not surrendered.

By being given a new name, one could say that the old self of Jacob died, at least symbolically, and that a new self, Israel, was born. His new name indicates a change of destiny, a new role in history, a new sense of vocation. The death of the one who was identified with the wrestler is a pre-condition for the birth or reanimation of the one identified as Israel. As a result of the dream/vision sequence, Jacob received a new identity, a new status, as the one who provides his people with a name—Israel (God-wrestlers). But when Jacob, in turn, asked the other his name, he was told that he must not ask. Angels do not reveal their names. While Jacob won the battle, the identity of his adversary must remain unknown.

How might these two events in Jacob's life be compared— the Bethel ("ladder") dream and wrestling with the "angel" at Peniel? In the first dream, Jacob was an observer, whereas in the second he was active. In the first he was running away from his brother Esau and from his home; in the second he was returning to each. In the first he was going to a new land; in the second he was given a new name. In both cases, it was Jacob's willingness to encounter the dynamic of his unconscious which allowed him to integrate a divinely-inspired invitation to expand beyond previous personal limitations, not only for Jacob's own benefit, but for the good of the people. In each dream it can be said that Jacob experienced a death to his previous identity and a birth to a new self-understanding.

EARLY CHRISTIAN VIEWS

While there are fewer references to dreams in the New Testament, and while there is no record of Jesus' dreams, the gospels (especially Matthew and Luke), Acts and Revelation continue to present the Jewish experience of God-inspired dreams. The common word in Greek for dream, *onar,* means "that which is seen in sleep and then remembered," and frequently it referred to the spiritual world.[24] Indeed, it was believed that sleep was a kind of temporary death during which the soul left the body. Dreams occur, thus, while the body rests.

The New Testament contains numerous dreams. To begin

with, the conception of Jesus was announced to Joseph, his foster father, in a dream. Certainly in Matthew's mind, he would have expected his readers (a largely Jewish audience) to see the connection between the original Joseph of Genesis (the dreamer and interpreter of dreams), and the Joseph who, according to Matthew's genealogy, was also the son of a man named Jacob. Matthew tells us:

> He had made up his mind to do this when the angel of the Lord appeared to him in a dream and said, "Joseph son of David, do not be afraid to take Mary home as your wife, because she has conceived what is in her by the Holy Spirit. She will give birth to a son and you must name him Jesus, because he is the one who is to save his people from their sins." Now all this took place to fulfill the words spoken by the Lord through the prophet: The virgin will conceive and give birth to a son and they will call him Emmanuel, a name which means "God-is-with-us." When Joseph woke up he did what the angel of the Lord had told him to do: he took his wife to his home and, though he had not had intercourse with her, she gave birth to a son; and he named him Jesus. (Matthew 1:20–25)

Betrothal, according to Jewish law (Deuteronomy 22:13ff), was a binding arrangement, and the penalty for fornication during this period was death to each party. No wonder Joseph agonized. How could this be? How could Mary be pregnant? His first thought was to divorce Mary secretly—in the presence of selected witnessess—and, in this way, to avoid scandal. But because of the dream, his resistance to Mary's pregnancy died into an acceptance of God's will.

Consider the entrance of the divine messenger in the dream. It is to be noted first that only a direct revelation of God's will can reshape Joseph's action and, second, that such a revelation comes through a dream. The word here for the divine messenger is *angelos* which can refer either to a physical person or a spiritual envoy sent by God. In either case, such an experience inspires awe and fear, and generates devout action. Joseph is told what is to occur, how it will occur, and what he is to name the child.

Joseph's Dream

Here again, we encounter the significance of receiving a God-given name in a dream. As the name Isaac ("he who will laugh") was given as a name for Abraham's son (Genesis 17:19–20), here the name Jesus ("Yahweh saves") is given by God to indicate the role to be played by Jesus. Moreover, Matthew reports that this was to fulfill a prophecy that a virgin would bear a son who would be named Emmanuel ("God is with us").

Matthew then tells us that wise men, who were attempting to locate the birth site, were warned in a dream to avoid Herod. Shortly thereafter, Joseph is warned, also in a dream, of Herod's plot to kill the newborn baby, in response to which the family flees to Egypt. In a subsequent dream, Joseph is told that Herod is dead, and finally, in yet another dream, not to go to Judea, which is being ruled by Herod's son. It is difficult to imagine this birth narrative, and that told by Luke, without the dream sequences in which the divine message is communicated.

One of the most unusual examples of this communicative device, not religiously but culturally, occurred (after the death of Jesus) to the apostle Peter. In Luke, the author of the book of Acts, a God-fearing Roman centurion named Cornelius (a man of prayer) has a vision in which he distinctly sees that the angel of God enters his house and tells him that he is to send a servant to Jaffa to fetch Peter. The next day, before his servants had arrived, Peter went to a housetop, where he was staying, to pray.

> He felt hungry and was looking forward to this meal, but before it was ready he fell into a trance and saw heaven thrown open and something like a big sheet being let down to earth by its four corners; it contained every possible sort of animal and bird, walking, crawling, or flying ones. A voice then said to him, "Now, Peter; kill and eat!" But Peter answered, "Certainly not, Lord; I have never yet eaten anything profane or unclean." Again, a second time, the voice spoke to him, "What God has made clean, you have no right to call profane." This was repeated three times, and then suddenly the container was drawn up to heaven again. (Acts 10:10–16)

As Peter is attempting to understand the trance-dream, the servants of Cornelius arrive to invite Peter to the home of Cornelius. The next day, they travel to Caesarea where Cornelius is waiting. The first thing Peter says is that he now knows (as a result of his dream) that no one can be called unclean or profane. "The truth I have now come to realize," he says, "is that God does not have favorites, but that anyone of any nationality who fears God and does what is right is acceptable to him" (Acts 10:34–35).

Peter, who was known to be narrow-minded about Jewish law, especially with regard to prohibitions against eating with Gentiles, is completely turned around by his dream. Like Jacob, who wrestled with the unnamed opponent, Peter (in a sense) dies to his old pro-legalistic, anti-Gentile attitude. He is given a new direction, a new understanding by the contents of the dream.

But without a doubt, the most powerful dream-vision in the New Testament appears in its last book, Revelation. Called the Christian apocalypse since it depicts in vivid imagery the second coming of the Messiah, the book opens with its purported writer, John, identifying himself as a close follower of Christ. John writes that he was "in the spirit," which some interpreters take to mean "in ecstasy," or "standing beside [or outside] oneself." Whether he was fully conscious or not, we cannot say. What we can say is that he was in an extra-normal state of awareness, dream-like, in which he hears a voice like a trumpet saying, "Write what you see in a book."

When he turns to see who is speaking, he sees the Son of Man—whose head is snow-white, whose eyes are like a flaming fire, whose feet glow like bronze, whose voice sounds like the roar of rushing waters—with a sharp two-edged sword issuing from his mouth, and his face shining like the sun.

> When I saw him, I fell in a dead faint at his feet, but he touched me with his right hand and said, "Do not be afraid; it is I, 'the First and the last'; I am the Living One, I was dead and now I am to live forever and ever, and I hold the keys of death and of the underworld. Now write down all that you see of present happenings and things that are still to come."
> (Revelation 1:17–20)

The voice John heard is behind him and when he turns to identify it, what he sees fells him, like one struck dead. We are reminded here of the passage, "No one can look upon the face of God and live," for it is as if he has seen the face of God by seeing the Son. As we have said of the other dreams and visions, in some sense the dreamer must die (a kind of dying-before-dying) if he or she is to receive the fullness of the divine revelation.

At this point, the Son touches him to calm his fear, and identifies himself—"I am the Alpha ('first') and the Omega ('last'), the Living One"—and then speaks of his victory over death: "I hold the keys of death and of Sheol ('the pit or underworld')," he says. The reader is reminded of the passage in Matthew (16:16ff) where Jesus gives the "keys of the kingdom of heaven" to Peter. The keys equal spiritual authority over the earthly realm. Just as Jesus gave Peter the authority to "bind" ("to exclude from the community") or to "loose" ("to readmit into the community"), here the living one, the risen Christ, because of the resurrection, has full power over death. By passing through death, by journeying into Sheol to preach to the damned, by reappearing to the apostles and disciples, and now by coming to John in his ecstatic dream-vision, Christ guarantees the faithful that they, too, will share in his resurrection.

"Indeed I was dead," the Son says, "but, behold, I live for all eternity." The parallel here between Christ and John is striking. Christ died and resurrected. John, upon seeing Christ, falls as if dead, but is resurrected by the message which comes to him through the ecstatic dream-vision. What John could not fully know in the light of human consciousness, he can receive in the half-light of extra-conscious awareness. And he is given a task, to write down everything that he sees. One could say that like Jacob, like Joseph and like Peter, John is called to a new identity which comes as a result of a death, in dream, to the dreamer's initial self-image. In each case, when the dreamer awakens, he is not the same person who, prior to the dream, fell asleep. And while the dreamer (in a sense) dies, the dreamer dies only to survive with a new vitality, a new purpose, a new calling.

ISLAM'S NIGHT FLIGHT

Like Judaism, and to some extent Christianity, Islam is a prophetic faith based on divine revelation. As such, its spirituality was influenced by the potency of dreams. In fact, it is reported that Muhammad frequently asked his disciples about their dreams, and that dream interpretation was widely practiced. A clear distinction between divine dreams and false dreams is drawn in the *Qur'an* where one finds a growing awareness that some dreams have physiological causes (e.g. wine and bad foods). From the *Qur'an* it is clear that Muhammad and his followers accepted principles of dream interpretation practiced in the Near East (i.e. awareness of the dreamer's age, occupation, religion and rank).

Second to the *Qur'an* in importance is the *Hadith,* or the "Sayings of the Prophet." One of the best-known is the "Night Journey" (*Lailatal-Miraj*), which is the story of the Prophet Muhammad's dream-journey into the mysterious nature of the celestial realms. The story begins with the Prophet sleeping between the hills of Meeva and Safa, when the angel Gabriel appears to him along with Elboraq (a half-human, white riding-beast whose every leap carried him as far as one could see). In an instant, they (Gabriel and Muhammad) reach Jerusalem, the spiritual center of the world. There, his mare lands on the rock-altar upon which Abraham had attempted to sacrifice his son Isaac at God's bidding. From that point, they push off, and soar on Elboraq through seven celestial spheres.

In the first sphere, Muhammad meets Adam. In succeeding spheres, he meets Jesus and John the Baptist (second heaven), Joseph (third heaven), Enoch (fourth heaven), Aaron (fifth heaven), Moses (sixth heaven), and Abraham (seventh heaven). Each greets Muhammad in the same way: "Welcome to the righteous son, the righteous prophet."[25] As Muhammad continues his ascent, he passes the two rivers of Paradise, the Nile and the Euphrates, where he is given a command for his community:

> Then there was laid on me the religious duty of performing fifty prayer services daily, and I departed. As I passed by Moses he asked: "With what have you been commanded?" "With fifty prayer services each day," I replied. "But your community," said he, "will never be able to perform fifty prayers a day. By Allah, I have had experience with people before you, and I had to strive hard with the Children of Israel. Return to your Lord and ask Him to lighten it for your community."[26]

Moses continues to send Muhammad back until he is bidden to perform five prayer services daily, to which, against Moses' objections, he submits. After this, Muhammad is brought to the place of the Throne of Allah. In the presence of a scintillatingly bright light, beyond words, he reports:

> My sight was so dazzled ... that I feared blindness. Therefore I shut my eyes, which was by Allah's good favour. When I thus veiled my sight Allah shifted my sight [from my eyes] to my heart, so with my heart I began to look at what I had been looking at with my eyes.[27]

At this, Muhammad requests a boon of Allah, that he will be given "a steadfast vision of Him" with his heart, a boon which

is granted. Then Allah draws near. As if a veil has been lifted,
His glory, His dignity, His majesty, His might, is revealed to
Muhammad.

> To those who believe
> And do deeds of righteousness
> Hath God promised forgiveness
> And a great reward.
>
> Those who reject faith
> And deny Our Signs
> Will be Companions
> Of Hell-fire.[28]

Allah then touches Muhammad between his shoulders and
he feels a cool sweetness on his heart that melts away all his
terrors.

> Then was I filled with joy, my eyes were refreshed, and such
> delight and happiness took hold of me that I began to bend
> and sway to right and left like one overtaken by slumber.
> Indeed, it seemed to me as though everyone in heaven and
> earth had died, for I heard no voices of angels, nor during the
> vision of my Lord did I see any dark bodies. My Lord left me
> there such time as he willed, then brought me back to my
> senses, and it was as though I had been asleep and had awak-
> ened. My mind returned to me and I was tranquil, realizing
> where I was and how I was enjoying surpassing favour and
> being shown manifest preference.[29]

Remarkably, as with Jacob and the John of Revelation,
there is a death experience here, of everyone on earth and in
heaven (presumably including Muhammad himself). Afterward,
he is revived, his mind is brought back and he enjoys surpassing
favor. And as with Jacob and John, Muhammad is then given a
direct command:

> I am sending you as a prophet to the white folk of the earth
> and the black folk and the red folk, to join and to men there-
> on, though never before you have I sent a prophet to the
> whole of them. I am appointing the earth, its dry land and its

sea, for you and for your community as a place for purification and for worship. I am giving your community the right to
booty which I have given as provision to no community before them.[30]

COMMENTARY

While we began this chapter with the suggestion that in the
west dream experiences occurred on three levels—revelations of
the deity, reflections of the dreamer's state of mind, and predic-
tions of forthcoming events—we saw that there were other types.
These included dreams in which a messenger of God brings the
dream, or in which the soul journeys out of its body in the underworld, or in which a gift, a power, a magical remedy or a charm is
given to the dreamer. For example, as the Babylonians viewed
dreams, they were the result of evil spirits, or brought a message
of doom and death (as in the case of Enkidu, Gilgamesh's friend).

In early Egyptian and Greek cultures, we noted the practice
of dream incubation which in Greece had four elements—the
dream temple, the dream gods, the incubation rituals, and the
dream interpretation. Interestingly, when one explores Greek
images of the underworld, a cluster of related, divine beings
emerges—Death, Night, Sleep, and various Dreams. It bears repeating that these share a common lineage. According to Greek
myth, Sleep (or *Hypnos*) and his twin brother Death (*Thanatos*)
lived in a dark, misty cavern through which the river of forgetfulness (called *Lethe*) flowed. Sleep was surrounded by an infinite
number of Dreams, sons of Sleep and the goddess Night (*Nyx*).
Death was, therefore, an uncle to all Dreams.

As for the three great monotheistic traditions—Judaism,
Christianity and Islam—dreams were viewed as one way in
which God encountered his people. Not only did God reveal
something of the divine nature, but in some cases the dreamer
was trans/formed, through a death of sorts. Each dreamer experienced a new perspective on reality, along with an expanded
view of the self.

Originally, the Jews viewed dreams as journeys of the soul;
later, they understood them as supernatural visitation in which
God communicated a life-trans/forming message. Early Christi-

anity, as it developed from its Jewish parent, took with it Hebrew attitudes toward dreams. Early Christians accepted the notion that some dreams had divine inspiration, and that the dreamer experienced, thereby, a death to one's former self-understanding, and a birth of a new identity. And, in the Islamic tradition, while there is an awareness that some dreams have physiological causes, the *Qur'an* speaks of divine dreams, and the *Hadith* tells of Muhammad's "Night Journey."

From a comparativist's standpoint, western cultures and religious traditions offer a much different view toward dreams than eastern traditions. While in each tradition a distinction is made between insignificant (inauspicious) dreams and significant (auspicious) dreams, in the eastern traditions auspicious dreams are those which assisted the dreamer toward enlightenment, while in western traditions they revealed a divine message from a holy other. Of interest to our study is the fact that in either case, death dreams provide significant clues to the meaning and purpose of life. While they may indicate the possibility of a life after death, this is not their final significance. Rather, whether through realization of true self-identity, or revelation of divine will and purpose, dreams in which the dreamer dies indicate a reordered, reanimated perception of reality. The dreamer, through the death experience, is shown a new relationship with truth or with the holy, one that illumines the possibility of a new self-identity in place of one's pre-dream self-understanding.

In fact, two distinctions have emerged over the last two chapters. First, in pre-historic and pre-literate cultures, death dreams were viewed as a function of the power of disembodied spirits (whether natural, ancestral or animal), whereas in the higher religions of the west, they were seen as a function of the dreamer's psychological condition, and/or either a demonic spirit or the holy other. Second, in the higher religious traditions, death dreams were to be either (1) *inauspicious* dreams, those which are merely illusory projections of an unenlightened mind (eastern), or demonically inspired temptations (western), or (2) *auspicious* or trans/formational dreams, those which point toward true self-realization (eastern), or the revelation of a divine message (western). In the latter cases, the dream is usually accompanied by the dreamer's receiving a new identity, or new name. The question which naturally arises is how to differentiate between these types of death dreams. Hence, the importance of the dream interpreter (e.g. the Shaman, the guru, the Masters of the Secret Things, the Greek Temple interpreters, and the rabbi or priest) cannot be underestimated.

Having reviewed two seemingly different, though in a way complementary, religious attitudes toward death dreams—the eastern view and the western view—in the next chapter we will examine ways in which philosophers, both ancient and modern, have discussed dreams of death. We will be interested to note similarities and differences between what philosophers say and what yogis and sages have said, and to wonder (with the philosophers) whether dreams are a product of the rational or the irrational mind.

NOTES

[1]John F. Priest, "Myth and Dreams in Hebrew Scripture," in *Myths, Dreams and Religion,* edited by Joseph Campbell (New York: E.P. Dutton & Co., 1970), 60. For a more detailed study of dreams in the ancient Near East, see A. Leo Oppenheim, "The Interpretation of Dreams in the Ancient Near East," in *Transactions of the American Philosophical Society,* 46 (1956), 179–373.

[2]Second Plague prayer of Mursih II, quoted in Michael Loewe and Carmen Blacker's *Oracles and Divination* (Colorado: Shambhala Publications, Inc., 1981), 143. The rite of dream incubation involved, among other practices, sleeping in a sacred temple in order to initiate auspicious dreams. That such places were commonplace in the classical world indicates how seriously dreams were taken by ancient peoples.

[3]*Ibid.*

[4]*The Epic of Gilgamesh,* translated by N.K. Sandars (New York: Penguin Books, 1960), 92–93.

[5]*Ibid.,* 93.

⁶Jackson Stewart Lincoln, *The Dream in Primitive Cultures* (London: Cresset Press, 1936), 4.

⁷See A.J.J. Ratcliff, *A History of Dreams* (Boston: Small, Maynard & Co., 1923), 36. For a popular account of dream incubation see Patricia L. Garfield's *Creative Dreaming* (New York: Simon and Schuster, 1974), especially Chapter Two, "Learn From Ancient Dreams." Garfield blends Greek, Egyptian, Chinese, yogic, and native American practices and suggests the following common elements: (1) a place of non-distraction, (2) a clear formation of the intended dream, (3) a concise positive phrase which summarizes the intention, (4) deep relaxation and dream suggestion, and (5) visualizing the dream at sleep onset.

⁸Lewis Spence, *Myths and Legends Series: Egypt* (New York: Avenel Books, 1986), 206–219.

⁹Thomas Bulfinch, *Bulfinch's Mythology* (New York: Avenel Books, 1979), 71–72. Other sources include Michael Grant & John Hazel's *Gods and Mortals in Classical Mythology* (New York: Dorset Books, 1985), and Edith Hamilton's *Mythology: Timeless Tales of Gods and Heroes* (New York: Mentor Books, 1964). The descendants of Chaos alone are Nyx (Night), Cer (Fate), Thanatos (Death), Hypnos (Sleep), and Oneiros (Dream).

¹⁰Bulfinch, *op. cit.,* 73.

¹¹Quoted in *The Power of Myth* by Joseph Campbell with Bill Moyers (New York: Doubleday & Company, Inc., 1988), 40. "The dream," Campbell remarks, "is an inexhaustible source of spiritual information about yourself." Speaking earlier about the connection between myth and/dream, Campbell writes in *The Hero with a Thousand Faces* (Princeton: Princeton University Press, 1949) that "Dream is the personalized myth, myth the depersonalized dream; both myth and dream are symbolic in the same general way of the dynamics of the psyche" (19).

¹²Submitted by Cinde Connor in a paper titled "The Dead Are Actually Alive in Dreams" as a final project for "Death, Dying & Religions" course, December 5, 1988. Cinde reports waking from this dream feeling rejuvenated, relieved, reassured, even excited.

¹³Furthermore, "the underlying idea seems to be that of contact with 'potnia cthion', Sacred Mother Earth, who sends the dreams." See C.A. Meier, *Healing Dream and Ritual: Ancient Incu-*

bation and Modern Psychotherapy (Switzerland: Daimon Verlag, 1989), 77.

[14]Will Durant, *The Story of Civilization: Part II, The Life of Greece* (New York: Simon and Schuster, 1966), 179.

[15]Quoted in Meier, 85–90.

[16]*Plato: The Last Days of Socrates,* translated by Hugh Tredennick (New York: Penguin, 1954), 183.

[17]Meier, 103.

[18]Christopher Evans, *Landscapes of the Night* (New York: Pocket Books, 1985), 48. Evans continues, "The snakes, which were of a harmless Mediterranean species, were looked on as the servants of the god Aesculapius (hence the serpent wound round the staff, which is now the international emblem of the medical practitioner) and were allowed to come and go as they pleased. In the morning the fortunate would have had their dream, hopefully replete with useful medical advice, while the unlucky remainder would prepare themselves for another night's stay. If they could afford it."

[19]Ratcliff, 48.

[20]Loewe and Blacker, 201. Also see Morton T. Kelsey's *God, Dreams and Revelation* (Minneapolis: Augsburg Publishing House, 1968), 19.

[21]It has been suggested by E.A. Speiser that the etymology of the term translatable as "ladder" suggests instead a ramp or a solid stairway. He likens this to the Mesopotamian ziggurats which, to Speiser, is the only way one can make sense of the angels ascending and descending, and to understand the later reference to the "gate of heaven." See E.A. Speiser's *The Anchor Bible: Genesis:* Vol. 1 (New York: Doubleday & Company, 1979), 218.

[22]Elie Wiesel, *Messengers of God: Biblical Portraits and Legends* (New York: Random House, 1976), 124. Wiesel adds that the other half was the side of Jacob that doubted, that felt undeserving and unworthy.

[23]*Ibid.,* 125.

[24]For a more detailed description of the various words used in the New Testament—night visions, waking visions, trance states, ecstatic states, sight, disclosure, and revelation—see Kelsey, 80–86.

[25]From al-Baghawi's *Masabih Al-Sunna,* quoted in *Sacred Texts of the World: A Universal Anthology,* edited by Ninian Smart and Richard D. Hecht (New York: Crossroad, 1982), 167–168.

[26]*Ibid.,* 168.

[27]*Ibid.,* 170.

[28]*The Holy Qur'an,* translated by Abdullah Yusuf Ali (New York: McGregor & Werner, Inc., 1946), Surah V: 10–11.

[29]Smart and Hecht, *op. cit.,* 171.

[30]*Ibid.*

Chapter 6 PHILOSOPHICAL TRADITIONS

I had a very vivid dream in the night. I was present at a funeral, and moved about in the house among the mourners without being in the least degree able to realize the death of my friend as a case for mourning. I saw the coffin placed in the hearse, and in due course I was marshalled to a place in the funeral procession, which proved to be not in the mourning-coach, but in my own carriage. By my side, in the shadow, sat a gentleman, who, after being silent for a short time, said to me in a well-known voice, "I agree with you that death ought not to be regarded as a subject for mourning, and that the trappings of woe are out of place on an occasion like this." I looked up to see who it was who had thus divined my own thoughts, and saw, without the least feeling of surprise or fear, that the speaker was no other than the friend whose body was then in the hearse on the way to the grave. It seemed to me to be quite natural that he should thus divine my thought, and that we should be together, he talking and I listening, as if death had not parted us. It also seemed quite natural that a moment or two later he should vanish away as he did, and I be left alone as I was, with a strong conviction that I ought to be able to come and go, divine and speak as he had done.[1]

If philosophy is the love of wisdom, and if wisdom is the quest for comprehensive meaning and values in the face of cultural fragmentation, then the study of death cannot be undertaken in isolation. Death, along with its significance and implications, is irretrievably linked with what we know consciously, as well as with what we know unconsciously. Just as this book cannot exist without its outer binding, neither can it exist without its inner pages. Likewise, if we are to arrive, philosophically, at a complete understanding of physical death, we will need to explore its outer (conscious) and inner (unconscious) meanings. That philosophers have been interested in dreams since antiquity is testimony to this necessity.

Whether considered as rational (Aristotle) or irrational (Plato), whether as the voice of consciousness (Socrates) or symbolic discourse (Artemidorus), whether thought to be a prophetic synthesis (Aquinas) or an expression of somatic stimuli (Hobbes and Kant), the function of dreams has always been of philosophical concern. This chapter will briefly review some of the main dream theories in the history of philosophy, especially those which conceptualize dreams as manifestations of our rational or irrational natures, or as revelations of a deeper truth. Underneath these theories, in fact their source, is the way philosophers characterize the nature of the self vis-à-vis the consciousness/ unconsciousness distinction. As a second-order function, standing apart from the realm of dreams, philosophers bring a reasoned analysis to the process of interpretation. In one sense, philosophy is less concerned with the meaning of death dreams than with the methods used for arriving at one's interpretation.

PLATO, SOCRATES AND ARISTOTLE

In the century before Plato (427–347 BCE), many Greek philosophers were skeptical about the dream world. Heraclitus (540–475 BCE), for instance, remarked that while dreaming, each person retires into a private world which had little significance since, according to him, each person should follow the Logos (reason) that is common to all. Centuries earlier, Homer (850 BCE) had assigned two gates to dreams: the gate of truth and the gate of error and delusion. Though Plato did not emphasize dreams, passages in the *Crito* (44) and the *Phaedo* (60)—on the last days of Socrates—depict two dreams. In the first, while discussing the coming of a ship from Delphi whose arrival meant his death, we read:

> **Socrates:** Then I don't think it will arrive on this day that is just beginning, but on the day after. I am going by a dream that I had in the night, only a little while ago. It looks as though you were right not to wake me up.
> **Crito:** Why, what was the dream about?
> **Socrates:** I thought I saw a gloriously beautiful woman dressed in white robes, who came up to me and addressed me

in these words: "Socrates, to the pleasant land in Phthia on the third day thou shalt come."
Crito: Your dream makes no sense, Socrates.
Socrates: To my mind, Crito, it is perfectly clear.[2]

And in the *Phaedo,* while speaking about turning to poetry during his last days in prison, Socrates said to Cebes:

> "Tell him the truth," said Socrates, "that I did not compose them to rival either him or his poetry—which I knew would not be easy; I did it in the attempt to discover the meaning of certain dreams, and to clear my conscience, in case this was the art which I had been told to practice. It is like this, you see. In the course of my life I have often had the same dream, appearing in different forms at different times, but always saying the same thing: 'Socrates, practice and cultivate the arts.' In the past I used to think that it was impelling and exhorting me to do what I was actually doing; I mean that the dream, like a spectator encouraging a runner in a race, was urging me on to do what I was doing already, that is practicing the arts; because philosophy is the greatest of the arts, and I was practicing it. But ever since my trial, while the festival of the god has been delaying my execution, I have felt that perhaps it might be this popular form of art that the dream intended me to practice, in which case I ought to practice it and not disobey; I thought it would be safer not to take my departure before I had cleared my conscience by writing poetry and so obeying the dream."[3]

Interestingly, it is not clear whether these are the opinions of Socrates alone, or whether Plato was also expressing his views. But more to the point, what might his dreams mean to him?

In each case Socrates attributes great importance to his dreams in that he noted them, interpreted them, and followed their suggestions. In the first dream he is told that on the third day he will come to Phthia (eastern Thessaly), the homeland of Achilles in the *Iliad.* Since Socrates refused to escape, and since he was certain of the dream's meaning, one can deduce that it pictured for him the land of the soul's afterlife. And in the second dream, somewhat surprisingly, Socrates speaks of a shift in attention from philosophy to poetry—a shift occasioned by the dream. All his life he had dreamed the same dream in various forms: to practice and cultivate the arts. All his life he thought it meant that he should practice philosophy. But as death approached, he arrived at a new interpretation for the dream, namely to practice poetry.

On the other hand in the ninth book of the *Republic,* Plato seems to take a different view. There he writes:

> ... When a man's pulse is healthy and temperate, and when before going to sleep he has awakened his rational powers, and fed them on noble thoughts and enquiries, collecting himself in meditation; after having first indulged his appetites neither too much nor too little, but just enough to lay them to sleep, and prevent them and their enjoyments and pains from interfering with the higher principle—which he leaves in the solitude of pure abstraction, free to contemplate and aspire to the knowledge of the unknown, whether in past, present or future: when again he has allayed the passionate element, if he has a quarrel against any one—I say, when, after pacifying the two irrational principles, he rouses up the third, which is reason, before he takes his rest, then, as you know, he attains truth most nearly, and is least likely to be the sport of fantastic and lawless visions.

I quite agree.

> In saying this I have been running into a digression; but the point which I desire to note is that in all of us, even in good men, there is a lawless wild-beast nature, which peers out in sleep. Pray consider whether I am right, and you agree with me.[4]

Speaking in a way which would seem to anticipate Freud—"in all of us, even in good men, there is a lawless wild-beast nature, which peers out in sleep"—Plato appears to temper Socrates' previously quoted remarks. Depending on the mood of the person when he or she falls asleep, in Plato's eyes dreams will be less or more irrational, but in either case the irrational nature will be dominant. What most troubled Plato was that sleep suspended the rule of reason and allowed desire and anger—the soul's other element—to break through.

Aristotle, on the other hand, took another approach. Since there is not a non-physical world from which dreams arise, he believed that dreams were the result of residual impressions experienced in the physical world and then reexperienced randomly. He was disinterested in prophetic or divinely inspired dreams; if the gods wanted to communicate with human beings, he argued, it would occur in daylight and then only to the wisest of humans. Dreams do not come from God, he argued, "but either through mere coincidence, or through the extreme sensitiveness of the mind in sleep, by which minute details, unnoticed by day, point to a probable future result, or through dreams dwelling on (the) dream so seriously that (it) brings about the result."[5]

In one of Aristotle's three treatises on dreams, *On Prophecy in Sleep—On Sleep and Waking* and *On Dreams* being the other two—Aristotle writes:

> This is plain in what often happens during sleep; for example, dreamers fancy that they are affected by thunder and lightning, when in fact there are only faint ringings in their ears; or that they are enjoying honey or other sweet savours, when only a tiny drop of phlegm is flowing down (the esophagus); or that they are walking through fire, and feeling intense heat, when there is only a light warmth affecting certain parts of the body. When they are awakened, these things appear to them in this their true character.

A bit later he continues:

> Most (so-called prophetic) dreams are, however, to be classed as mere coincidences, especially all such as are extravagant, and those in the fulfillment of which the dreamers have no initiative, such as in the case of a sea-fight, or of things taking place far away. As regards these it is natural that the fact should stand as it does whenever a person, on mentioning something, finds the very thing mentioned come to pass.[6]

Since the soul is more sensitive during sleep, it is able, Aristotle believed, to detect sensations from the outside world not ordinarily perceivable. Beyond dreams that were simply accidents, and therefore virtually meaningless, of those meaningful dreams, some may actually be the causes of a future action which the dreamer may take when awake. Aristotle reached this conclusion by starting with the fact that people often dream at night the same experiences which occurred earlier in the day. As well, it is possible that a person may dream of having a specific experience, and then awake to find himself or herself having that same experience.

In addition to the potential predictive nature of dreams, Aristotle also felt that dreams enabled people to experience in magnitude the subtler things in life. For example, two people may be having a conversation in the same room where someone is sleeping. Hearing the voices, the person sleeping may then dream of being in a large auditorium filled with people. Or, if it is slightly cold in the room, a person may dream of being at the North Pole. Again, as with Socrates, there is a relationship between the occurrences, or between waking-life and dream-life.

ARTEMIDORUS AND CICERO

If for Plato dreams were a product of irrational forces, and if for Aristotle they were a natural, rationally explainable phenomenon, for Artemidorus of Daldis (second century CE) dreams were always symbolic. It is Artemidorus who, in his *The Interpretation of Dreams* (a 1644 translation of which exists in the Houghton rare-book room at Harvard University), has bequeathed us with the most systematic theory of dreams from ancient times. Concerned with whether dreams were sent by the gods or not, he composed five little handbooks based on his observation of people's lives in which he suggested that there are six elements to be found in all dreams: "nature, law, custom, professional skill, art, and name."[7] Before undertaking an interpretation, he required that complete information in these six areas be supplied so that he could then synthesize them as part of his analysis. To his credit, he avoided the application of a static symbol system, but rather acknowledged that dream symbols change over time.

After spending much of his life collecting all the information about dreams that he could find (by visiting incubation

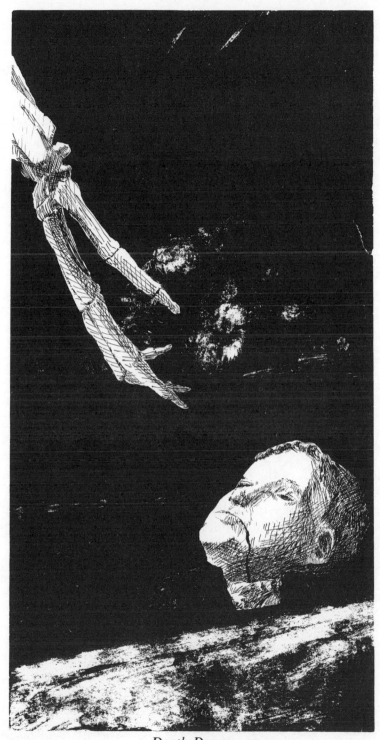

Death Dream

centers, buying old manuscripts, interviewing dream interpreters, and traveling to the Royal Babylonian Library at Nineveh), Artemidorus wrote his *Oneirocritica* (*Oneiros* is Greek for dreams). Of its five books, three were lexicons of dream interpretation, while the other two contained information about the proper decorum of the dream interpreter. He writes:

> There are Five Sorts of Dreams, that have different qualities. The first is a Dream: the second a Vision: the third an Oracle: the fourth a Phantasy or vain Imagination: the fifth an Apparition.

He continues:

> There are two principal kinds of dreams: First, Speculative or Contemplative. The second is Allegorical or Figurative.

> Speculative dreams have an immediate event; but the Allegorical not so soon, for there is a day or two between a Dream and the event thereof. Sometimes there are Dreams which cannot possibly happen; as when you dream that you fly, have horns, go down into Hell, and the like: These are allegorical, and carry a different significance.[8]

For Artemidorus, dreams are a symbolic expression ("under a hidden figure") of the dreamer's own rational insights. Dreams in which God's will is revealed through an angel, he calls an "Oracle." We notice in his list that all dreams are evaluated predominantly in terms of actual future events which will determine whether they have a favorable outcome.

With this as a background, what about death dreams? When writing of death dreams, Artemidorus often stated his interpretation without any discussion. For example:

> It is bad for a sick man to dream that he is kissing the dead, since it portends his death.

> If a sick man dreams that he is wearing white clothes, it portends his death, since the dead are carried off in white clothes.

Simply to see the dead without doing or suffering anything noteworthy signifies that the dreamer will be affected in a way that corresponds to the relationship that existed between the dreamer and the dead while they were alive.

If dead men return to life again, it signifies disturbances and losses. For one must hypothetically imagine the kind of confusion that would result if the dead were to come back to life again. They would naturally demand their possessions back, which would bring about losses.[9]

At the same time, in other places in his remarkable text, Artemidorus demonstrates a subtle discernment of several variables. Addressing those who classify dreams in neatly arranged categories, Artemidorus challenges these diversions by referring to death dreams. In response to the category of "personal" dreams, he suggests that dreams do not always come to fruition for the dreamers themselves. For example: a man dreamed he died but in real life his father (his second self) died. "Another man dreamt that his mistress dies. And shortly afterwards, robbed of the acquaintance dearest to him, he himself died."[10]

In his most sustained treatment of death dreams (in Book 2), he based his interpretation on the identity of the dreamer. He writes:

To dream that one is dead, that one is being carried out for burial, or that one is buried foretells freedom for a slave who is not entrusted with the care of the house. For a dead man has no master and is free from toil and service. But for a slave who has been entrusted with the care of the house, it signifies that death will rob him of his trusteeship.

It signifies marriage for a bachelor. For both marriage and death are considered to be critical points in a man's life and one is always represented by the other. And so, if a sick man dreams that he is being married, it portends death. For the same things befall a groom and a dead man as, for example, a procession of friends, both male and female, wreaths, spices, unguents, and written records of their possessions.

If a married man dreams that he is dead, it means that he will be separated from his wife. It also indicates that associates, friends, and brothers will part and be separated from one another. For the dead do not dwell with the living, nor do the living dwell with the dead. It signifies that a man who is living in his native land will travel abroad, since a dead person no longer remains in the places that he previously inhabited. But it signifies that a man who is abroad will return to his native land. For the dead are lowered into the earth, which is the common fatherland of all men.

A death dream, moreover, signifies victory in the games for athletes. For like victors, the dead have also, as it were, completed the course. It is also auspicious for literary men and fathers. For they will leave behind a memorial of their lives— fathers in their children and literary men in the written works that contain their wisdom.

I have observed that a death dream means good luck both for those who are distressed and for those who are afraid. (For the dead know no fear and no grief.) It also indicates good luck for those who are engaged in lawsuits that involve land disputes and for those who wish to buy land. For the dead are masters of the land. But in regard to other lawsuits, dying is a bad sign.[11]

At the same time, there are death dreams which yield a similar interpretation no matter who the dreamer is. To dream of being buried alive, for instance, is beneficial to no one. And to dream of being strangled, or of hanging oneself, signifies "oppression and distress" no matter who dreams it. He writes:

If anyone dreams that he has committed suicide, the good or bad fortune that death signifies will come true for him, since he has been the cause of his own death. But if he dreams that he has been killed by someone else, the fulfillments will come true for the murderer, since he was the cause of the death. All deaths resulting from a judge's verdict indicate that the good or bad fortune signified by the dream will be more intense. At this point, it would be profitable to treat the matter thoroughly.[12]

Cicero (106–43 BCE), on the other hand, would have rejected this kind of interpretation. Writing in a Roman culture which was attracted to divination of all kinds, in his *On Divinations* he expressed annoyance with the popular conviction that dreams might be prophetic. He compared such interpretation to a soothsayer's trickery which, if he had his way, should be "jeered off stage." In fact, he insisted, the only reason that dreams are highly regarded is because they have been "taken under the wing of philosophy."

The following passages from *On Divinations* illustrate how seriously he was opposed to the whole phenomenon:

> The first thing for us to understand is, that there is no divine energy which inspires dreams; and this being granted, you must also grant that no visions of dreamers proceed from the agency of the gods. For the gods have for our own sake given us intellect sufficiently to provide for our own future welfare . . .

> Again, let me ask you, if God gives us visions of a prophetic nature, in order to apprise us of future events, should we not rather expect them when we are awake than when we are asleep? . . .

> If, then, dreams do not come from God, and if there are no objects in nature for which they have a necessary sympathy and connection, and if it is impossible by experiments and observations to arrive at a sure interpretation of them, the consequence is that dreams are not entitled to any credit or respect whatever.[13]

Here then the lines are drawn between several positions in the ancient world: that dreams are irrational or that dreams are rational; that dreams can be divinely inspired or that dreams are certainly not divinely inspired; and that dream interpretation is significant enough to become a science or that it is irrelevant at best and folly at worst. Two questions arise: How were these lines of thought developed as philosophical thought developed through the centuries? And, more specifically, in what ways do modern philosophers interpret dreams of death and beyond?

HOBBES, DESCARTES AND PASCAL

Modern dream interpretation (i.e. since the seventeenth century) has essentially expanded upon, with some variations, the dream theories of antiquity (e.g. the belief that dreams were the result of somatic stimuli). Thomas Hobbes (1588–1679), in the *Leviathan,* assumes that all dreams are the result of physical factors such that if a person sleeps in a draft, he or she may dream of being in a blizzard. Hobbes writes:

> And seeing dreams are caused by the distemper of some of the inward parts of the body; divers distempers must needs cause different dreams. And hence it is, that lying cold breedeth dreams of fear, and raiseth the thought and image of some fearful object (the motion from the brain to the inner parts, and from the inner parts to the brain being reciprocal) and that, as anger causeth heat in some parts of the body, then we are awake, so when we sleep, the overheating of the same parts causeth anger, and raiseth up in the brain the imagination of an enemy. . . . In sum, our dreams are the reverse of our waking imaginations; the motion when we are awake, beginning at one end; and when we dream, at another.[14]

Apparently, from this we can assume that Hobbes would not have been troubled, as some have been, by the question of who dreams whom. For Hobbes, dreams are the reverse of waking. He is quite satisfied to know that when he wakes, he is not dreaming, and that what he dreamed was not real. One suspects therefore that if he ever dreamed of his own death, or the death of a friend, upon waking he would dismiss it as a dream caused by an irrational fear.

In France, the rationalist philosopher René Descartes (1596–1650) theorized that dreams were the result of activity in the sleeper's organs, and that they were expressed in terms which responded to the sleeper's desires. For instance, between 1614 and 1619, Descartes had been struggling to find a way or method which would enable him to pursue truth as a life occupation. Wrestling with the existential question "What way of life shall I follow?" he found the answer in a dream. As if receiving a compelling command from heaven, his answer arrived: "Search for the truth, by applying the mathematical method (i.e. analytical geometry) to all other studies."[15]

At the same time, for Descartes the question of who's dreaming whom was more difficult to answer. In *Discourse on Method* he wrote:

> ... that there is sufficient reason to exclude entire assurance, in the observation that when asleep we can in the same way imagine ourselves possessed of another body and that we see other stars and another earth, then there is nothing of the kind. For how do we know that the thoughts which occur in dreaming are false rather than those others which we experience when awake, since the former are often not less vivid and distinct than the latter?[16]

One wonders how Descartes reconciled these thoughts with his famous dictum, "I think therefore I am!" Does thinking include dreaming for him? If he dreamed that he died, how would that affect the way he thought about himself?

In a similar fashion, Blaise Pascal (1623–1662), French mathematician, physicist, and religious philosopher, in his *Pensées* wrote:

> If we dreamt the same thing every night, it would affect us as much as the objects we see every day. And if an artisan were sure to dream every night for twelve hours' duration that he was a king, I believe he would be almost as happy as a king, who should dream every night for twelve hours on end that he was an artisan ...

> But since dreams are all different, and each single one is diversified, what is seen in them affects us much less than what we see when awake, because of its continuity, which is not, however, so continuous and level as not to change too; but it changes less abruptly, except rarely, as when we travel, and then we say, "It seems to me I am dreaming." For life is a dream a little less inconstant.[17]

What connects life and dreams for Pascal is the fact that dreams are always shifting; continuity is thus a continuity of change, albeit more abruptly than in life. The only difference, therefore, for Pascal between life and dreams is consistency—"life is a dream a little less inconsistent."

BERGSON

One of the most creative, philosophic approaches to dreams is one taken by Henri Bergson (1859–1941). Like philosophers before him, he too accepted the theory of somatic stimuli but, like Freud, he suggested that the dreamer draws upon a vast storehouse of memories. For Bergson, dreams are a web of forgotten memories which the unconscious fits to the somatic stimuli. From all our past life, he writes, everything that happens to us is preserved in the minutest detail—all thoughts, perceptions, emotions, and volitions—as "invisible phantoms."

> So, then, among the phantom memories which aspire to fill themselves with color, with sonority, in short with materiality, the only ones that succeed are those which can assimilate themselves with the color-dust that we perceive, the external and internal sensations that we catch, etc., and which, besides, respond to the effective tone of our general sensibility. When this union is effected between the memory and the sensation, we have a dream.[18]

To Bergson, the birth of a dream, therefore, is no mystery since it "resembles the birth of all our perceptions." He depicts the dream mechanism with a striking illustration. Suppose a person dreamed of speaking before a political assembly when, in the midst of the audience, a murmur arose and became a roar which issued into cries of "Out! Out!" When the dreamer awoke he or she heard a neighboring dog baying. To the dreamer, each "wow wow" seemed identical to the "Out! Out!" Bergson writes:

> The waking ego, just reappearing, should turn to the dreaming ego, which is still there, and, during some instants at least, hold it without letting go. "I have caught you at it! You thought it was a crowd shouting and it was a dog barking.

Now, I shall not let go of you until you tell me just what you were doing!" To which the dreaming ego would answer, "I was doing nothing; and this is just where you and I differ from one another."[19]

To correct this mistake, Bergson proposed that what in fact occurs is that one's entire memory is brought "to converge upon a single point, in such a way as to insert exactly in the sounds you heard that one of your memories which is the most capable of being adapted to it."[20]

Accordingly, we could speculate, based on Bergson's theory of memory, that when one dreams of dying two elements coalesce: first, an event/situation in waking life like someone's death or near-death, and, second, the coupling of remembered thoughts, feelings or perceptions one has about one's own death. As a tailor pulls together pieces of cloth to fit a person's body, so are memories pulled from one's unconscious storehouse to fit an external stimulus.

FOUCAULT

By far the most profoundly original philosophical work in the area of death dreams has been done by Michel Foucault (1926–1984). Influenced by Martin Heidegger's *Being and Time,* Foucault applied Heidegger's notions of space and time to form the theoretical foundation of a psychiatry not limited to mental representations. In his essay, "Dream, Imagination and Existence," more than any of the works already considered, Foucault shifts the conversation about dreams from the anthropological, even from the psychological, into the ontological realm. Foucault invites his readers, as we do here, "to follow for a moment this path of reflection, and to see whether the reality of (humankind) may not prove to be accessible only outside any distinction between the psychological and the philosophical."[21] It is, he asserts, rather through various interpretations and forms of human existence that one can come to understand humanity.

Originally written as an "Introduction" to Ludwig Binswanger's "Dream and Existence," Foucault remarks that he will not retrace Binswanger's analysis. Instead, he underscores the significance of the coincidental publication of Husserl's *Logical Investigations* (1899) and Freud's *Interpretation of Dreams* (1900). He sees their connection in and through "symbolic value," whether of phenomena or dream images. Foucault then brings his focus to a single point: "the dream, like every imaginary experience, is an anthropological index of transcendence; and in this transcendence it announces the world to (humankind) by making itself into a world, and by giving itself the species of light, fire, water, and darkness."[22]

What Foucault means to signify by the "transcendence of the dream" cannot be discovered in the classical dichotomies of immanence and transcendence. Rather, for him "the cosmogony of the dream is the origination of existence," that is, the origin of the human soul. It is for this reason that dreams bear the "deepest human meanings." While there is no way to capture the heart of Foucault's profound reflection on death and dreams, we will quote the following paragraphs (interspersed with brief commentaries) to provide the reader with a taste of his profound insights. He writes:

> But does not the dream thus reflect a contradiction just where one might succeed in discerning the cipher of existence? Does it not designate at one and the same time the content of a transcendent world and the original movement of a freedom? The dream is deployed, we said earlier, in a world which secretes its opaque contents and the forms of a necessity which cannot be deciphered. Yet at the same time it is free genesis, self-accomplishment, emergence of what is most individual in the individual. This contradiction is manifest in the content of the dream when it is deployed and offered to discursive interpretation. It even bursts forth as the ultimate meaning in all those dreams that are haunted by the anguish of death. Death is experienced as the supreme moment of that contradiction, which death constitutes as destiny. Hence the meaningfulness of all those dreams of violent death, of savage death, or horrified death, in which one must indeed recognize, in the final analysis, a freedom up against a world.[23]

Foucault can best be understood here according to a series of distinctions, the largest being between death dreams as a *contradiction* and as a *reconciliation*. The "ultimate meaning," he writes, especially in all death dreams, is the contradiction between the *transcendent* world and the movement of *freedom*. On the one hand, the death dream can never be understood or correctly interpreted, yet, on the other, its context is "free genesis, self-accomplishment, emergence of what is most individual in the individual." Death, he suggests, is both the "supreme moment of the contradiction," and also "constitutes our destiny." He continues:

> If consciousness sleeps during sleep, existence awakens in the dream. Sleep, itself, goes toward the life that it is preparing, that it is spelling out, that it favors. If it is a seeming death, this is by a ruse of life, which does not want to die; it "plays dead" but "from fear of death". It remains of the order of life. The dream is no accomplice of sleep, it ascends again the slope that sleep descends, towards life, it goes towards existence, and there, in full light, it sees death as the destiny of freedom. For the dream, as such, and by virtue of the meanings of existence it bears with it, kills sleep and life that falls asleep.[24]

A second distinction for Foucault is that between *consciousness* and *existence*. While dreaming, one's consciousness sleeps, but one's existence awakens. Here one needs to follow Foucault closely. If this is so, then: (1) the dream ascends while sleep descends, (2) the dream moves toward existence while sleep moves toward life, and (3) the dream, in full light of existence, "sees death as the destiny of freedom." It is not sleep which makes dreaming possible, but "the dream that makes sleep impossible by waking it to the light of death."
Foucault writes:

> In depth of this dream, what man encounters in his death, a dream which in its most inauthentic form is but the brutal and bloody interruption of life, yet in its authentic form, is his very existence being accomplished.[25]

Here Foucault posits another distinction, between *inauthentic* and *authentic*. If the depth of human dream is marked by death, then there are two ways to respond. The inauthentic response is to interpret death as the "brutal and bloody interruption of life." The authentic response is to view death dreams as one's "very existence being accomplished."

> ... But death can also appear in dreams with another face: no longer that of contradiction between freedom and the world, but that in which their original unity and their new alliance is woven. Death then carries the meaning of reconciliation, and the dream in which the death figures is then the most fundamental of all: it no longer speaks of life interrupted, but of the fulfillment of existence, showing for the dreamer the moment in which life reaches its fullness in a world about to close in. Hence, in all the legends, death as reward of the wise man, as happy declaration that henceforth the perfection of his existence no longer requires the movement of his life; in announcing death, the dream exhibits the fullness of being which existence has now attained. In this latter form, as in the former one, the dream of death appears as what existence can learn that is most fundamental about itself.[26]

The second major type of death dream for Foucault (the contradiction between freedom and the world being the first) is that of reconciliation with an original unity. Death dreams, for Foucault, are the most fundamental dreams available to humans since they are no longer about life in its various interpretations, but now about the "fulfillment of existence," the moment in which life simultaneously reaches its fulfillment.

Still more centrally, by announcing death, the dream "exhibits the fullness of being which existence has now attained." It is what is most fundamental about all human existence. He concludes:

> ... In this death, anguished or serene, the dream fulfills its ultimate vocation. Nothing could be more mistaken, therefore, than the naturalistic tradition according to which sleep would be a seeming death. It is rather a matter of dialectic of

the dream itself insofar as it is a kind of explosion of life toward existence, which discovers in this light its destiny of death. The recurrence of dreams of death, which for a moment caused Freudian psychoanalysts to hesitate, the anguish which accompanies them, exhibit a death encountered, refused, cursed as a punishment, or as a contradiction. But in the serene dreams of fulfillment, there, too, is death: whether with the new visage of resurrection, for the healed man, or as the calming, at last, of life. But in every case death is the absolute meaning of the dream.[27]

Therefore death dreams, whether anguished or serene (a final distinction), fulfill the dream's ultimate vocation. Returning to an earlier distinction—between death dreams seen as a contradiction (as Freud did), and death dreams seen as a serene fulfillment (whether a resurrection, a healing, or a calming)—he concludes with confidence: "But in every case death is the absolute meaning of the dream."

COMMENTARY

Philosophers have offered various interpretations of dreaming, and of death dreams in particular. For Plato dreams were rational; for Aristotle, irrational. To Socrates, dreams were important, especially in his last days when he interpreted them prophetically. Artemidorus, among the early philosophers, addressed death head-on in his *The Interpretation of Dreams*. He provided a fairly sophisticated way (for his times) of interpreting death in dreams. Aside from general remarks (e.g. "if dead men return to life again, it signifies disturbances and losses"), he based his interpretation on the identity of the dreamer. The same dream of dying (more or less) might be interpreted differently according to who dreamt it (that is, whether the dreamer was a slave, a bachelor, a married person, or an athlete).

Descartes, it will be remembered, arrived at the methodology upon which he based his philosophy in a dream. To Bergson, dreams are a web of forgotten memories triggered by somatic stimuli. But it was in Foucault's work where we found the most profound, if not original, understanding. In an essay "Dream Imagination and Existence," Foucault argues that dreams bear the "deepest human meanings" and that in death dreams, especially violent ones, one can recognize "a freedom up against a world." On the one hand a death dream cannot be understood; on the other hand, it constitutes human destiny. The most authentic way, he concludes, to respond to death in a dream is to view it as one's "very existence being accomplished."

From a comparativist's viewpoint, philosophers make a much needed contribution to the study of death dreams. As a second-order function, standing apart from the realm of dreams, philosophers bring a reasoned analysis to the process of interpretation. Less concerned with the meaning of death dreams than with methods for arriving at one's interpretation, philosophers themselves are not in total agreement about the nature of dreaming, or about the meaning of dream symbols. Given that there are a multitude of approaches to death dreams, and that even among philosophers there is no final agreement about the way to interpret them, how can the subject be investigated in the clearest way?

One of the more noted philosophers of the twentieth century, Ludwig Wittgenstein, offers a very helpful suggestion for understanding occurrences to which a single meaning cannot be attributed, namely that of "family resemblances." Like the concept "game," which has many functions (depending on the game being played, the players playing it, and the skills required), death dreaming too has no single function or meaning. Rather, the different kinds of death dreams overlap, partially intersect and are mutually significant in the same way that members of a family both resemble, and are different from, one another. Death dreams in this sense belong together in a network whose "family resemblances" provide a model for investigation. It could be suggested, for instance, that dreams in which the dreamer dies are related to, and should be viewed against, dreams in which the dead return.

From a philosophical standpoint, for example, it would be insufficient to analyze (a) just one death dream, (b) just one type of death dream, and/or (c) just one method of studying death dreams. To do so would be to decontextualize the dream or dream type studied, to ignore the structural correpondences among and between types, and to overlook valuable interpretative implications contained in the fuller context. The way in which one understands a dream in which the dreamer dies, for instance, will be clarified and amplified by one's understanding of dreams in which others die, and dreams in which the dead return. By virtue of their resemblances, in spite of their differences, meanings which might have otherwise remained unnoticed will rise to the surface.

Wittgenstein concluded his *Tractatus Logico-Philosophicus* by writing:

> My propositions serve as elucidations in the following way: anyone who understands me eventually recognizes them as nonsensical, when he has used them—as steps—to climb up beyond them. (He must, so to speak, throw away the ladder after he has climbed up it.) (6.54)

In a sense, the same can be said about the interpretations of dreams found in this chapter, if not in the entire book. They can be used as steps to be climbed up on, and then to be climbed beyond. At some point, philosophically speaking, the interpretations presented here become the ground and source for newer, more personal interpretations. The philosophic tradition encourages, as Socrates taught, to search out truth for oneself, and in so doing to question and challenge all received viewpoints. This is not to say that the views presented in this chapter are necessarily inadequate, or for that matter necessarily correct, rather that they must be existentially engaged by the reader before they can be validated or dismissed.

With the philosophical context behind us, we are better prepared now to shift our attention to the psychological domain. As will become apparent, philosophical discourse and psychological discourse, while related by virtue of phenomenological and existential pursuits, are dissimilar in terms of applied methodology. Our question in the following chapter will be simple, though its answer will be varied: What new understandings does the study of psychology bring to the subject of death in dreams?

NOTES

[1]C.B. Radcliffe, "A Speculation About Dreaming," in *The Contemporary Review,* 40 (1881), 105, and Horatio King, "On Dreams," in *The New England Magazine,* 2, No. 3 (1890), 329.

[2]*Plato: The Last Days of Socrates,* translated by Hugh Tredennick (New York: Penguin, 1954), 80–81.

[3]*Ibid.,* 103.

[4]Plato, *The Republic,* translated by Benjamin Jowett (New York: The Modern Library, 1941) 330–331.

[5]A.J.J. Ratcliff, *A History of Dreams* (Boston: Small, Maynard & Co., 1923), 45.

[6]*The Works of Aristotle,* translated by W.D. Ross (Oxford: The Clarendon Press, 1908), Chapter I.

[7]C.A. Meier, *Healing Dream and Ritual: Ancient Incubation and Modern Psychotherapy* (Switzerland: Daimon Verlag, 1989), 122.

[8]Artemidorus of Daldis, "A Soothsayer's Dream Book," in *The New World of Dreams,* edited by Ralph L. Woods and Herbert B. Greenhouse (New York: Macmillan Publishing Co., Inc., 1974), 135–136.

[9]Artemidorus, *The Interpretation of Dreams,* translated by Robert J. White (New Jersey: Noyes Press, 1975), 83–84, 129, 130.

[10]*Ibid.,* 16.

[11]*Ibid.,* 126.

[12]*Ibid.,* 127.

[13]Cicero, "No Divine Energy Inspires Dreams," *The New World of Dreams,* 171–173.

[14]Thomas Hobbes, *Leviathan* (London: George Routledge & Sons, 1885), 6.

[15]Lancelot Law Whyte's, *The Unconscious Before Freud* (New York: Basic Books, Inc., 1960), 90.

[16]René Descartes, *Discourse on Method,* translated by John Veitch (Chicago: Henry Regnery Co., 1949), 35.

[17]Blaise Pascal, *Pascal Pensées* (New York: E.P. Dutton & Co., 1958), 104–105.

[18]Henri Bergson, *Dreams* (New York: B.W. Huebsch, 1914), 35.

[19]*Ibid.,* 46.

[20]*Ibid.,* 47.

[21]Michel Foucault, "Dreams, Imagination, and Existence," in *Dream & Existence,* edited by Keith Moeller (a special issue from *The Review of Existential Psychology & Psychiatry,* Vol. XIX, No. 1), 32.

[22]*Ibid.,* 49.

[23]*Ibid.,* 54. Interestingly, Foucault notes: "It is doubtless no accident that Freud was halted, in his dream interpretation, by the recounting of dreams of death. They marked, in effect, an absolute limit to the biological principle of the satisfaction of desire; they showed, Freud sensed only too keenly, the need for a dialectic."

[24]*Ibid.*

[25]*Ibid.*

[26]*Ibid.,* 55.

[27]*Ibid.*

Chapter 7 PSYCHOLOGICAL TRADITIONS

I was walking barefoot on a wooden lattice, which was floating in the sky, and inlaid with smooth round stones. If I looked down through the lattice, I could see the deep blue sky going on forever.

I walked across the lattice into a grey, dusty rock quarry on my left. A crowd of unfamiliar people were there. All of us were milling around the southern wall of the quarry. A large black Mafia staff car came roaring up, and several black-clad gangsters jumped out of the car and machine gunned us to death. We all died simultaneously.

I recall that in the dream I experienced the actual sensation of dying. Although I can't consciously remember exactly how it felt, I do recollect that the death process involved sensations of dispersion and dissolution, and that it was pleasant, not at all frightening, and was quite freeing both in a physical and emotional sense.

After we (the group) died, I remember a momentary lapse of consciousness. When I came to, all of us had lost our human bodies, and each person consisted of a brightly colored column of light. No two people had the same color. All of us were laughing and talking to each other (telepathically, I assume), very much enjoying the death experience. We were all floating upwards. As we floated, our separate colors became increasingly less distinct as we diffused and merged into each other. This was accompanied by a profound sense of gradual loss of individual identity and fusion into one group consciousness. It was an incredible feeling which I can't describe anymore, except to say that it was happy and peaceful. As we realized that we were all about to lose our individual identities for good, we called out goodbye to each other. It wasn't a sorrowful leave-taking; rather, it was a joyous farewell to one way of being and a welcome to another.

Finally we all completely lost individual identity. After this happened, we saw a brilliant white column of light in front of us. We shot up alongside the column, moving faster and faster. Somehow we knew that this column was the source of all things.[1]

Perhaps in none of the chapters of this text are dreams considered to be as significant, and as crucial for understanding human behavior, as in this one. And, at the same time, few of the chapters evidence as much variety and disagreement as this does, for every psychologist has his or her own theory for interpreting dreams. Already this situation was evident in post-biblical times where, reportedly, there were twenty-four interpreters of dreams in Jerusalem. It is said that one day a man had a dream. He decided to take it to each of the twenty-four interpreters. None of them interpreted his dream in the same way and yet, as the story goes, each interpretation was fulfilled in one way or another. Thus arose the saying: "The dream follows the mouth (of the one who interprets it)."[2]

In some ways it is like that in the field of psychology today, except that the twenty-four interpretations have been replaced by at least two hundred and twenty-four more. According to much of the vast literature on the subject, the images and ideas which arise in dreams are said by various theorists to be caused by:

- the unconscious workings of the brain;
- psychosomatic disturbances;
- sensory stimulation (e.g. sounds and light);
- internal brain stimulations (e.g. physiological abnormalities);
- repressed conflicts or real-life struggles;
- illness, fever, severe sicknesses;
- deep grief, trauma, mourning or extreme elation;
- pre-natal, intra-uterine regression;
- the need for creative problem solving; and
- a spiritual quest for deeper meaning in life.[3]

Our purpose in this chapter will be neither to provide materials in support of the major dream theorists, nor to evaluate and select some of them over others. Rather, we will focus our attention on the two most significant theorists of the twentieth century—Freud and Jung—and then mention more recent work being done in the field of death dreams, especially Marie-Louise von Franz and James Hillman, each of whom views death dreams in a trans/formational context.

SIGMUND FREUD

Shortly after Christianity gained control of European culture (under church-inspired thinkers who linked sexuality, sin and demons together with the unconscious), dreams fell from grace, so to speak, and were considered to be untrustworthy. During the nineteenth century this began to change with the advent of a more scientific approach to the human personality. As a result of encountering patients with apparent physical disorders, such as paralysis (with no seeming organic causation), Freud developed a new approach to treatment which he called psychoanalysis. Basically, this approach consisted of encouraging patients to "free associate" in response to set questions, thereby to uncover underlying symptoms which Freud felt were rooted in some form of sexual difficulty. This method lead Freud to realize the utter significance of dreams as the "royal road" to the unconscious mind.

In 1900, Freud published six hundred copies of *The Interpretation of Dreams,* about which he wrote in a 1931 Foreword: "Insight such as this falls to one's lot but once in a lifetime."[4] What insight? First and foremost, that "*The content of the dream is . . . the fulfillment of a wish; its motive is a wish.*"[5] That dreams were produced by suppressed or repressed wishes seeking fulfillment was the cornerstone of Freud's theory. To illustrate this point, he referred to a Hungarian proverb told to him by one of his students. It asked: "What does the goose dream of?" and answered: "Of maize." Freud remarked: "The whole theory that the dream is the fulfillment of a wish is contained in these two sentences."[6]

In response to foreseen criticism of his view, Freud distinguished between "dream-content" and the "thought-content" which lay behind the dream. There are, he continued, two levels of the dream: its *manifest* content (that which is consciously remembered), and its *latent* content (unconscious wishes and fantasies which have been denied expression). Of these two languages, separated by what Freud called "the censor" (the force of repression), it was latent content which had priority over manifest content. What was radically new about Freud's approach was that whereas previous interpreters of dreams concerned themselves only with the remembered, manifest content, Freud traced "relations between the latent dream-thoughts and the manifest dream-content, and the processes by which the latter has grown out of the former."[7]

Given this theoretical context, what does Freud write about death dreams? In his fifth chapter, "The Material and Sources of Dreams," Freud turned his attention to typical dreams among which are what he called "Dreams of the Death of Beloved Persons." He began by distinguishing two classes of such dreams: those in which the dreamer is unmoved by the death, and those in which the dreamer is "profoundly grieved." The former dreams he ignored since they were intended to mask something else such as the wish to see the beloved person again. Death dreams which affected the dreamer profoundly, however, to Freud signified "the wish that the person in question might die."[8] Since he anticipated a strong reaction to this theory, he then attempted to prove it.

He began by suggesting that the wish fulfillment was not always a current wish but may have been a bygone, buried and repressed wish. He added:

> If anyone dreams that his father or mother, his brother or sister, has died, and his dream expresses grief, I should never adduce this as proof that he wishes any of them dead now. The theory of dreams does not go as far as to require this; it is satisfied with concluding that the dreamer has wished them dead at some time or other during his childhood.[9]

Though many people love their brothers and sisters now, they may harbor unconscious, hostile wishes which survive from an earlier time. Freud pointed out for instance that children around the age of four are capable of extreme jealousy and hostility toward siblings.

The death itself may also be disguised. For example, one of his female patients, who denied ever having a death dream, once told Freud a dream she dreamed repeatedly:

> A number of children, all her brothers and sisters with her boy and girl cousins, were romping about in a meadow. Suddenly they all grew wings, flew up, and were gone.

To this, Freud added the following interpretation:

> ... we can hardly fail to recognize it as a dream of the death of all the brothers and sisters, in its original form, and but little influenced by the censorship. I will venture to add the following analysis of it: on the death of one out of this large number of children—in this case the children of two brothers were brought up together as brothers and sisters—would not our dreamer, at that time not yet four years of age, have asked some wise, grown-up person: "What becomes of children when they are dead?" The answer would probably have been: "They grow wings and become angels." After this explanation, all the brothers and sisters and cousins in the dream now have wings, like angels and—this is the important point—they fly away. Our little angel-maker is left alone: just think, the only one out of such a crowd! That the children romp about a meadow, from which they fly away, points almost certainly to butterflies—it is as though the child had been influenced by the same association of ideas which led the ancients to imagine Psyche, the soul, with the wings of a butterfly.[10]

If the death-wish a child had for brothers and sisters was a function of childish egoism, how could Freud explain the same wish for the child's parents who raised the child lovingly? In response, Freud noted that dreams in which a parent died usually, though he admitted not always, referred to the parent of the same sex as the dreamer. It was as though at an early age the boy regarded his father, like the girl regarded her mother, "as a rival in

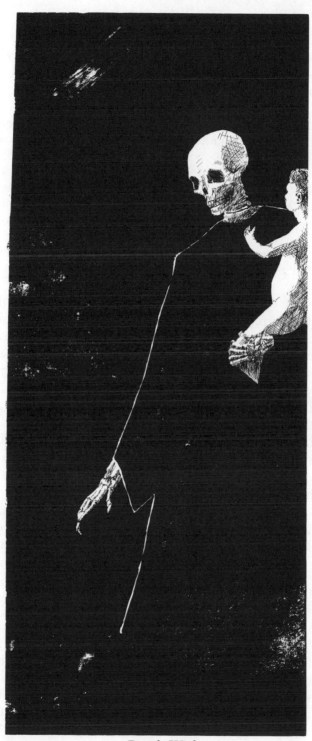

Death Wish

love." Further, the sexual wishes of the child awakened at an early stage with the earliest affection of the girl-child directed toward the father, the boy-child toward the mother. Freud writes:

> For the boy the father, and for the girl the mother, becomes an obnoxious rival, and we have already shown, in the case of brothers and sisters, how readily in children this feeling leads to the death-wish. As a general rule, sexual selection soon makes its appearance in the parent; it is a natural tendency for the father to spoil his little daughters, and for the mother to take the part of the sons. . . . Thus the child is obeying its own sexual instinct, and at the same time reinforcing the stimulus proceeding from the parents, when its choice between the parents corresponds with their own.[11]

Drawing upon legends from antiquity, Freud reinforced his theory. He referred to the play *Oedipus Rex* of Sophocles in which Oedipus, the son of King Laius and Queen Jocasta, through a tragic fate killed his father and married his mother. Freud suggested that "there must be a voice within us which is prepared to acknowledge the compelling power of fate in the *Oedipus*," a voice which is "nothing more or less than a wish-fulfillment—the fulfillment of the wish of our childhood."[12]

With Freud's *The Interpretation of Dreams,* the study of dreaming was resurrected from the periphery of cultural concern, and shifted to a central place in attempts to understand the human personality. What was radically new about Freud's approach to dreams was his insistence that *latent* dream content is more significant than *manifest* dream content, and that dreams are therefore the fulfillment of wishes, either current or bygone ones.

CARL JUNG

The Swiss psychiatrist Carl Jung, born in 1875, was a student of Freud's and a very close friend between the years 1907 and 1913. Like Freud, Jung studied dreams, but for him they revealed far more than personal wishes or repressed fears. They were linked to universal, archetypal symbols. A split between Freud and Jung developed after Jung published his first important book, *The Psychology of the Unconscious* (1912), which was critical of Freud's emphasis on the function of sexuality in personal development. Jung's approach, called analytic psychology, distinguished two major attitudes: *extroversion* (when a person is oriented toward the objective, external world), and *introversion* (when a person is oriented toward the subjective, inner world). The psyche for Jung was a self-regulating system which maintains its equilibrium (between introversion and extroversion) and is comprised of both consciousness and the unconsciousness.

To illustrate Jung's analysis of consciousness, we will briefly describe its four functions—thinking, feeling, intuition and sensation—which counter-balance each other. If thinking is extroverted, feeling is introverted. If intuition is introverted, sensation is extroverted, and vice versa. To picture this movement, one can think of a wheel on the circumference of which thinking is opposite feeling and sensation is opposite intuition. The psyche results from a tension of these opposites, with the conscious and the unconscious dependent on each other. Psychic energy emerges from this tension. The degree of conflict here determines the amount of energy that is expressed, and its intensity.

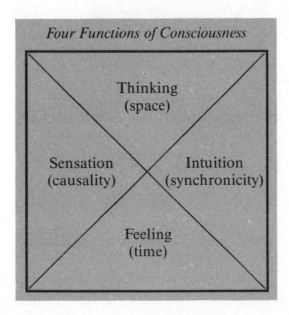

Four Functions of Consciousness

Thinking
(space)

Sensation
(causality)

Intuition
(synchronicity)

Feeling
(time)

Considering an organism as a unity, the fundamental process tends always to reestablish a wholeness (or equilibrium) in the following way: "Sensation" is the way individuals meet the outside world; through "thinking" one moves to understand whatever the senses bring into consciousness; through "feeling" a decision must be made about whether an experience is pleasurable or not, accepted or rejected; and through "intuition" the implications or overtones of insight are known.

While all four functions are experienced by every individual, they are not always evident to the same degree. Any one of the four can be dominant. For some, one function may be more highly developed than others. Whichever function is dominant rises to a conscious level. A person uses just one function as a means to experience the world and as a basis of organizing personality. However, there are many variations since the functions overlap. Ideally, the opposites will balance one another and maintain a constant interrelationship.

When we examine Jung's analysis of the unconsciousness, we come to another distinction which must be balanced, one between the *personal* (or individual) unconsciousness, and the *collective* (or archetypal) unconsciousness. For Jung the collective unconsciousness (which contains pre-historic inherited images shared with all other humans) operates at a deeper level than Freud's unconscious, and manifests itself in archetypal images and ideas (universal patterns or motifs which are the fundamental content of morals, mythologies, legends and fairy tales). These archetypes, varied though they be, occur in what Jung called "big" dreams. Distinct from "little" dreams ("the nightly fragments of fantasy coming from the subjective and personal sphere"), what he calls "big" dreams "employ numerous mythological motifs that characterize the life of the hero of that greater man who is semi-divine by nature."[13]

While Freud, relying mostly on free association, understood dreams as expressions of infantile, irrational desires, Jung interpreted them as expressions of the wisdom of the unconscious. While Freud relied only on a single dream cause to formulate his interpretation (i.e. wish fulfillment), Jung emphasized that it was necessary to study a series of dreams—the symbols for which were never static but always in the process of formation. While Freud viewed dreams as a repression-releasing device, for Jung dreams awakened the dreamer to a blind spot in the dreamer's self-awareness. While Freud viewed dreams as a depression of mental imagery through which he approached his patient's neuroses, to Jung dreams were a healthy expression of the unconscious. And while Freud used a purely personal approach to dream interpretation, Jung applied the collectivity of humanity's common history. Therefore, Jung was unable to accept Freud's reduction of all dreams to mere wish-fulfillments.

> As against Freud's view that the dream is essentially a wish fulfillment, I hold with my friend and collaborator Alphonse Maeder that the dream is *a spontaneous self-portrayal, in symbolic form, of the actual situation in the unconscious.*[14]

Essentially Jung gave a different value to the unconscious than Freud had, a value which enabled Jung to make claims which would have been inconceivable to Freud. About 1930, Jung wrote:

> In this respect I go several steps further than Freud. For me the unconscious is not just a receptacle for all unclean spirits and other odious legacies from the dead past. . . . It is in very truth the eternally living, creative, germinal layer in each of us, and though it may make use of age-old symbolical images, it nevertheless intends them to be understood in a new way.[15]

To understand Jung's view of death more clearly, and in the process his understanding of dreams, we now turn to two specific texts—*The Soul and Death,* and his autobiography *Memories, Dreams, Reflections.* In his writings, Jung repeatedly refused to state without qualification that there is life after death. However, he usually provided copious evidence that it was so. Clearly, Jung himself believed in a continuation of individual existence beyond physical death, though the nature of that existence remained undefined.

In *The Soul and Death,* Jung compared the fear of death in old age with fear of life in youth, and found both fears to be equally neurotic.

> Many young people have at bottom a panic-fear of life (though at the same time they intensely desire it), and an even greater number of the aging have the same fear of death. Yes, I have known those people who most feared life when they were young to suffer later just as much from the fear of death. When they are young, one says they have infantile resistances against the normal demands of life; one should really say the same thing when they are old, for they are likewise afraid of one of life's normal demands. We are so convinced that death is simply the end of a process that *it does not ordinarily occur to us to conceive of death as a goal and a fulfillment,* as we do without hesitation the aims and purposes of youthful life in its ascendance.[16]

Jung described what he called the "curve of life" which ascended in youth and declined with old age. However, the curve of our psychological development generally lags behind the curve of our physical development, so that, as we grow to maturity, we tend to cling to our childhood and, as our bodies decline in old age to death, we reminisce about the achievements of mid-life. In both cases, we are out of touch with our natural life, and this dysfunction causes a loss of vibrancy and vigor. He stated, "From the middle of life onward, only he remains vitally alive who is ready to die with life."[17]

The dreams and fantasies of the young are generally preoccupied with the future, as they should be. In the elderly, however, dreams are more frequently concerned with the decline of body and the approach of physical death. Thus our psyche seems to know and prepare us for the natural course of our lives. More astonishing is the fact that the psyche, as evidenced in dreams, behaves as if it will continue beyond physical death. Again, Jung offers evidence for the existence of life after death without conclusively affirming it. Trying to maintain some semblance of scientific objectivity, and to ward off charges of "mysticism," he writes:

We may establish with reasonable certainty that an individual consciousness as it relates to ourselves has come to an end. But whether this means that the continuity of the psychic process is interrupted too remains doubtful, since the psyche's attachment to the brain can be affirmed with far less certitude today than it could fifty years ago. Psychology must first digest certain parapsychological facts, which it has hardly begun to do as yet.[18]

What then can we say about death dreams in a Jungian context? First and foremost, for Jung death dreams revealed far more than a person's fears or anxieties about dying; more often they are to be linked with a universal, primordial imagery or set of archetypes. As well, he insisted on interpreting dreams in a series in order to understand their fullest context. In his autobiography, *Memories, Dreams, Reflections,* Jung provides a series of death dreams—dreams he experienced at the time of his mother's death, as well as his own dreams at the time he was near death. For instance:

> While I was working on this book (*Wandlungen und Symbole der Libido*), I had dreams which presaged the forthcoming break with Freud. One of the most significant had its scene in a mountainous region on the Swiss–Austrian border. It was toward evening, and I saw an elderly man in the uniform of an Imperial Austrian customs official. He walked past, somewhat stooped, without paying any attention to me. His expression was peevish, rather melancholic and vexed. There were other persons present, and someone informed me that the old man was not really there, but was the ghost of a customs official who had died years ago. "He is one of those who still couldn't die properly." That was the first part of the dream.[19]

When he analyzed this dream, Jung associated the word "censorship" with the "border" that appears in the dream—the border between the conscious and the unconscious on the one hand, and Freud and himself on the other. Since, at that time, Freud's authority had lost much of its impact for Jung, Freud was represented by the customs official. Jung wondered whether this dream indeed represented a death wish which Freud had suggested Jung felt toward him.[20]

In a dream that Jung called one of the most important in his life, he was in an unknown, two-story house that belonged to him. Fine rococo oil paintings covered the walls of the upper level. When he descended the stairs to explore the lower levels, he discovered the rooms to be older, darker, the furnishings medieval, the floors of red brick. Passing through a heavy door, he descended a stone stairway which led to a vaulted, ancient room in the cellar. The walls dated from Roman times. Descending another stairway, he entered a low cave cut in the rock.

> Thick dust lay on the floor, and in the dust were scattered bones and broken pottery, like remains of a primitive culture. I discovered two human skulls, obviously very old and half disintegrated. Then I awoke.[21]

When Jung told the dream to Freud, Freud urged him to focus on the two skulls and to find a wish associated with them by which Jung knew Freud implied a death-wish. But he found none. Rather, to Jung the house represented an image of the psyche in which each level (of the house) represented different layers of historic consciousness—the upper representing normal consciousness, and the lowest representing the primitive, or archetypal, within himself. It was during this time that Jung came to feel how keenly he experienced the difference between himself and Freud.

The following dreams are associated with his father's and then his mother's death:

> Six weeks after his death my father appeared to me in a dream. Suddenly he stood before me and said that he was coming back from his holiday. He had made a good recovery and was now coming home. I thought he would be annoyed with me for having moved into his room. But not a bit of it! Nevertheless, I felt ashamed because I had imagined he was dead. Two days later the dream was repeated. My father had recovered and was coming home, and again I reproached myself because I had thought he was dead. Later I kept ask-

ing myself: "What does it mean that my father returns in dreams and that he seems so real?" It was an unforgettable experience, and it forced me for the first time to think about life after death.[22]

Later, Jung reports, he continued to ponder the meaning of his dead father's return in dreams; he seemed so real.

Equally important to him were dream experiences he had before his mother's death.

> The night before her death I had a frightening dream. I was in a dense, gloomy forest; fantastic, gigantic boulders lay about among huge jungle-like trees. It was a heroic, primeval landscape. Suddenly I heard a piercing whistle that seemed to resound through the whole universe. My knees shook. Then there were crashings in the underbrush, and a gigantic wolfhound with a fearful, gaping maw burst forth. At the sight of it, the blood froze in my veins. It tore past me, and I suddenly knew: the Wild Huntsman had commanded it to carry away a human soul. I awoke in deadly terror, and the next morning I received the news of my mother's passing.[23]

What shook Jung about this dream was a superficial consideration that it was the devil which took her. But upon further reflection, he realized it was the "Wild Huntsman" who, in the season of January storms, could have been Wotan (the god of the Alemannia forefathers), who had taken his mother to her ancestors—"negatively to the 'wild horde'," but positively to "the blessed folk." Thus, to Jung, the dream indicated that the soul of his mother was taken to "that greater territory of the self," taken into that "wholeness" of nature and spirit where all contradictions are resolved.

If there is to be an afterlife existence for Jung, it would likely continue on the level of consciousness attained while alive. Jung came to this conclusion through analyzing dreams in which the dead appeared.

> I had another experience of the evolution of the soul after death when—about a year after my wife's death—I suddenly awoke one night and knew that I had been with her in the south of France, in Provence, and had spent an entire day

with her. She was engaged on studies of the Grail tree. That
seemed significant to me, for she had died before completing
her work on this subject.[24]

It was extremely reassuring to him to think of his wife continuing
her work, begun while alive, after her death.

A final dream, one which concerns the problem of the relationship between the eternal and the earthly self, begins on a
hiking trip.

> I was walking along a little road through a hilly landscape;
> the sun was shining and I had a wide view in all directions.
> Then I came to a small wayside chapel. The door was ajar,
> and I went in. To my surprise there was no image of the
> Virgin on the altar, and no crucifix either, but only a wonder-
> ful flower arrangement. But then I saw that on the floor in
> front of the altar, facing me, sat a yogi—in lotus posture, in
> deep meditation. When I looked at him, more closely, I real-
> ized that he had my face. I started in profound fright, and
> awoke with the thought: "Aha, so he is the one who is medi-
> tating me. He has a dream and I am it." I knew that when he
> awakened, I would no longer be.[25]

Jung's analysis of this dream, which occurred in 1944 after
an illness, in a way highlights the crucial elements of his dream
theory. In the dream, his "self" meditates his earthly form, and
assumes a three-dimensional shape. The yogi represents his
"unconscious prenatal wholeness." At first, from the standpoint
of his ego-consciousness, he just sees the yogi. But when he looks
again, more deeply, he sees himself. Rather than ego generating the unconscious, the unconscious is the generator of his
empirical personality. The unconscious images, for Jung, have
a spontaneous reality of their own. One can recall Chuang
Tzu's butterfly dream at this juncture. Is it possible, from Jung's
perspective, that the butterfly represented Chuang Tzu's true self
which generated, as Jung's yogi did, Chuang Tzu's empirical
self? For Jung is convinced that "the unconscious produces the
idea of a deified or divine [person]," which he explains not as
regression, but as a spiritual development which can be traced in
ancient, mythic symbols.[26]

MARIE-LOUISE VON FRANZ

Just before he died, Jung was interviewed by the British Broadcasting Corporation (BBC), and was asked by the interviewer if he believed in life after death. Replying that he did, Jung gave as a reason the fact that the dreams of people on the verge of death seem to ignore death as if it were a relatively unimportant event.

Those who follow Jung's thought, especially recent Jungian analysts, provide a slightly different interpretation of a dying person's dreams. Robert Bosnak, for example, in his *Dreaming with an Aids Patient,* traces the dreams of a client stricken with this deadly illness. The dreams are increasingly filled with images of physical entropy, as well as glimmers of hope (e.g. a little girl who looked like a "picture of summer" and who readily played with the dreamer). Even more clearly, Jane Wheelwright, in her *The Death of a Woman,* writes of the trans/formational effect evident in the dreams of a dying cancer patient. While Sally, the patient, did not specifically dream of her own death, the dreams convinced Wheelwright that "when death is the issue, the unconscious takes up in dreams whatever is unresolved."[7]

Marie-Louise von Franz is another dream analyst who, to a large extent, follows Jung's basic approach to dreams. She asserts that there are dreams which symbolically indicate the explicit continuation of a "psychic life" after death. In 1987, an English translation appeared of her *On Dreams and Death* which expanded and applied Jung's dream insights specifically in the realm of death dreams. Agreeing with Jung, von Franz states that the message from our unconscious, "that death is a 'cure' and that there is an afterlife," cannot be mere wish-fulfillment, "for at the same time the end of physical existence is also predicted, quite brutally and unequivocally."[28] Because dreams are the "voice of nature within us" and are not under our control, von Franz believes that they prepare us for our own death. She suggests that when people are aware of their impending death, or even when they are unaware of it, dreams may play out the drama quite bluntly. While the physical body dies, she writes, simultaneously certain dreams contain elements and symbols which point to an afterlife. In her book, von Franz comments

largely upon archetypal death dreams which she amplifies
through depth psychology, alchemical symbolism and parapsychological research.

The most intriguing aspect of von Franz's approach is
the variety of trans/formational archetypes she finds in death
dreams. Prominent among these archetypal symbols for life after
death is the image of vegetation which frequently occurs in the
dreams of people who are close to death. Vegetation refers to a
continuation of the life process which, symbolically, outlines the
opposites of life and death.

While the death of vegetation often appears as an image of
human death, at the same time it is also a symbol for resurrection. According to Egyptian belief, resurrection is not a simple
matter of restoration of the dead body, but a complete recon-
struction of it. The ancient Egyptians believed, along with the
early alchemists, that resurrection occurs from the remains of the
dead body, not just from the soul but from transformed matter
as well.

Another widespread motif, she writes, is the "death-wedding."
In Greece, Artemidorus wrote that dreaming of a wedding could
mean death since weddings are regarded as turning points in

Egyptian Death Dream

human life. In ancient Greece, von Franz likewise notes, the innermost coffin chamber was the *thalamos,* or bridal chamber. Other dream images of life after death include: the image of a dark, narrow birth passage (such as tunnels, pipes, and heavy dark spots), clouds, black holes, tombs, revolving doors, a journey beyond the sun, and a burglar, or someone unfamiliar, who unexpectedly enters one's present life. Von Franz adds:

> From my own experience, it seems to me that the terror-filled, uncanny aspect of the "other" appears especially when the dreamer has as yet *no relation to death or does not expect it.* Basically, the figures of personified death (death, devil, Yama, Jesus, Hades, Hel, etc.) seem to be nothing other than *a dark side of the god image.* It is actually God, or a goddess, who brings death to (humans) and the less familiar (one) is with this dark side of the divine the more negative (one's) experience will be.[29]

In the second half of *On Dreams and Death,* von Franz shifts her attention more to the psyche and the body, to union and transformation (here I spell the word as she does without the slash). Quoting the Komarios text (one of the oldest texts of Greco-Egyptian alchemy, dating back to the first century), before spirit and soul can return to the body, the soul must undergo a transformation; a dissolution or sacrifice of the old body must occur. Von Franz indicates that sacrifice usually means surrendering something to a higher authority, whether a god or gods (e.g. a sacrifice of the body in the Egyptian mummification ritual). In psychological terms, the body is transformed into collective unconsciousness, and into the Self. Thus we have a joining of both the individual self and the collective unconscious into the transformed body.

When she shifts to near-death experiences, von Franz states that ego and Self are almost completely united. When Jung was near death, she recalls, he described a change in his everyday ego whereby everything of his earthly existence was stripped away, but something remained, as if he now carried along with him everything he had ever experienced or done. Jung felt that he was a bundle of what had been accomplished existing in an objective form. Von Franz further adds that at death, together with the cessation of affects, desires, and emotions, much of what one calls the ego seems to disappear.

Reflecting on the phenomenon of shifting ego-identity, von Franz notes that she has often observed in some people that a "second consciousness," or a "deeper consciousness," was present as they were dying. On the one hand, a person's ordinary consciousness continued to make future plans while, occasionally, a more serious consciousness broke through which was well aware of the impending death. In dreams occurring at this time, one often can see, von Franz writes, a transformation that leads to a union of body and psyche, or of ego and Self.

Addressing the final resurrection as the reunion of psyche and the body, the Komarios text again is quoted:

> And the soul (is) united with the body, since the body had become divine through its relation to the soul and it dwelt in the soul. For the body clothed itself in the light of divinity, and the darkness departed from it, and all were united in love, body, soul and spirit, and all became one; in this the mystery is hidden.[30]

Von Franz states that what appears to be the reunion of soul and body is no longer a union of opposites, since body has become psyche as well—the body-*soul*. She writes that one finds the motif of an eternal house in the Beyond in many grave rituals (e.g. the stupas of Buddhist cultures), and she notes that tombs are not dwelling places for the dead, but rather a substitute for the mortal frame of the deceased. Jung himself, two months before he died, dreamt that the "tower" (which he had built for himself) was now completed and ready for habitation. Von Franz concludes:

> *All of the dreams* of people who are facing death indicate that the unconscious, that is, our instinct world, prepares consciousness not for a definite end but for a profound transformation and for a kind of continuation of the life process which, however, is unimaginable to everyday consciousness.[31]

According to von Franz, this transformational continuation of the life process compares with various religious teachings about life after death. Each employs mythic images, the structural correspondences of which prove surprising.

JAMES HILLMAN

Plowing the same field of the psyche and dreams as did Freud and Jung, James Hillman approaches them from a different angle. Rather than selecting one theorist over the other, he recognizes the contributions of each, blends them together and then moves beyond them. From Freud he inherits three views of the dream: the *romantic* (that dreams contain hidden, personal messages from another world), the *rationalist* (that the manifest dream images were worthless and needed to be deciphered into latent content), and the *somaticist* (that dreams reflect physiological processes which for Freud had to do mainly with sexuality). And from Jung he inherits the notion that the dream is a *compensation.* That is, Jung approached psychology in terms of opposites which were either converted, regulated, unified or seen as identical. Dreams, for Jung, were always partial, always incomplete without the dayworld, without a compensated interpretation which sought to locate its hidden balance. In that sense, death dreams can never be broken apart from life-meaning.

Starting with Freud and Jung—each of whom assumed that dream figures were interior psychic possibilities—Hillman reverses the usual procedure of translating dreams into the ego-language of the dayworld. Instead, he proposes translating the ego into dream-language. To accomplish this, Hillman grounds his dream theory in underworld mythology. Recalling the affinity between sleep and death, and the ancient people's understanding that in sleep the soul wanders away from the body, he writes: "Like Hermes with Hercules, we take the dream-ego as an apprentice, learning to familiarize itself with the underworld by learning how to dream and learning how to die."[32]

Looking at the word "death" etymologically, Hillman indicates that its root means "hidden" (i.e. buried, shrouded, concealed, secret, black, forbidden, subterranean). This underworld, for Hillman, is the realm of the psyche, or, more bluntly, *is* psyche. The transformative work of dreams, he states, is to construct the "House of Hades, one's individual death" upon which each dream builds. Therefore, "each dream is practice in entering the underworld, as preparation of the psyche for death."[33] To interpret dreams, from this point of view is to recognize that dreamwork is really death-work. By death, Hillman does not mean literal physical death, but metaphoric, mythic death. In this way, Hillman has attempted to bring death back from its cultural exile by reminding dreamers that each morning is a return from death.

If for Hillman dreams are the material of the underworld, itself the mythological abode of death (in various personae), it would seem to follow that death is the backdrop of all dreams. But this is not the case for Hillman—the soul is. Rather than focusing on death as the content of dreams, death is seen as the most radical metaphor for expressing a shift in consciousness from dayworld to dreamworld. Therefore, when Hillman discusses the interpretative implications of his theory, what he calls "deepening a perspective," he does not present clues to death dreams. To assume that a dream of a black dog or a leaky jar was predictive of imminent death would be to reduce the dream to rational, dayworld meanings. For Hillman the key is to "assume the underworld perspective," thus to "release radically different insights from what one usually expects."[34]

Resisting the temptation, as so many books on dreams do, to tell readers what certain types of dreams mean, Hillman concludes by listing several dream images (e.g. black, sickness, animals, roundness, ceremonial eating, door and gates, ice, and space) which initiate one into the underworld perspective. From this perspective, a killer in one's dream is neither merely a shadow element of the dreamer which seeks integration into the dream's personality, nor simply a signal that some aspect of the dreamer's ego must be overcome. For Hillman, "there is a divine death figure in the killer, either Hades, or Thanatos, or Kronos-Saturn, or Dis Pater, or Hermes, a death demon who would *separate consciousness from its life attachments.*"[35]

COMMENTARY

One of the major concerns flowing through this chapter is an attempt to identify the underlying cause of dreams. Do dreams originate, as Freud argued, from the eruption of repressed wishes and desires seeking to find their fulfillment? Or do dreams, on the other hand, arise from the reservoir of the collective unconscious in archetypal images and symbols, as Jung argues? Freud was convinced that there are two levels of the dream—its *manifest* content and its *latent* content. It was the latter which, for Freud, had priority over the former. Death dreams therefore were interpreted as a death wish, either in the present or at some time in the past.

Like Freud, Jung valued dreams; however he interpreted them much differently. Jung differentiated between the *personal* unconscious (little dreams) and the *collective* unconscious (archetypal dreams). For Jung, death dreams, when they are of the latter type, are to be linked with a universal primordial imagery of trans/formation. He interpreted a dream about his mother's death as in indication that her soul had been taken into that wholeness of nature and spirit which he calls the Self.

For von Franz, who follows Jung's lead, death dreams are transformational. When one dreams of his or her own death, von Franz writes, the soul and the body are reunited and become the body-*soul*. In a sentence she writes: "All the dreams of people who are facing death indicate that the unconscious . . . prepares consciousness not for a definite end, but for a profound transformation of the life process." And for Hillman, since the underworld is psyche, and each dream is the dreamer's entering this underworld, each dream so to speak prepares the psyche for its own death. The transformative work in dreams is the construction of the "House of Hades, one's individual death," upon which each dream is built.

From a comparativist's viewpoint, clearly not *all* death dreams are trans/formational in nature. At the same time, it is clear that many death dreams may have a trans/formational intention which, however, is not recognized as such. It is also clear that "big dreams," as Jung called them, or deep dreams of death may indeed represent shifts in self-awareness: from a self which is problematic (e.g. self-deceived, out of balance, incomplete) to a self which is trans/formed (i.e. liberated, more wholly integrated, illumined). In mythic language, one could say that when the experience of death is fully accepted, it naturally (even cosmically) leads to an intense experience of rebirth. It goes without saying that this rebirth may take a variety of forms and culturally differing expressions.

One of Jung's foremost critics, it should be noted, was the Jewish philosophical anthropologist Martin Buber. Buber met Jung in 1934 when he took part in the "Eranos" Conference in Switzerland. In 1952, Buber published his *Eclipse of God,* in which he stated that the key question for Jung was this: "Is God merely a psychic phenomenon or does (God) also exist independently of the psyche of (humans)?"[36] Buber located Jung's answer in the unconscious, since Jung ascribed all statements about God to the *psyche.* Western religions, as we have seen, distinguish between psychic states to which a super-psychic reality "corresponds," and psychic statements to which none corresponds. Buber's concern was that Jung had overstepped the legitimate boundaries of psychology when he suggested that God cannot exist independently of humans and when he reduced God to an "autonomous psychic content." Obviously, one's answer to the question of the source or origin of death dreams (i.e. whether a transpsychic Holy Other is evoked, or an intrapsychic activity) may depend on how one understands this disagreement.

Our point here is to introduce the reader to, and perhaps encourage the reader to further evaluate, the Jung–Buber dialogue, especially since the issues it raises are central to the meeting between religion and psychology. It is not our intention to validate or invalidate either viewpoint. Rather, we are interested in pursuing pathways which take each into consideration, and which may even lead beyond their dialogue. With this in mind, we now turn our attention to ways in which death dreams appear in various literary forms. As we shall see, the literary expression of death dreams opens surprising avenues of interpretation which may otherwise have gone unnoticed.

NOTES

[1]Kyra Gordenev, a free-lance writer, Santa Cruz, California. She was thirteen years old when she had this dream.

[2]Quoted in *The New World of Dreams,* edited by Ralph L. Woods & Herbert B. Greenhouse (New York: Macmillan Publishing Co., Inc., 1974), 158.

[3]See Robert Van de Castle's *The Psychology of Dreaming* (New York: General Learning Press, 1971), 11ff.

[4]Sigmund Freud, *The Interpretation of Dreams* (New York: The Modern Library, 1950; originally copyrighted 1938, copyright renewed 1964 by Gioia B. Bernheim and Edmund Brill, reprinted by permission), "Foreword," dated March 15, 1931. Interestingly, in a footnote in the very beginning of his discussion on "The Method of Dream Interpretation," Freud writes that Artemidorus "has furnished us with the most complete and careful elaboration of dream-interpretation as it existed in the Greco-Roman world" (10).

[5]*Ibid.,* 30.

[6]*Ibid.,* 42–43. A Jewish version of the same proverb asks: "Of what does the hen dream?" and answers, "Of millet."

[7]*Ibid.,* 174. How did Freud work with this latent material? The process by which latent content is inserted in the dream is fourfold: condensation, displacement, considerations of representability, and secondary revision. *Condensation* is the mechanism whereby several latent images are compressed into one (e.g. one's father may also be a teacher, an analyst, a boss, etc.). *Displacement* refers to the transference of an emotion from one situation to another in order to distract the dreamer's attention. *Representability* was Freud's way of saying that of the various unconscious thoughts and images, the preferred ones are those which "admit of visual representation." And *secondary revision* is the process of unconsciously altering the recalled dream in order to make sense of it.

[8]*Ibid.,* 147.

[9]*Ibid.,* 148. He continues that this is so because old wishes are not dead like persons who have died, "but rather like the shades in the Odyssey which awaken to a certain degree of life so soon as they have drunk blood."

[10]*Ibid.,* 152.

[11]*Ibid.,* 156.

[12]*Ibid.,* 161.

[13]Carl G. Jung, *Dreams,* translated by R.F.C. Hull (Princeton: Princeton University Press, 1974), 76, 79.

[14]*Ibid.,* 49. Interestingly, Freud and Jung often shared their dreams. When asked by an interviewer to disclose the content of Freud's dreams, Jung said that he would not betray a confidentiality. When the questioner said, "Since he's dead now, perhaps . . ." to which Jung replied, "Oh no, dreams are stronger than death." Quoted from the film "Face to Face with Dr. Jung," filmed by the BBC in 1958.

[15]Carl G. Jung, *Collected Works,* Vol. 4, translated by R.F.C. Hull (Princeton: Princeton University Press, 1961), 330.

[16]*Wirklichkeit der Seele,* 1934, translated by R.F.C. Hull, in *The Meaning of Death,* edited by Herman Feifel (New York: McGraw-Hill Book Company, Inc., 1959), 4. Italics are added.

[17]*Ibid.,* 6.

[18]*Ibid.,* 12. This characteristic of the psyche is discussed thoroughly in *Synchronicity: An Acausal Connection Principle* (1952), in *Collected Works,* Vol. VIII (Princeton: Princeton University Press, 1967), translated by R.F.C. Hull.

[19]C.G. Jung, *Memories, Dreams, Reflections,* translated by Richard and Clara Winston (New York: Vintage Books, 1965), 163.

[20]In 1909, in Bremen, Jung shared his interest in so-called "bog corpses" with Freud—pre-historic bodies buried in marshes that contained humic acid which acted as a natural mummification agent. At one point a vexed Freud, while at dinner with Jung, suddenly fainted. Afterward, Freud said he was convinced that Jung's chatter about the bog corpses meant that Jung had death-wishes toward him. *Ibid.,* 156.

[21]*Ibid.,* 159.

[22]*Ibid.,* 96–97.

[23]*Ibid.,* 313.

24*Ibid.,* 304.

25*Ibid.,* 323.

26C.G. Jung, *Collected Works,* Vol. XI, translated by R.F.C. Hull (New York: Pantheon Books, Bollingen Series, 1958), 96. In response to this, Maurice Friedman has suggested that there is a danger in Jung's "divinization of the unconscious" in that it may leave him at the mercy of "dark, irrational forces." See *To Deny Our Nothingness* (New York: Delta, 1967), 166.

27Jane Hollister Wheelwright, *The Death of a Woman* (New York: St. Martin's Press, 1981), 48

28Marie-Louise von Franz, *On Dreams and Death,* translated by Emmanuel Kennedy and Vernon Brooks (Boston: Shambhala, 1984), ix.

29*Ibid.,* 72.

30*Ibid.,* 120.

31*Ibid.,* 156.

32James Hillman, *The Dream and the Underworld* (New York: Harper & Row, 1979), 117.

33*Ibid.,* 133.

34*Ibid.,* 143.

35*Ibid.,* 166.

36Martin Buber, *Eclipse of God* (New York: Harper Torchbooks, 1952), 133–134.

Chapter 8   LITERARY TRADITIONS

Lying in a hearse as big as a furniture van, she was surrounded by dead women. There were so many of them that the back door would not close and several legs dangled out.

"But I'm not dead!" Tereza cried. "I can still feel!"

"So can we," the corpses laughed.

They laughed the same laugh as the live women who used to tell her cheerfully it was perfectly normal that one day she would have bad teeth, faulty ovaries, and wrinkles. Laughing the same laugh, they told her that she was dead and it was perfectly all right!

Suddenly she felt a need to urinate. "You see," she cried. "I need to pee. That's proof positive I'm not dead!"

But they only laughed again. "Needing to pee is perfectly normal!" they said. "You'll go on feeling that kind of thing for a long time yet. Like a person who has an arm cut off and keeps feeling it's there. We may not have a drop of pee left in us, but we keep needing to pee."

Tereza huddled against Tomas in bed. "And the way they talked to me! Like old friends, people who'd known me forever. I was appalled at the thought of having to stay with them forever."[1]

Until recently, the subject of dreams and literature, if discussed at all, involved the application of psychoanalytic categories to literary texts. Literature, in this enterprise, was converted into "evidence" used to confirm psychological hypotheses about the dreams of fictional characters as well as "real" ones. However, in the last decade, voices have been raised against this reductionist, mechanistic approach. Commenting on the relation between psychoanalysis and literature, Shoshana Felman writes that it is time "to explore, bring to light and articulate the various (indirect) ways in which the two domains do indeed *implicate each other,* each one finding itself enlightened, informed, but also affected, displaced by the other."[2] Following this suggestion, there are at least five categories within which this interrelation can be explored: "a) dreams in literary texts; b) literary texts as dreams; c) the dreamed text; d) the literariness of dream treatises;

e) the dream-likeness of literary texts."[3] In this chapter we will be interested primarily in the irreconcilable variety of dreams and dream-like episodes or images embodied in literature.

To the phenomenon of dreams, which the psychoanalytic tradition examines on a case study basis, literature brings an extra element—the creative imagination. Not restricted by the principles of a scientific methodology, the literary artist is able to bypass the imprint of imitation (e.g. the dream as *remembered*), by creating an imaginable gestalt (e.g. the dream as *recreated*). In this way, ambiguity, suspended expectations and abrupt shifts in purpose—as life itself would present them—can be represented inventively. Free too from the confines of textual literalism, the literary imagination adds to dream recall powerfully formed images of things not seen or experienced in waking consciousness. Therefore, when dreams appear in literary texts, especially death dreams, they challenge the reader's sense of reality in two ways: with a fresh and vivid presentation of the unconscious force behind dreams, and with a more detailed reanimation of the dream narrative.

In *The Unbearable Lightness of Being* (quoted at the beginning of this chapter), for instance, Tereza dreams that she has died and is lying in a hearse surrounded by other dead women. Rather than receiving only fragmented images, the author recreates the dream in the same narrative style, with the same attention to detail, as one finds in the rest of the novel. The reader, therefore, is able to penetrate more deeply into Tereza's psyche. She is appalled at how similar her post-death consciousness is (even still needing to pee) to her pre-death, waking consciousness. In this chapter we will examine ways in which death dreams appear in three literary genres: first, fiction; second, drama; third, poetry. In each section we will focus upon the imagistic details of post-death consciousness, details often unavailable in ordinary dream recall, and details which resist, to the end, any final interpretation.

FICTION: POST-MORTEM CONSCIOUSNESS

When we consider fiction, especially the area of short story, we encounter an extraordinary facet of our study which some literary critics have called "post-mortem consciousness." Actually, the term is a misnomer because it does not mean, as one might suppose, the possibility of an awareness of reality after death. Rather, it connotes a "definite attempt made by the dying self in the last second *before* death consumes it, but also in the first second *after* death can possibly be averted, to impose its own rule upon the universal order in place of the inevitable fate [death] that is coming to pass."[4] It refers to a surging, hypersensitive consciousness in the dying moment.

Here we will use the term slightly differently. By post-mortem consciousness we will mean a consciousness (however partial) of after-death realities as they are brought back (from the future so to speak) in the dream state. That is, in our dreams it is possible to picture episodes or instants in the landscape of death which point to what we think (or fear, or hope) may happen after we indeed die. In this section we will briefly review two works—Hemingway's "The Snows of Kilimanjaro" and Dostoyevsky's *The Dream of a Queer Fellow*—each of which depicts the geography of death in dreams.

Ernest Hemingway begins one of his best-known short stories, "The Snows of Kilimanjaro," with the circumstances of Harry's impending death. While on a safari, the hero suffers from a gangrenous leg wound which the buzzard-like birds, circling overhead, can smell. Eventually the birds land nearby, waiting for the expected corpse.

Harry seems resigned to his inevitable fate. Knowing that it is unwise, under such deteriorating physical conditions, he drinks liquor. But he is not beyond caring. As Hemingway writes: "Since the gangrene started in his right leg he had had no pain and with the pain the horror had gone and all he felt now was a great tiredness and anger that this was the end of it."[5] Harry had wanted to write about his experiences, but now it seemed likely that the stories within him would remain unwritten. All that remained was a calculated, measured acceptance.

Helen, however, his "rich bitch" wife, would not support Harry's willing acceptance of death. She was terrified. She loved Harry, but not the thought of losing him. When he sleeps, fitfully, Hemingway shifts to italics to indicate Harry's entry into the dream realm. There are five such interludes which appear closer together as death nears. One way to look at each of the dreams is to realize that they depict a potential scene from Harry's afterlife—which, as *The Tibetan Book of the Dead* states, is a state filled with scenes from one's lifetime.

The first dream-episode pictures a railway station at Karagatch, surrounded by snow on the Bulgarian mountains. (The dreams collectively, it should be noted, are comprised of the memories which Harry had always hoped to write, but had never started.) When he awakens, he asks Helen about Paris and about where they had stayed. The dialogue between them is testy, and often quarrelsome. She persists in not dealing with Harry's illness: "If you have to go away," she asks, "is it absolutely necessary to kill off everything you leave behind?" Harry replies, "I don't like to leave things behind." One suspects that Harry's *dreams* may be his attempt to take life's unfinished business with him to the other side of death.

At one point, Harry watches Helen begin to prepare a broth from a ram she had shot. When she leaves to bathe, Harry falls asleep again. In yet another interval of dreaming, he relives the war and his subsequent return to Paris. That his dreams always contain the elements of travel or movement seems to prepare him for the coming journey into death.

In the next dream episode, Harry remembers the first dead man he'd ever seen, "wearing white ballet skirts and upturned shoes with pom-poms on them." After awaking, he accepts the broth offered by Helen and, looking upon her, "felt death come again." Pondering the wonder of his own approaching death, he is fully conscious that he does not want to spoil "the one experience that he had never had."

In successive dreams, Harry is taken to Paris and to the surrounding countryside. In an intervening conversation in the interval, two things are evident: his desire again for whiskey-soda (as an anesthetic to numb his secretly death-fearing soul?) as well as his increasing fatigue. Death, it becomes evident, would be a real release, and would bring an end to the pain he fears. In his last dream:

> He remembered long ago when Williamson, the bombing officer, had been hit by a stick bomb some one in a German

patrol had thrown as he was coming in through the wire that night and, screaming, had begged every one to kill him. He was a fat man, very brave, and a good officer, although addicted to fantastic shows. But that night he was caught in the wire, with a flare lighting him up and his bowels spilled out into the wire, so when they brought him in, alive, they had to cut him loose. Shoot me, Harry. For Christ sake shoot me. They had had an argument one time about our Lord never sending you anything you could not bear and some one's theory had been that meant that at a certain time the pain passed you out automatically. But he had always remembered Williamson, that night. Nothing passed out Williamson until he gave him all his morphine tablets that he had always saved to use himself and then they did not work right away.[6]

In this dream, he remembers being present at an officer's extremely painful death. He recalls a discussion about the Lord never sending one more pain than one can bear, and the theory that at a certain point pain would automatically pass you out. In the officer's case, it did not work. Or did it? In fact, Harry was able to finally "pass him out" with morphine tablets he had been saving for himself. The dream reminds Harry of how excruciatingly painful death can be, and of how difficult it is to let life go.

The seemingly endless amount of time death is taking bothers Harry, yet he tells "it" to come closer. Helen continues to resist, and urges him to send "it" away. It is during this time, when her denial is at its zenith, that death finally arrives.

> Because, just then, death had come and rested its head on the foot of the cot and he could smell its breath.
> "Never believe any of that about a scythe and a skull," he told her. "It can be two bicycle policemen as easily, or be a bird. Or it can have a wide snout like a hyena."
> It had moved up on him now, but it had no shape any more. It simply occupied space. "Tell it to go away."
> It did not go away but moved a little closer.
> "You've got a hell of a breath," he told it. "You stinking bastard."
> It moved up closer to him still and now he could not speak to it, and when it saw he could not speak it came a little

closer, and now he tried to send it away without speaking, but it moved in on him so its weight was all upon his chest, and while it crouched there and he could not move, or speak, he heard the woman say, "Bwana is asleep now. Take the cot up very gently and carry it into the tent."

He could not speak to tell her to make it go away and it crouched now, heavier, so he could not breathe. And then, while they lifted the cot, suddenly it was all right and the weight went from his chest.[7]

In the last two sentences, we are told that he died (yet not as quickly as they thought he did), and that he stopped breathing (yet that his last sensation had not left him). With this device, Hemingway creates another interval so that readers can come to terms with his death, as Harry had long ago. The circling birds with which the story began are replaced with the eerie noise of a hyena outside the tent.

Whereas Hemingway describes a five-dream series of a dying man, Dostoyevsky in *The Dream of a Queer Fellow* depicts one extended dream, clearly of an afterlife existence. In it, Dostoyevsky describes, with uncanny persuasion and precision, the consciousness of one who passes through death to the bright radiance of that other earth. "I am a queer fellow," Dostoyevsky begins. Quickly, the unnamed protagonist rehearses his life of anguish and alienation in which he suffered the humiliation of feeling that everyone laughed at him. Emerging from this perception was his conviction that "it is all the same," and that it always would be the same, anywhere.

As a consequence of learning this truth, all of his questions disappear, along with his desire to live. He proposes to kill himself that night. Standing in the street, hungry, after a day-long rain, mist ascending from every stone and every person, a little girl, terrified, grabs his arm and cries: "Mother, Mother!" But he is incapable of helping her. Later, in his room, he questions himself: "Why did I not help this little girl?" Ruminating upon this question makes him realize that the little girl had saved him from killing himself. He then falls asleep in his easy-chair, "quite unconsciously."

In an extraordinarily strange dream, he takes a revolver, points it at his heart, and quickly pulls the trigger. Feeling no pain, he says, "it seemed to me that with the report, everything in me was convulsed, and everything suddenly extinguished." Everything became terribly black. "I became as though blind and numb," he recounts. He can neither see nor make a sound, and as he is carried off in a coffin, for the first time he becomes aware that he is dead. As is usual in dreams, he notes, "I accept the reality without a question."[8]

Suddenly his grave opens and a dark being, unknown to him, takes him into deep, dark space. Just as suddenly, he is left by his companion on the other earth, as beautiful as paradise and where people are unpolluted by transgression, yet with knowledge deeper than earth's science. His description of the post-death existence is colorful:

> The grass was aflame with brilliant and sweet scented colors. Flights of birds wheeled in the air, and fearlessly settled on my shoulders and my hands, joyfully tapping me with their dear, tremulous little wings. At last I saw and recognized the people of that happy land. They came to me themselves, thronged me about, and kissed me. Children of the sun, children of the sun—oh, how beautiful they were! Never on earth have I seen such beauty in man. In our children alone, in their very earliest years, one could perhaps find a remote and faint reflection of that beauty. The eyes of those happy people shone with a bright radiance. Their faces gleamed with wisdom, and with a certain consciousness, consummated in tranquility; but their faces were happy. In their words and voices sounded a childlike joy.[9]

What he remembered most in hindsight was the depth of their love. They were completely at home in their nature. Trees and animals understood them. It seemed to him as if they were connected to the stars, as if they drew energy from them. There were no quarrels among them, neither jealousy nor disease, and when people died, they "died quietly, as though they fell asleep."

> One could have believed that they still had communion with their dead even after death, and that their earthly union was not severed by the grave. They hardly understood me when I asked them concerning eternal life, but they were evidently so convinced of it that it was no question to them.[10]

Hand–Body

In a fascinating way, at the heart of the dream, the dreamer steps outside of the dream into the future to look back. He tells of the future critics' negation of his story: that it is impossible to dream in such detail, that the dream was a function of his delirium, and that he created the particulars in waking consciousness. While he agrees that they may all be partly right, he suggests that the real images of his dream were "perfected to such a harmony, were so enchanting and beautiful," that he was obligated to unconsciously "compose the details afterwards."[11] In this way the dream images and the imaginary images implicate and inform each other—the former initiates, the latter completes. Then, as if toying with his audience, he remarks that he will impart a secret—"perhaps all this was not a dream at all!"

When we are taken back into the dreams, we discover that something very profound has happened—he has introduced jealousy and disunion into their world. He has taught them to lie, and soon they love it. As a result, science and religion appear. When he tries to warn the people of their mistakes, they threaten to put him in a madhouse. Then he awakens. An ineffable rapture exalts his being. He has realized the truth of living love.

In that moment, trans/formed by the power of his death dream, he vows to preach the truth that he had seen. But the critics do not understand or believe in him. They say:

> "He saw a dream, a delirious vision, a hallucination." Ah, but is this really wise? A dream? What is a dream? Is not our life a dream? I'll say more! Let it be that this will never come to pass and there will be no paradise—that at least I understand—well, still I will preach.[12]

And in the last sentence we learn that he has decided to find the little girl again. In the queer fellow's dream, we are given a glimpse of a realm usually reserved for visionaries, mystics and saints, a glimpse of an altogether transcendent reality—one which brings about a conversion of faith and understanding.

Taking an inclusive viewpoint, that both the dreamer (for whom the dream was real) and his detractors (who insist that his dreams were hallucinated visions) are each partially right, raises a question about the nature of consciousness. If by consciousness one means the subjective, self-reflective awareness, as well as awareness of the objective world, where does consciousness begin and end? In the story of a queer fellow it begins in anguished, suicidal self-awareness, shifts into the unconsciousness of sleep and dream, slips further into what Mircea Eliade has called "transconsciousness" (the dream paradise in which people fall from innocence into corrupted consciousness), and awakens into rapturous awareness (consciousness transformed by the living image of love). Human consciousness, in other words, cannot be limited merely to our daily thoughts and feelings. Neither can our study of dreams be limited to fragments of recalled dream images. By adding the imaginal connectors and associations, a more complete dream narrative emerges, and, along with it, previously unthought-out signposts become evident which enlarge our view of the unconscious.

DRAMA: THE DEAD VOICES

If fiction focuses upon the society and the characteristics of the persons described, then drama elevates and develops their dialogue; if fiction enunciates the anatomy of the social world, then drama highlights the architecture of interactive situations. Drama, rather than dwelling on characterization, is more interested in the conflict of ideas, actions and feelings. Just as the narrative descriptions in novels and short stories provide detailed *persona,* both outside and within dreams, the speech and action of dramatic descriptions concretize the visionary abstractions of the dreamworld. Consider, for example, a tragicomedy of Samuel Beckett.

All three—death, dreams, and the uncertainty which they occasion—coalesce in Beckett's *Waiting for Godot.* Each character in the play (Vladimir, Estragon, Pozzo, Lucky, and even the messenger), have an air of dream-like uncertainty about them, such that the audience is never quite certain about what there is to be certain about. One has the feeling throughout the play that each in his own way is waiting, and in the meantime being overtaken by the long, slow process of dying.

The undramatic action occurs largely between two characters, Vladimir (Didi) and Estragon (Gogo), who are waiting for the arrival of Godot, who they hope will save them from their absurd situation. Whoever Godot is, and several interpretations have been suggested (e.g. God, death, Christ), Godot never comes. Instead, the practical, persistent, intellectual Vladimir badgers the volatile, forgetful, lethargic Estragon. Just as they are tied to waiting for Godot, they are tied to each other. They cannot stand to be without each other, yet, at the same time, they cannot stand to be together. Because of these opposites, there is an endless bickering which produces a series of threatened departures. Each character needs the other and yet, because of their uncomplementary natures, each annoys the other "to death."

Their repetitive waiting is punctuated by Pozzo (the sadistic, attention-seeking master) and Lucky (his slavish luggage-bearer). Just as Vladimir and Estragon are psychologically tied to waiting for Godot, Lucky is tied to Pozzo by a rope around his neck which Pozzo controls. Ultimately, what can be said about one can be said about all four: each is afflicted with pain, physical as well as psychological, each is a social outcast and a vagabond, each fails to relate to the others because of fear and mistrust, each is caught in meaningless activity, and each struggles to achieve an identity through the quiet despair of waiting.

The second act repeats the first; there is "nothing to be done," nothing happens and nothing is certain. It begins with an absurd nursery rhyme:

> A dog came in the kitchen
> And stole a crust of bread.
> Then cook up with a ladle
> And beat him till he was dead.
> Then all the dogs came running
> And dug the dog a tomb. . .

At this Vladimir pauses, ruminates, and then resumes:

> And wrote upon the tombstone
> For the eyes of dogs to come . . .[13]

He then repeats the entire lyric until it becomes a picture within a picture—that is, a self-contained repetition of itself.

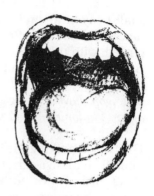

Mouths

As absurd as their situation becomes, Vladimir and Estragon still keep up the pretense of having a conversation:

> **Estragon:** In the meantime let us try to converse calmly, since we are incapable of keeping silent.
> **Vladimir:** You're right, we're incxhaustible.
> **Estragon:** It's so we won't think.
> **Vladimir:** We have that excuse.
> **Estragon:** It's so we won't hear.
> **Vladimir:** We have our reasons.
> **Estragon:** All the dead voices.
> **Vladimir:** They make a noise like wings.
> **Estragon:** Like leaves.
> **Vladimir:** Like sand.
> **Estragon:** Like leaves.
> *Silence.*
> **Vladimir:** They all speak at once.
> **Estragon:** Each one to itself.[14]

The dead voices are not only in nature, but also are: the voices of the living who live "as if" already dead, the voices of those who are bored to death, the voices of those who need something to give them the impression they exist, the voices of those born in the grave-digger's forceps. In perhaps the most revealing lines of the play, Vladimir penetrates toward the heart of his absurd predicament:

> **Vladimir:** Was I sleeping, while the others suffered? Am I sleeping now? To-morrow, when I wake, or think I do, what

shall I say of to-day? That with Estragon my friend, at this place, until the fall of night, I waited for Godot? That Pozzo passed, with this carrier, and that he spoke to us? Probably. But in all that what truth will there be?

(Estragon, having struggled with his boots in vain, is dozing off again. Vladimir looks at him.)

He'll know nothing. He'll tell me about the blows he received and I'll give him a carrot. (*Pause.*) Astride of a grave and a difficult birth. Down in the hole, lingeringly, the grave-digger puts on the forceps. We have time to grow old. The air is full of our cries. (*He listens.*) *But habit is a great deadener.* (*He looks again at Estragon.*) At me too someone is looking, of me too someone is saying, He is sleeping, he knows nothing, let him sleep on. (*Pause.*) I can't go on! (*Pause.*) What have I said?[15]

What he has said, the insight into his condition which comes through his words, is not heard because Vladimir (like Estragon, Pozzo and Lucky) has died psychologically. They are all in the chorus of "dead voices." Each is the victimizer and the victimized. All joy, expectation, hopefulness and excitement have been numbed by the enslaving habit of waiting.

But is there a deeper level to this tragi-comedy, one which lies within the channel of our concern in this section? In the speech by Vladimir we just quoted, Vladimir remarks:

Was I sleeping while the others suffered? Am I sleeping now? To-morrow, when I wake, or think I do, what shall I say of to-day?[16]

Vladimir's uncertainty about the borderline between sleeping and waking is an uncertainty that extends to whether and/or when Godot will come, to time and place and even to the names of the characters themselves (which range somewhere between Adam and Mr. Albert). It is this blurring between all boundaries that leads us to a deeper insight, namely that the entire play is a dream—and a deathly dream at that.

The evocative possibility that *Waiting for Godot* is itself a dream has been suggested by Thomas Cousineau, who writes that "Vladimir's and Estragon's actions frequently exhibit the unnatural quality of dreams."[17] Dreams, like the dramatic action of the play, often turn into nightmares without apparent provocation. The most persuasive occasion of this is what he calls the "suspension of the law of contradiction." A simple example occurs when Estragon asks Vladimir for a carrot. Vladimir gives him a turnip. Estragon bites it and is angry. "It's a turnip!" he says. Vladimir responds: "I could have sworn it was a carrot."[18] To Vladimir, it's all the same. And when, at the end of Act II, the boy-messenger enters (the same boy who entered at the end of Act I), the boy denies that he's ever been there. "The suspension of the law of contradiction," Cousineau writes, "permits Beckett to dramatize the truth of unconscious experience, which ignores the existence of such law," much like what happens to us when we dream.[19]

In a world where nothing is certain, where Vladimir and Estragon neither can tolerate each other, nor the thought of departing from one another, Vladimir cannot convince Estragon that only the day before they had contemplated suicide as a way out of their intolerable situation.

> **Vladimir:** [*Estragon looks at the tree.*] The tree, look at the tree.
> **Estragon:** Was it not there yesterday?
> **Vladimir:** Yes of course it was there. Do you not remember?
> **Estragon:** You dreamt it.
> **Vladimir:** Is it possible you've forgotten already?
> **Estragon:** That's the way I am. Either I forget immediately or I never forget.[20]

What Beckett has achieved in *Waiting for Godot* is to masterfully present death, dream, and life in a non-distinguishable triad, such that we are no longer sure if there is a difference, or if there is none. Even if there is, we are not sure whether we can detect it, and, if we can, whether it has any significance. Whether we forget or remember, whether we are alive trying to avoid death or already dead and dreaming life, what difference does it make? To whom? Or what difference would the possibility that it makes no difference at all make? The reader is left without a solid foundation upon which to stand, as if in a nightmare from which one does not awake. By dramatizing death in a dream-like way, Beckett forces the reader to interact with death and the question of life's meaning all over again in the process.

POETRY: DREAMS FULL OF DEATH

While dreams have a vividness of their own, when expressed in poetry—which adds the dimension of language stretched beyond its ordinary, prosaic usage—that vividness is intensified. It is this vividness that has inspired artists and poets to transfer dream glimpses into luminescent symbols, and into images no less haunting than the dreams themselves. What happens when the poetic imagination is coupled with the language of dreams is like shining a searchlight into a dimly-lit cave. Images that were hidden, or only partially exposed, are brought into the foreground, and that which would have otherwise remained undistinguished is intensified. The uncertain distinction between life and death, between waking and dream consciousness, is clarified.

Walt Whitman, for example, in "The Sleepers," pierces the darkness of night in a dream vision which takes him from bedside to bedside:

> I dream in my dream all the dreams of the other dreamers,
> And I become the other dreamers.[21]

Whitman not only takes these dream-reveries upon himself, but he also becomes hypersensitive to those who are dying. In "Old War-Dreams," he begins:

> In midnight sleep of many a face of anguish,
> Of the look at first of the mortally wounded, (of that
> 　　indescribable look,)
> Of the dead on their backs with arms extended wide, I dream,
> 　　I dream, I dream.[22]

In this same poem, death and dream are juxtaposed with beauteous scenes of fields and mountains, in night, under an "un-

Death Dream

earthly" moon that helps the dreamers dig their barren trenches ("shining sweetly," no less).

In "Of Him I Love Day and Night," Whitman achieves perhaps his deepest death-dream juxtaposition:

> Of him I love day and night I dreamed I heard he was dead,
> And I dream'd I went where they had buried him I love, but he
>   was not in that place,
> And I dream'd I wander'd searching among burial-places to
>   find him,
> And I found that every place was a burial place;
> The houses full of life were equally full of death (this house is
>   now),
> The streets, the shipping, the places of amusement, the Chicago,
>   Boston, Philadelphia, the Manhattan, were as full of the
>   dead as the living . . .[23]

Amazed at the indifference and blindness of the populous, as well as his former self, Whitman later concludes the dream-poem with the comforting prospect that:

> . . . [I]f the memorials of the dead were put up indifferently everywhere, even in the room where I eat or sleep, I should be satisfied.

And, conversely, he adds:

> And if the corpse of any one I love, or if my own corpse, be duly render'd to powder and pour'd in the sea, I shall be satisfied . . .[24]

The poet who willfully contradicts himself, saying "I am large—I contain multitudes," and the poet who celebrates himself with "I Sing the Body Electric," is also a poet dedicated to the beauty of death. Not that accepting death came easily—it did not. Yet Whitman discovered how inseparable life and death (and we could add waking reality and dreaming reality) are. He writes:

> And I will show that whatever happens to anybody, it may be turn'd to beautiful results—and I will show that nothing can happen more beautiful than death.[25]

So for Whitman, the dream is a tool for trans/formation, as well as for knowing himself.

This American hero (rough, bearded, sunburned), who prefers to look with his soul, and who is granted a vision of life and death, and of "life in death," is to some extent the reader as well: "What I assume you shall assume." Whitman's *persona* invites the reader into the *Leaves of Grass* world, into the world of dreams and death in order to explore, for himself or herself, whether what Whitman's "I" has realized is, in fact, true for the reader.

Consider also Edgar Allan Poe, whose prose, poetry, and short stories are rich with dream imagery and with spirits of the dead. For example, he dedicates his work, in the Preface to a long essay entitled *Eureka,* to dreamers and to those who put faith in dreams. Indeed, Poe often longs for the "reality" of the dream-world—"Oh! That my young life were a lasting dream!"—which to him seems "better than the cold reality/Of waking life." In "Dreams," from which these lines come, he writes:

I have been happy, tho' [but] in a dream.
I have been happy—and I love the theme:
Dreams! in their vivid coloring of life,
As in that fleeting, shadowy, misty strife
Of semblance with reality which brings
To the delirious eye, more lovely things
Of Paradise and Love—and all our own!
Than young Hope in his sunniest hour hath known.[26]

Consider the contrast Poe draws between "vivid coloring" and "shadowy . . . semblance," each of which is dream-occasioned and which brings a happiness to the poet beyond that of youthful hope. No wonder his poems are filled with the stuff of dreams and, as he writes in "Dream-Land," the "wild weird clime that lieth, sublime,/Out of SPACE—out of TIME."[27]

This out-of-space, out-of-time land, we are told, opens out into uncharted territory by an obscure route—that which leads to death. It is as if the dreamer, or the dreamer's soul—for "the traveller travelling through it,/May not—dare not openly view it"—is taken into the Kingdom of Death, "Haunted by ill angels only." Poe is well aware of the seemingly contradictory feelings of attraction and repulsion which are associated with death. Throughout his poetry, he exploits this contradiction through dream imagery.

> Bottomless vales and boundless floods,
> And chasms, and caves, and Titan woods,
> With forms that no man can discover
> For the dews that drip all over;
> Mountains toppling evermore
> Into seas without a shore:
> Seas that restlessly aspire,
> Surging, unto skies of fire;
> Lakes that endlessly outspread
> Their lone waters—lone and dead—
> Their still waters—still and chilly
> With the snows of the lolling lily.[28]

The poet then describes what the traveller meets there, "the Ghouls/By each spot the most unholy," and perhaps worse still, "Sheeted Memories of the Past." Yet despite this glimpse, into the death-like kingdom, it is merely a glimpse, for the traveller "May not—dare not openly view it" since its mysteries are never fully exposed. While the dream provides him entry into a place that waking consciousness does not, it leaves him looking as if "through darkened glasses."

When we read the next poem—"A Dream Within a Dream"— our comparative reasoning is immediately kindled. Why? With what does this poem ask to be compared? It begins with the voice in the poem departing with a kiss from an unnamed companion. The departure brings him to avow that his "days have been a dream," for he states, "All that we see or seem/Is but a dream within a dream." But then he writes:

> I stand amid the roar
> Of a surf-tormented shore,
> And I hold within my hand
> Grains of the golden sand—
> How few! Yet how they creep
> Through my fingers to the deep,
> While I weep—while I weep!

O God! can a tighter clasp?
O God! can I not save
ONE from the pitiless wave?
Is all that we see or see
But a dream within a dream?[29]

Now his initial statement has become a series of questions: Whose dream is it, if life is a dream within a dream? Who is the dreamer and who is the dreamed? And is there an awakening from the dream within the dream? Perhaps, as literary critic David Saliba has written, the answer to questions like these lies in Poe's view of death. He writes:

> For the conscious side of man to be able to yield itself to "death" it must allow the unconscious side to lead it away from physical reality. Only by breaking the fetters of consciousness, putting aside a strong will, can the psyche experience the death–rebirth cycle or metamorphosis of the unconscious mind.[30]

Finally, let us consider a poem of T.S. Eliot—noted playwright, literary critic, and poet of *The Waste Land.* In a dreamlike poem, "Sweeney Agonistes," Eliot writes that he did not know if: 1) he was alive and his companion was dead; or 2) she was alive and he was dead; or 3) both were alive; or 4) both were dead.[31]

This same ambiguity appears in a later poem, "Little Gidding" in the *Four Quartets.* The scene is set in London during World War II. Eliot, serving as an air raid warden, is walking the early morning London streets searching for fires (caused by German bombing raids). There, the poet describes a dream-like sequence in which he is visited by a dead master who is characterized as a "compound ghost." He writes that he suddenly saw some "dead master" whom he half-recalled. The former teacher had the look of a "familiar compound ghost," both recognizable and yet unidentifiable.[32]

Unfortunately, at this point most criticism leads the reader far from the heart of the matter by attempting to justify this or that identification of the compound ghost (e.g. William Butler Yeats, Dante, Shakespeare, or Irving Babbitt). In all such speculations a vital possibility is overlooked. Whoever the compound

ghost is (if he is at all), he is very much like the central consciousness, that is, a poet and philosopher. In fact, since Eliot's dialogue occurs within the poet himself, the ghost is also an aspect
of the speaker.

The narrator assumes a double part, both his old self who
"met one walking," and a new one, the one who was blown toward him to compel recognition. If one follows the pronouns, we
move from "I" to "you" to "we" to "I" to "myself" to "he." As Eliot
intimated in "Burnt Norton" ("My words echo/thus, in your
mind")—where the philosopher-poet is able to transpose himself
into the mind of the other and to know what the other is thinking—here he becomes another's voice (as one does in the dream
state), while yet remaining himself. At this intersection of time
with the timeless, the dialogue takes place "nowhere, no before
and after," as they "trod the pavement in a dead patrol." The
philosopher-poet is, in a sense, dead to himself, and the ghost is a
compound of dead masters, who die to being dead in order to live
into the conversation.

The "I" begins: "The wonder that I feel is easy, yet ease is
cause of wonder. Therefore speak." And he, the "I's" double part,
tells the "I" that he is not eager to rehearse forgotten theories or
last year's language, but that he prays they will be forgiven by
others "as I pray you to forgive" what others have written. He
continues that there is no longer a hindrance between the two
worlds (consciousness and unconsciousness) because they have
become like each other.

Thus the doorway into the realm of death is opened, making
a two-way transit possible, from the side of the living and from
the side of the dead. And in the crossing, each partner in the
dialogue finds ". . . words I never thought to speak/In streets I
never thought I should revisit/When I left my body on a distant
shore." Death enters the dialogue from each side of the relationship, for it is through the doorway of death that each finds a new
voice. Passage through this doorway requires, in one way or another, that each leave his body (whether physical, intellectual,
psychic, or spiritual) behind, that is, become detached from all
attachments which would prevent such a dialogue.

Passing from his world into the world of the philosopher-
poet, the compound ghost recalls their common concern—"To

purify the dialect of the tribe." He then discloses "The gifts reserved for age" which, ironically, will also crown his lifetime's effort. Three "gifts" are identified: first, "the cold friction of expiring sense . . . As body and soul begin to fall asunder"; second, impotent rage "At human folly, and the laceration/Of laughter at what ceases to amuse;" and third, "the rending pain of re-enactment/Of motives late revealed . . . Which you once took for exercise of virtue."[33]

For Eliot, death is imaged as leaving one's body behind, the surrender of one's composite personality. In the process the philosopher-poet not only discovers the gifts reserved for age, but as well that there is a language beyond the language of the living in which he discovers a redemptive alternative. Life moves from "wrong to wrong" unless "restored by the refining fire/ where you must move in measure, like a dancer." With the pregnant remark, "he left me" and disappeared "on the blowing of the horn," the dreamer awakes into language.

In the beginning of the chapter, it was mentioned that in literature the dream is both *remembered* as well as *recreated*. We conclude this chapter by presenting a death dream which, in part, was triggered by a children's story. The dreamer, Julianne S., relates that before sleeping she listened to her husband as he read the story of *Badger's Parting Gifts* to their son. In the story, on the same night that he died Badger dreamed that he was running through a long passageway until he began tumbling freely in the air. "It was as if he had fallen out of his body."[34] Then Julianne had the following dream:

> I can't believe this is happening to me. What is going on? Why are all these people being killed? Where am I? There is a man coming toward me wearing a black shirt, black pants, and a red sash, carrying a large curved sword. He has a strange smile on his face. I'm not afraid; this really isn't happening to me. He slashed my abdomen! I did not feel it but I know he did. Wow, I'm falling. This feels great! I don't think I'm alone but all I see is this beautiful golden light. Wait a minute. Something is wrong. I am falling through a passage of light. I heard this is what happens when you die. Could this be death? That's what Ivan Ilyich said when he was dying. What are some of the things I learned in class about

death? What should I be thinking? Should I be praying? I'm
not prepared for death. I don't know what I should be doing. I
learned that this is supposed to be a wonderful moment and
that I should not be afraid, but I am afraid. There is no one
here to help me. I don't want to die! I can't seem to get my
body turned around. There is nothing but golden space. I am
back lying on the ground. There is another man dressed in
black with a red sash standing above me. He is holding a
knife, a double-edged knife. He is looking right at me with a
devilish smile. I wonder if it is better to slash my wrists or my
throat? If I slash my wrists there is the chance that it won't
work. The throat is a sure thing. I'm holding up my right
hand. He slits my throat. Where am I? I can hardly walk.
Everything is white. Is this a hospital? If so, where is everyone? My clothes are white, the table is white, the walls are
white, the floor is white. There is no blood on me. I know
I was slashed with a sword and with a knife, but I don't feel
any pain. Who took care of me? I feel I should protect my
wounds, but they seem to be healed. There is no sign of any
injury. No pain.[35]

COMMENTARY

In this chapter we have examined literary representations
of death dreams and some of their implications. Like Paul
McCartney's response to receiving a musical award for twenty-
five years of achievement—"Welcome to my dream!"—we have
seen that the line between waking consciousness and sleeping
consciousness was continually challenged. It was as if the page
you are reading now represents waking consciousness. Its flip
side, then, would represent dreaming consciousness which is
always just beneath our awareness and as accessible, in this
moment, as falling asleep.

For some, dream reality was exalted; for others it was dis-
counted as no different from waking reality. With the exception
of Beckett, in most cases the experience of death that came in
dreams clearly had a trans/formative effect on the subsequent
life of the dreamer or, as in Harry's case, pointed to what he was
going to bring with him into the next life. For Walt Whitman, the
dream was a mystical code of consciousness. "I dream in my

dreams all the dreams of the other dreamers," he writes, "And I become the other dreamers." For Poe, dreams were haunted by the Kingdom of Death. They were where the traveler met the "lone and dead." And for Eliot, entering into a dialogue with a dead master revealed to him the "gifts reserved for age."

Though each literary work provided a unique slant on the death dream, is there a common ground which connects them? It has been suggested that to the ordinary, fragmentary recall of dream images, literature adds the element of imagination. Therefore, when dreams (especially death dreams) appear in literary works, they reanimate and expand the dream narrative. As we saw in "The Dream of a Queer Fellow," the "real" images of his dream—so enchanting, so beautiful, so true—became blurred upon his awaking. Thus he had to compose the details afterward such that the original dream images and the imagined images implicated and informed each other—the former initiates, the latter completes.

Of Beckett's *Waiting for Godot,* we suggested that the entire play can be viewed as a death dream in which the characters are doomed to a long, slow process of dying. It becomes thus the theater of nightmare in which dreaming or awaiting the reality of death's presence is the same. In Dostoyevsky, on the other hand, the death dream of the queer fellow transported him into a paradise-like existence of innocence where he learned the true meaning of love and service.

From a comparativist's viewpoint, one could say, as Maurice Friedman has (in *To Deny Our Nothingness*), that literature is the real homeland of authentic existence since it provides concrete, unique exemplifications of what it means to be human, which the more abstract disciplines (e.g. the social sciences) cannot. Because the images and characterizations of human life (and death) presented in fiction, drama and poetry are so extremely close to actual life situations, readers are compelled—as in few other forms of expression—to enter into a dialogue with both the author, and with his or her idiom. This is especially true of the dreams expressed in literary works where the unconscious and imagination intersect. If anything, the reader must come face-to-face with expressions which elude all attempts at reduction into interpretive categories.

Since literary depictions of death dreams embody layers of meaning, the reader is denied any final, objectifying viewpoint from which to understand these dreams. Instead, the genius of literary expression—its interplay of characterization and situation, of image and symbol—is to disclose human consciousness without closing off its unending mystery. Dreams of death, in this mode, while given a more intricate, more detailed, and more provocative presentation, do not provide final guidance, but rather return the reader to his or her dialogue both with the text and with his or her own dreams. From a literary viewpoint, more significant than cognitive interpretations is felt experience, and more important than figuring dreams out is an ongoing dialogue which deepens one's sensitivities of their nuances.

Having looked at the contributions of philosophy, psychology and literature to death dream studies, in the following chapter we will shift our gaze to dream-related occurrences such as near-death experiences, out-of-body travels and especially lucid dreaming. Our interest will be to see to what extent, if any, these analogous experiences contribute to our growing understanding of the phenomena of death dreams.

NOTES

[1]Milan Kundera, *The Unbearable Lightness of Being,* translated by Michael Henry Heim (New York: Harper & Row, 1984), 18–19.

[2]Shoshana Felman, "To Open the Question," in *Yale French Studies,* Number 55/56 (1977), 9.

[3]Carol S. Rupprecht, "Dreams and Literature: A Reader's Guide" in Jayne Gackenbach's *Sleep and Dreams: A Source Book* (New York: Garland, 1986), 363.

[4]John Kenny Crane, "Crossing the Bar Twice: Post-Mortem Consciousness in Bierce, Hemingway, and Golding," *Studies in Short Fiction,* 6 (1969), 361. Crane isolates four phases of post-mortem consciousness: the slowing down of time, extreme

hypersensitivity, the imposition of a *temporary reality* upon the universe, and at the most real, most ultimately satisfying moment, the arrival of death.

[5]Ernest Hemingway, *The Short Stories of Ernest Hemingway* (New York: Charles Scribner's Sons, 1938), 54.

[6]*Ibid.,* 73.

[7]*Ibid.,* 77–75.

[8]Fyodor Dostoyevsky, *The Dream of a Queer Fellow* (London: George Allen & Unwin, 1961), 18.

[9]*Ibid.,* 22–23.

[10]*Ibid.,* 24.

[11]*Ibid.,* 25.

[12]*Ibid.,* 30.

[13]Samuel Beckett, *Waiting for Godot* (New York: Grove Press, 1954), 37. See my *Sacred Art of Dying: How World Religions Understand Death* (Mahwah: Paulist Press, 1988), 19–22.

[14]Beckett, 40.

[15]*Ibid.,* 58.

[16]*Ibid.*

[17]Thomas Cousineau, *Waiting for Godot: Form in Movement* (Boston: Twayne Publishers, 1990), 40.

[18]*Ibid.,* 14.

[19]*Ibid.,* 39.

[20]Beckett, 39.

[21]Walt Whitman, *Leaves of Grass* (New York: Signet, 1980), 331.

[22]*Ibid.,* 370.

[23]*Ibid.,* 345.

[24]*Ibid.*

[25]Walt Whitman, *The Portable Walt Whitman,* edited by Mark van Doren (New York: Viking Press, 1945), 17.

[26]Edgar Allan Poe, *Edgar Allan Poe,* edited by Margaret Alterton and Hardin Craig (New York: Hill and Wang, 1935), 11.

[27]*Ibid.,* 44.

[28]*Ibid.*

[29]*Ibid.,* 13.

[30]David R. Saliba, *A Psychology of Fear: The Nightmare Formula of Edgar Allan Poe* (Maryland: The University Press of America, 1980), 155.

[31]T.S. Eliot, *The Complete Poems and Plays: 1909–1950* (New York: Harcourt Brace Jovanovich, Publishers, 1971), 84.

[32]*Ibid.*, 141.

[33]*Ibid.*

[34]Susan Varley, *Badger's Parting Gifts* (New York: Mulberry Books, 1984), pages unnumbered.

[35]Dreamed by Julianne Saia, a student in my "Death, Dying & Religions" class at SJSU.

Chapter 9 ANALOGOUS EXPERIENCES

My near-death experience was caused by an overdose of cocaine—approximately one-half an ounce. I was aware of what was happening to me, but I would not let anyone take me to a hospital. It first started with my muscles flexing involuntarily. The whole time I was trying to rationalize the experience. But as I went into epileptic seizures, I was losing control; when I was trying to control my muscle spasms, my mind was brought into a new level. I could see myself making the same choices, over and over, with all the same mistakes. I felt that I was trapped, that there was no way out and I would see this for an eternity.

Then I felt that I was in control of the past, that I could change it. I didn't because I couldn't know what would be happening in the present . . . I was still stuck seeing all of the mistakes of the past . . . Now I just wanted this to stop, but it wouldn't. I was stuck, very much like a computer stuck in a loop . . . It was a game. I had to break the events leading me to hell. Or I could give up and go there . . .

Many other things happened at the same time, including my senses being suppressed into feelings of intense pleasure and pain, seeing intense light and complete blackness, and the feeling of security and panic.

I cannot remember very much else of what happened afterward, except that I wanted to back out and I kept thinking of different things to try. Then I found that it was some type of computer program holding me back. I could not find a way to break into it. Somehow I was able to "list" the program but the information was going by too fast. I then re-entered a line of information which changed the program. I deleted a lot of what I felt to be useless information . . . Now I was able to stop, regain consciousness, and control my life.[1]

During the course of our research for this book, it has become strikingly clear that there exists a collection of experiences and states of consciousness which, while not technically called "dream states," nonetheless share significant similarities with dreams. Moreover, some of the implications of recent electrophysiological studies of dream states and other states of consciousness (e.g. meditation and yoga) point to provocative similarities. Such studies suggest a continuum between them and dreams in that each activates a deautomatization of one's motor apparatus, which affects the body's psycho-sensory, and organizational patterns.

In this chapter we shall discuss experiences which may be considered analogous to the dreaming experience, especially what has been called ASCs ("altered states of consciousness"), NDEs ("near-death experiences"), and OBEs (or "out-of-body experiences"). Not only are elements of each of these experiences found in death dreams, but more significantly those who have these experiences, as is also true of some death dreamers, report a renewed sense of aliveness and a trans/formed attitude toward death as a result. After a brief mentioning of meditation-induced experiences, which possess qualities of all three, we will conclude with a discussion of lucid dreaming.

ALTERED STATES

In 1901, around the time Freud published his landmark work, *The Interpretation of Dreams,* William James published a book which has become, in its own way, a classic—namely, *The Varieties of Religious Experience.* In it, James writes that ordinary consciousness is continuous with other states of non-rational consciousness (e.g. our dreams), and with what he calls "a wider self." He writes:

> Our normal waking consciousness, rational consciousness as we call it, is but one special type of consciousness, whilst all about it, parted from it by the filmiest of screens, there lie potential forms of consciousness entirely different. We may go through life without suspecting their existence; but apply the requisite stimulus, and at a touch they are there in all their completeness, definite types of mentality which probably

somewhere have their field of application and adaptation. No account of the universe in its totality can be final which leaves these other forms of consciousness quite disregarded.[2]

James calls these second types of mental forms "non-rational." Since they are both so close, as well as so discontinuous, with our ordinary conscious state, the question for James (and for us in this chapter) is how to regard them.

There are several ways to approach this issue. Instead of the term "non-rational," for instance, Charles Tart uses the phrase "altered state of consciousness." By "normal state of consciousness," Tart means simply the one in which a person spends the majority of waking hours. By "altered state of consciousness," he means one in which a person "clearly feels a *qualitative* shift in his pattern of mental functioning." This shift is:

> . . . not just a quantitative shift (more or less alert, more or less visual imagery, sharper and duller [imagery], etc.), but also that some quality or qualities of his mental processes are different. Mental functions operate that have no normal counterparts . . .[3]

Given the wide variety of ASCs, along with the range of ways in which they are generated, one would expect these experiences to be fundamentally different from one another. But as Arnold Ludwig has pointed out, most altered states of consciousness share certain traits which are characteristically similar to their other ASC counterparts. ASCs tend to include:

- Alterations in thinking
- Disturbed time sense
- Loss of control
- Change in emotional expression
- Body image change
- Perceptual distortions
- Change in meaning or significance
- Sense of the ineffable
- Feelings of rejuvenation
- Dissolution of self boundaries[4]

According to Tart, two types of dream experiences (hypnagogic and hypnopompic) also qualify as ASCs. The "hypnagogic" period is the borderline stage which occurs at the onset of sleep, while the "hypnopompic" is the transition stage which occurs just as we begin to awaken from sleep. For most people, the perceptual material experienced during these periods is quickly forgotten, yet "this may be a period of enchantment, with beautiful visions, sweet music, and insights . . . [yielding] material as rich as any nocturnal dream."[5]

Another type of altered dream (or ASC) is what Tart calls the "high dream." In it the dreamer experiences the ineffable, as if influenced by psychedelic chemicals. From Tart's perspective, a high dream occurs when one, during sleep, finds oneself in the dream-world and is aware of being in an altered state of consciousness similar to that induced by psychedelic drugs. Tart gives, as an example, the high dream of a psychologist friend:

> I was standing in the country-side talking with a friend of mine, Bill. In the dream he had recently returned from San Francisco, and he told me that he had obtained a new psychedelic drug there. He gave me a small white pill and we took the pills together. . . . Shortly after swallowing the pill I began to feel the effects. I was looking at the green grass and green hills of the country-side. Slowly the green changed into lavender, then violet, then purple. Soon I was enveloped in a purple cloud. My entire body was deep purple. It was an extremely pleasant sensation. It resembled sleeping between covers of purple velvet, an experience which I had at one time in my life and which was very sensuously enjoyable. There was no difference between inner and outer sensation: I felt the purple on the inside as well as on the outside. When I awakened I remembered this experience very clearly as it was very sensual, very unique, and very pleasant. The dream differed from my usual dreams in terms of the mental processes employed: most of my dreams include a great deal of conceptual activity, but by the end of this dream I was involved in a sheer sensing function. For example, I could see purple but I did not think "I am seeing purple." I put the experience in verbal terms only upon awakening.[6]

While on the one hand this is a dream, it is unlike his normal dreams in that "conceptual activity" was replaced by a "sheer sensing function." Clearly, many of Ludwig's list of ASC traits can be seen in this dream.

Researchers have also found that chemical substances taken before sleep may elicit "high dreams." The dreams produced with opium, for example, are as voluptuous as they are grandiose. Perhaps the best known example of such dreams are those of Thomas de Quincy, "the English Opium-Eater," as he called himself. His opium-induced dreams seemed to him like a descent—literally into dark chasms below consciousness. He writes:

> The waters now changed their character—from translucent lakes, shining like mirrors, they now become seas and oceans. And now came a tremendous change, which, unfolding itself slowly like a scroll, through many months, promised an abiding torment; and, in fact, it never left me until the winding up of my case. Hitherto the human face had mixed often in my dreams, but not despotically, nor with any special power of tormenting. But now that which I have called the tyranny of the human face began to unfold itself. Perhaps some part of my London life might be answerable for this. Be that as it may, now it was that upon the rocking waters of the ocean the human face began to appear; the sea appeared paved with innumerable faces, upturned to the heavens; faces, imploring, wrathful, despairing, surged upwards by thousand, by myriads, by generations, by centuries—my agitation was infinite—my mind tossed and surged with the ocean.[7]

Again, this dream exemplifies traits of an altered state of consciousness. This association raises two points of interest for our study: (1) Can ASC experiences in the non-dreaming state be identical with those in the dreaming state? (2) What do ASC experiences reveal about the death process? In the two dreams just considered, the dreamer passes from a separatistic, ego-centered identity into a more cosmic one. Personal self dies, so to speak; a transpersonal self is born in its place.

NEAR-DEATH EXPERIENCES

Closely associated with the ASCs, at least in terms of imagery and life-trans/forming attitudes, is what has been called the NDE, or near-death experience. As a distinct discipline, attention to NDEs began with the appearance of Dr. Raymond Moody's *Life After Life* in 1975. The NDE can be defined as "the sequence of conscious experience that continues in spite of the fact that the subject is showing no external signs of life in terms of skin resistance, breathing, heartbeat and, occasionally, flat [sic] EEG."[8]

In his initial research, Moody studied three categories of experiences: persons who were resuscitated after being pronounced clinically dead, persons who came close to physical death for whatever reason, and persons who reported their experiences of dying as they died. Based on the data he collected, Moody identified more than a dozen "points of likeness" which include: ineffability or a sense of peace, learning *the news,* feeling peaceful, hearing *the noise,* moving through a dark tunnel, being out of the body, meeting others and the being of light, the life-review, *the border,* coming back, and telling others. To illustrate these characteristics, the following is a "composite" or "ideal" NDE offered by Moody:

> A man is dying and, as he reaches the point of greatest physical distress, he hears himself pronounced dead by his doctor. He begins to hear an uncomfortable noise, a loud ringing or buzzing, and at the same time feels himself moving very rapidly through a long dark tunnel. After this, he suddenly feels himself outside of his own physical body, but still in the immediate physical environment, and he sees his own body from a distance, as though he is a spectator. He watches the resuscitation attempt from this unusual vantage point and is in a state of emotional upheaval.
>
> After a while, he collects himself and becomes more accustomed to his odd condition. He notices that he still has a "body," but one of a very different nature and with very different powers from the physical body he has left behind. Soon other things begin to happen. Others come to meet and

to help him. He glimpses the spirits of relatives and friends who have already died, and a loving, warm spirit of a kind he has never encountered before—a being of light—appears before him. This being asks him a question, nonverbally, to make him evaluate his life and helps him along by showing him a panoramic, instantaneous playback of the major events of his life. At some point he finds himself approaching some sort of barrier or border, apparently representing the limit between earthly life and the next life. Yet, he finds that he must go back to the earth, that the time for his death has not yet come. At this point he resists, for by now he is taken up with his experiences in the afterlife and does not want to return. He is overwhelmed by intense feelings of joy, love, and peace. Despite his attitude, though, he somehow reunites with his physical body and lives.[9]

It is significant to note that every one of these near-death characteristics have also been reported, either independently or compositely, in the death dreams we have amassed in preparation for this book. Not one of these characteristics is different from those which are produced in a "normal" night's sleep. Two possibilities emerge: either NDEs can be discredited because they are really dreams, or dreams can be credited for tapping into the same psychic/spiritual awareness present in NDEs.

In a later book, *Reflections of Life After Life,* Moody outlined five major stages of the near-death experience which, considered in sequence, form a coherent pattern: peace, bodily separation, entering the darkness, seeing the light, and entering the light.[10] According to Moody's studies, the one element which is the most common—and the element which has the most profound effect—is the encounter with "the bright light." Typically, after journeying through a dark tunnel, a light appears very dimly at first, then grows in intensity until it reaches an "unearthly brilliance." Described variously as "white," or "clear," or "dazzling," it is said to have a Beingness of love, an irresistible presence which is usually depicted in religious terms. One person described it this way:

I heard the doctors say that I was dead, and that's when I began to feel as though I were tumbling, actually kind of

Near Death

floating, through this blackness, which was some kind of
enclosure. There are not really words to describe this. Everything was very black, except that, way off from me, I could see
this light. It was a very, very brilliant light, but not too large at
first. It grew larger as I came nearer and nearer to it.

I was trying to get to that light at the end, because I felt that it was Christ, and I was trying to reach that point. It was not a frightening experience. It was more or less a pleasant thing. For immediately, being a Christian, I had connected the light with Christ, who said, "I am the light of the world." I said to myself, "If this is it, if I am to die, then I know who waits for me at the end, there in that light."[11]

Compare this to an experience had by a San Jose State University student who also went through a near-death experience.

I feel I have experienced death. Two years ago on a hot summer day I was lying down in the backyard trying to get a tan. I was reading James Clavell's novel, *Shogun,* when suddenly I fell asleep. I must have been asleep for the longest time, for when I woke up, my body was red like a tomato. As I made an effort to sit up, I felt a little dizzy and very thirsty. I felt my head going in circles and at the same time I was seeing little bright stars. Suddenly, as I started to stand up, I felt a blackout. Right away I called my mother. I yelled and yelled until she heard and rushed out to the yard. I was about to fall on the concrete when she grabbed me and prevented the fall. She dragged me under a tree and sat me on a small chair. She noticed that my eyes rolled back and now all she could see was the white part. She kept calling my name again and again. . . . By this time, my mother was very scared because I was not breathing. So they took me to the emergency room at the Alexian hospital.

During all this time, I was like a dead person. Everything was dark and I could not see, feel or hear anything. The nurses came to the car and took me into a room where many machines were attached to my body. They thought I was already dead. The heart monitor was measuring a straight line which meant I had no life. Suddenly, the doctor began to give me electric shocks. My body jumped up and down on the bed. It was very weird. My mother says that I had all types of wires attached to my body and both of my legs were tied to the bed. I could not feel anything. For six hours the nurses and doctor were by my side and no reaction was observed.

Suddenly, after being in a very dark atmosphere, I experienced something very unusual. I felt that a part of me was leaving my body. It was something that I can't really explain. Out of the darkness, I saw a bright light which carried or lifted an image with a white sheet. My body was still on the bed, but something was floating on top of me. I kept feeling something very strange.

I must have experienced this for a very long time. Suddenly, I began to hear things, meaning I could hear the nurses talking and my mother crying next to my bed. I wanted to move, but I couldn't. I wanted to talk, but nothing would come out. I wanted to tell my mom to calm down, that I was okay, but I couldn't. It was very frustrating. I could hear the nurses say, "It's no use, she's already dead." But the doctor kept insisting to keep giving me electric shocks. A miracle happened; the heart monitor began to beep again and I started to breathe. Suddenly, I heard my mother cry, "Please give me a sign that you're alive!" Since I tried yelling and moving and nothing would happen, I began to cry. One teardrop rolled out of my eye and my mother said to the doctor, "See she is alive; that is the sign she gave me to prove that she is alive!" At this point, the doctor kept giving me electric shocks for a very long time. Finally, after eight hours of being in a coma, I came back to life. That was an experience I will never forget.[12]

Many critics argue that experiences such as these are merely hallucinations or wish fulfillments. Moody responds to these critiques by arguing that NDEers report basically similar experiences, and that whereas a wish fulfillment keeps one's situation as it is (due to the psyche's self-preserving mechanism), "a near-death experience is quite different in that it is a breakthrough which enables people to face their lives in a way that they have never done before."[13]

Along these lines, it is significant to raise another question: Are NDEs like dreams? And if so, in what ways? These are questions which have been asked by Kenneth Ring in his *Life at Death*. He suggests that one of the first questions usually brought to the NDE is whether it could have simply been a dream. The possibility is quite improbable to him because, as Moody had argued earlier, it would be unlikely that so many people would have such a common dream. Rather, he prefers responses collected from twenty-two people who experienced the near-death phenomenon; ninety-four percent stated that their experience was unlike dreaming. Only one person said her experience was dream-like. As for others, the NDE was too *real* to merely be a dream.[14] At the same time, it should be noted that similar experiences are reported by death dreamers (e.g. bodily separation, entering a darkness and seeing the light, wanting to communicate with those in bodies but not being able to, and feelings of elation and peace). Perhaps a better question than "Are NDEs like dreams?" is "What is the significance of the similarities between NDEs and death dreams?"

OUT-OF-THE-BODY EXPERIENCES

Another type of analogous experience is depicted by Robert A. Monroe in *Journeys Out of the Body* which reports the Virginia businessman's experiences of leaving his physical body, without willing it, and traveling via a "second body." It was as if his first body was uninhabited by time, space or even death. In the introduction to the second edition of the book, Charles Tart isolated five characteristics of OBEs (out-of-the-body experiences):

1. They are a universal human experience, cross-cultural, pan-historical.

2. They are generally once-in-a-lifetime experiences usually happening spontaneously.

3. They are one of the most profound experiences of a person's life and have life-altering consequences.

4. They are generally extremely joyful.

5. In some cases they describe what is happening in a distant place with more accuracy than can be explained by coincidence.[15]

For Monroe, such experiences usually involve a vibration and a shaking like an electric shock racing throughout his entire body. One night while in bed, he reports, after the vibrations, he looked and discovered that the wall had no windows and was not his bedroom wall. The wall was a ceiling and he was floating up against it. He looked down and saw his wife sleeping next to a strange man until he realized that *he* was the strange man in the bed!

> My reaction was almost instantaneous. Here I was, there was my body. I was dying; this was death, and I wasn't ready to die. Somehow, the vibrations were killing me. Desperately, like a diver, I swooped down to my body and dove in. I then felt the bed and the covers, and when I opened my eyes, I was looking at the room from the perspective of my bed.[16]

Such experiences (and there is no end to their reports) seem to be of two varieties: the type where one's consciousness moves into what may be called "ultra-physical realms" without any body, and the type where one moves into another non-physical body. Often such experiences will be occasioned by the threat of death. The following account appeared in the *Sunday Times* of March 25, 1962:

> During the war in the Western Desert, I was knocked unconscious by a bomb blast and had the peculiar sensation of being out of my body viewing the scene from a point about 20 feet above the ground. . . . I could hear the aircraft as it came in on another attack and the voices of my companions. I could see the dust clearing away from the explosion that had knocked me unconscious and my own body lying there on the gravel.
>
> . . . I remember the thought, "I've got to get back", and then . . . I was back in my body consciously trying to force my eyes open. An odd thing was that, although I could hear perfectly while I was unconscious and could tell my comrades what they had said during that period, when I recovered consciousness I was stone deaf and remained so for two weeks afterwards. . . .

> This experience has convinced me that there is a part of the
> person that survives after death. . . . I am certain that when I
> do eventually die, or rather when my body dies, part of me
> will carry on, to where or to do what I do not know.[17]

Similarly, Hemingway once wrote of such an experience to a
friend: "I felt my soul or something coming right out of my body,
like you'd pull a silk handkerchief out of a pocket by one corner."
And then he added, "It flew around and then came back and
went in again and I wasn't dead anymore."[18]

What exactly are out-of-the-body experiences? And what is
one to make of them? Are they merely subjective hallucinations
or psychic disturbances, or are they caused by chemical imbal-
ances in the body? And is there a higher reality, an ultra-physical
element, a psi-component which needs no body and yet which
contains consciousness?

As might be imagined, opinions fall on both sides: one
group suggests that consciousness is not necessarily localized
(that like electromagnetic fields it exists beyond the body), while
another group argues that experiences which cannot be objectively verified should be dismissed as subjective fantasies. Our
interest, however, is not to prove or disprove the out-of-the-body
phenomenon, but to look at its relationship to dreams. For us the
obvious question is: How do out-of-the-body experiences compare to death dreaming?

One of the most sustained responses to these questions is
found in Jan Currie's *You Cannot Die* in which she states that
comparing out-of-the-body experiences to dreaming has several weaknesses:

1. In dreams, we do not see our own bodies objectively from
   outside them, while this is a characteristic of OBEs.

2. In OBEs, surroundings are seen as they are in normal
   consciousness.

3. Dreamers, upon awakening, realize that they have been
   dreaming. But no such realization accompanies the end
   of an OBE. The firm conviction that the experience was

real, rather than a dream, holds not only while the experience is occurring, but when it is thought about later.[19]

While we understand the rationale behind these arguments, we must raise some counter-possibilities. To suggest, as Jan Currie does, that in dreams we do not see our own bodies (which is characteristic of OBEs) is to discount, or ignore, lucid dreams (in which the dreamer is able to do that) and some death dreams (in which the person who has died often is able to view his or her own dead body). Then, to suggest that upon awakening dreamers realize that they have been dreaming is to overlook Chuang Tzu's experience, and others like it, in which the dreamer is not certain of the difference between the waking and the dreaming state (see Chapter 4). Also, to suggest that in an OBE one's surroundings are "more vivid," or "more real," or "more convincing" is to make a subjective judgment which can easily be countered by contradictory subjective judgments. We are not suggesting that some, or all, dreams are identical to OBEs, but rather that the door between them should be left open to accommodate experiences often described in similar language.[20] (The reader will at least want to keep an open mind until after he or she has read the next section on lucid dreaming, a variety of dream experience largely different from most of what we have discussed.)

LUCID DREAMING

What about the phenomenon of lucid dreaming? Being lucid in dreams means being "aware" that one is dreaming while maintaining the dream. One may suddenly become aware, for instance, that there is something unreal in what one is experiencing and therefore deduce that it must be a dream. Some lucid dreamers find themselves flying freely through the air or they find themselves in a familiar room and then realize that the windows are missing or the door is in the wrong place, at which point they become "conscious" that they are dreaming. The first serious research into lucid dreaming, indeed the coining of the term itself, is attributed to a Dutch psychiatrist, Frederik van Eeden.

In 1913 van Eeden presented a paper, "A Study of Dreams," to the Society for Psychical Research in which he reported on over 352 of his own lucid dreams. In his description of lucid dreams, van Eeden characterizes them as ". . . undisturbed, deep and refreshing." Van Eeden gives examples of dreams where he fights demons and takes away their terror, leaving him with a sense of being refreshed and pleased with himself. He reports:

> On Sept. 9, 1904, I dreamt that I stood at a table before a window. On the table were different objects. I was perfectly well aware that I was dreaming and I considered what sorts of experiments I could make. I began by trying to break glass, by beating it with a stone. I put a small goblet of glass on two stones and struck it with another stone. Yet it would not break. Then I took a fine claret-glass from the table and struck it with my fist, with all my might, at the same time reflecting how dangerous it would be to do this in waking life; yet the glass remained whole. But lo! when I looked at it again after some time, it was broken.[21]

Most recently, research on lucid dreaming leads to two names which stand out both for their accomplishments in research and for the quantity of their published works—Stephen La Berge and Jayne Gackenbach. Stephen La Berge started his work on lucid dreaming in the fall of 1977 at the Stanford University Sleep Research Center. In 1978 La Berge was able to prove that lucid dreams do occur by signaling laboratory researchers with pre-arranged signals whenever one was having a lucid dream. As he continued his research, he also developed a method by which one could induce lucid dreams. He called this method the "mnemonic induction of lucid dreams" (MILD). In his book *Lucid Dreaming,* La Berge outlined four steps, or techniques, to enable one to dream lucidly: (1) in the morning, memorizing one's dreams, (2) returning to sleep saying—"Next time I'm dreaming," (3) visualizing oneself realizing that one is dreaming, and (4) repeating steps two and three while falling asleep again.[22]

La Berge suggests that emotional detachment is important for lucid dreaming because any type of emotional stirring in the dream threatens to awaken the dreamer. Lucid dreamers have intense brain activity, which probably correlates with the extreme perceptual vividness that is apparent in such dreaming. When entering into a lucid dream, critical thinking is most important because if one believes that one can do it, the more possible it becomes. A good indicator of lucid dreaming is the ability to fly in one's dream. It is as if the dreamer, as one psychologist notes, integrates dream objects and persons into a "detached self-awareness" which is aware of one's actual context. In other words:

> ... If Chuang Tzu had been lucid when he dreamed of being a butterfly, he would have known that he was Chuang Tzu, and if he had experienced an OBE dream that he thought was real, he would have realized that his physical body was in bed but he would have thought he was awake. Another possibility would be if he had had an OBE-lucid dream. Then he would have seen his physical body in bed, but he would have recognized that he was dreaming. This last variation is probably the most accurate.[23]

When one introduces the realm of death and afterlife into the discussion of lucid dreaming, we are taken through the doorway of lucid dreaming and beyond. It can be suggested that just as one moves from non-lucid dreaming to lucid dreaming, one can move from lucid dreaming to a state beyond ordinary lucid dreaming. In lucid dreaming, the dreamer is dominant. As we shall see in the following conversation, there is also a witnessing dream in which an "inside I" observes (or witnesses) the "outside I" of the dream. The difference between lucid dreaming and a witnessing dream is the difference between manipulating characters and creating situations in the dream, and stepping back to observe what is transpiring in the dream without being attached to it.

THE LUCID DREAMER

Because of the special nature of lucid dreaming, we conclude this chapter by quoting fragments of an interview with John Williamson, a young lucid dreamer who, upon hearing of our research, offered to share his experience with us. About himself Williamson said:

> My background is basically American Indian. I moved into a neighborhood that was known as "Cheyenne Harlem" in Oklahoma City. Both my parents have American Indian blood. But my mother, particularly, was well experienced in that she was brought up with American Indians. So, I have to say that my experience of life is not altogether white, Anglo-Saxon.

The first part of the interview focused on the phenomenon of lucid dreaming, in which he described three levels: first, being aware that one is dreaming in a dream; second, being able to control the dream; third, seeing the dreamer and witnessing the dream without participating in it. As distinct from non-lucid dreaming, in which one is not aware of dreaming until waking up, Williamson likened lucid dreaming to watching a television show and thinking that one is participating in it. In this first level of lucid dreaming, one is in the midst of a TV show without realizing what is happening when, at a certain moment, one wakes up (so to speak) in the dream. Williamson said:

> I generally don't have any trouble remembering a dream, in that same fashion of remembering early childhood experiences. Often I had dreams when I was much younger that in no way resembled my waking life. In other words, the set of the story was very different from my waking life. So it was not at all difficult for me to know that this is a dream—it's that I didn't do anything about it. I just saw that "Oh, this is a dream," and kind of "played along." That's a good phrase to use, actually. I kind of just "played along" with it. I knew it was a dream, but it was fun, and it was an escape from, in a sense, my waking life.

If the first level of lucid dreaming is being aware of dreaming while dreaming, at the second level the dreamer becomes aware that he or she can alter the dream. For Williamson, dream-control (like changing channels) occurs in at least two ways—either one's situation in the dream is changed (e.g. from fleeing a threatening situation to facing it fearlessly), or the entire dream scene is changed. Initially, what dream-control required for Williamson was having dreams that almost mirrored reality. For instance, he grew up in a large house, which had a front and back yard, an alley behind the back yard, an attic and a basement. This house became a very profound symbol for him in his dreaming state. Nightmares would often take place in the basement, or in the backyard, where there were no lights. Positive experiences would occur in the front yard in the daylight, on the porch. Williamson said:

> But if I were, for instance, having a nightmare, it was taking place in the basement. I would go, "Excuse me," turn around, walk up the stairs and walk into an entirely different dream situation, either in the kitchen where the basement went, or— I learned very quickly not to go out the backyard if it was dark. So I had territory, known territory, and could, in a sense, through controlling myself, control my dreams.
>
> But, you had to be lucid in the dream to do that. I mean, you had to go, "Oh, this is a nightmare—excuse me," and walk out of it.

For Williamson, the segue from calmly excusing himself to walking up the steps and entering another dream was gradual. He mentioned that when he walked through the doorway from the dark basement to the kitchen, there was a change of "camera angle," in a sense, so that he was walking onto a different set entirely. While he recalled the new set that he had willed, and a new set of circumstances, he did not recall taking the step from one dream to the next. The transition, that fine line, was never consciously crossed. It would happen like this, he said:

> I had a kind of a funny situation that happened. I was walking down a country road, and I came to this rather ominous-looking tree. Clouds began to gather and shapes began to form in the tree that were living and monstrous. And this voice from the tree said something quite foreboding, something like, "This is the end of you." And I went, "No it's not, bye!", and took a step. Literally, from that step, there was no

more storm, there were more clouds, and that was that. I mean, it was gone. That whole scene was gone, and I was in another dream.

Without addressing the third level of lucid dreaming, at this point the conversation shifted directly to reflect our theme:

KK: What about death dreams? What about life after death? What about when someone says to you, "Look, death isn't it." At some point along the line in your development, you must have encountered this idea: "When you die, you don't die."

JW: Actually, yes, very early on.

KK: Very early on? Is that something you have had the opportunity to explore as in: "Well fine—I'll die in a dream and see what happens."

JW: Let's talk about death. Now I still believe that you can die in your dreams, though I know more about the mechanics of that. . . . I'll just say this: that you can *actually* die in your dreams through circumstances in your dreams. Several voodoo and kahuna practitioners would stake their reputations on that fact. And I've met a couple of them.

KK: Have you died in your dreams?

JW: I've died in my dreams, in a dream scenario, in a sense, but I woke up.

KK: Can you have a dream in which you die and you don't wake up?

JW: That can be induced. In other words, for a lucid person it's more difficult to experience physical death. The only mechanics I'll mention is that not only do you have to know that you're dreaming, but also you cannot be aware of the fact that you're dreaming in order to have the environment in which you could actually lose your life in that situation.

I'd like to go into the mechanics of another situation—the guru appearing in the dream. When we talk about dreams, when we talk about all of that, we're talking about "higher consciousness." The dream area that we most commonly deal in isn't that much higher. As a matter of fact, it's about one rung above "lower mental."

KK: Which is why, parenthetically, that lucid dreaming, in and of itself, is not that significant.

JW: It ain't that big a deal! But it's the first step to those other stages in making sense out of what comes in. The fact that someone else can take some of that mental substance in your lower mind into the shape of the guru, and then communicate through that, is a power that some people have. Likewise, there are those on the other side who have gone over—who are dead—who can do the same thing, and *do* do the same thing. We just don't recognize it.

For instance, I have a dream about my aunt who died but I don't think that much about it, because she is dead, so I dismiss it. Well the thing is, that dream could have very well been the intelligence of my aunt. The thing is, though, and this is an ideal situation, the energy it takes to generate that form in your mental substance is tremendous. The guru has a great deal of energy at his disposal, and can do that very simply. It's almost a parlor trick.

But a "deceased person," and that's in quotes because what we're talking about is an intelligence that has transcended this intelligence, who may have even gone further and further, but has dipped down a portion of itself to take a form, to bring a message in some fashion. Or there may still be some connection to you, but if there is that connection, that person hasn't progressed out very far.

KK: A Muslim student of mine once told me this dream. He was sitting with me in a Mosque, in Syria (Damascus). I was telling him in Arabic about death, and then about how I named my first daughter Leila. All of a sudden, and from nowhere, his mother (who had been dead for two years) appeared. She called to him and he left me to go to his mother. His mother said to him: "Tell your teacher that the crying sound his daughter made after she was born—'ALLA'—is the Islamic word for God, and it is not what he thought." He told her, "Mom, I am sure he knows that." But she replied, "Just tell him that." He said, "Mom, you tell him." But she said, "He cannot see me. Remember, I am dead." The issue for me is—was that just a projection, or does it have an objective basis in reality?

JW: Of what? His own mind?

KK: Of his own mind. In other words, he sat in my class, heard me say something, remembered some other teaching which contradicted that, went to sleep, and put this whole thing in the guise of his mother, whom he trusted and loved. Maybe she was a wisdom figure for him. So he projected the whole thing, and received his own message. This would be opposed to the dream's being independent of his own projections.

JW: Well, certainly, there's no way you'll resolve that situation. And here's the thing—they both can be correct.

KK: Now, let's look at it in terms of directions. In our studies of 700 death dreams, the majority of the dreams occur either with the dreamer being alive, experiencing death, and *crossing-over,* or with the dreamer being alive, staying alive, and then having someone who has already died returning or *crossing-in* (if we could say that, instead of "crossing over"). So it seems to me that the majority of death dreams take one or the other direction. My question has to do with the relationship between those different scenarios . . . different messages.

JW: Very different. The only common thread they may have is that they are both dealing with death. But that may be the only common thread. Now, as I spoke earlier, I would say of your approximately forty percent (death dreams in which the dreamer dies), maybe roughly ten percent were actual experiences of someone who passed on. That's a possibility to consider. The other, however, would be just in coping with that whole situation of death, or the attachment to a loved one who's passed on.

Experiencing death, and coping with death in a lucid dream, would be a great prelude to lucid dying. I would think that the most appropriate training to prepare one for death, would be the ultimate use of this. Besides, of course, the yogi is seeking to die while he's still alive, which simply means experiencing those higher states of consciousness that you can experience once you die, only coming back to tell about it, as it were. And many of them have, which is obvious from what many of them have been able to bring back into the world. Unfortunately, that's mostly in the east; we haven't experienced it that much in the west.

A lucid dreamer has several opportunities. There is a hierarchy of intelligence that deals with the whole *deathing* process, but, unfortunately, they are spread rather thin. In other words, there's a lot of folks dying, and there aren't that many on the other side who can help out. That's why the relatives are called into a situation like that. Experiencing someone coming through—an intelligence that can help you with the dying process, that can work with you in your dreams—prepares you for what that is, even marches you through it. They take you through it, step by step.

There are intelligences all along the way to help you through. But as I said, they're spread a little thin. And for anyone who developed consciously (for instance, at a level of the teacher that I had and some of the yogis that I've known), part of their job is to join in the fun, helping people to cross.[24]

KK: Are you saying that dreaming—especially dreaming of death—can help prepare one for dying?

JW: Until you're dead, dreaming has significance; particularly when you're dead, you're gonna find out that dreaming has a lot more significance than you ever gave it credit for, and, chances are, the only thing that will keep you close to this earth is regret—for not having gotten yourself better at the whole thing, because that's the thing that happens in your dreams. That's what you can do in your dreams—you can prepare yourself for the inter-mittent time afterward, before you move into those realms where you don't have to deal with it.

Here's the other thing. If this person is actually experiencing causally, that's where they should go when they die. You see that? Ideally, if you have a natural death, and you see the first door, and you step through, or even in a very short time, if you miss all the doors, you will gravitate to the causal level because that's the level you consciously reached in waking life.

If, however, you didn't ever reach that level, chances are you're gonna end up on on a similar one for quite a while, and slowly work into the higher realms, a step at a time. And time does pass, but it's relative. Actually, "arc" is a much better image. An arc can be quite a distance, or an arc can be sharply upward and come back down, and the line that we're talking about (that the arc lands on) is time.

So, in other words, I can die today and I can go to a very high level and spend a lot of time there, and come back and be born tomorrow—not very likely—or I can die and gradually go up, and arc and arc . . . and come down years from now, or come down in the next century. Now, this is taking reincarnation and looking at it in a more practical sense, taking into consideration a lot of other factors. It's a very practical thing. It explains time and separation, that is, that time is just one dimension of a much broader scheme.

KK: So, given what you just said, in a sense, we've had our focus a bit too narrow here. Meaning, my original assumption was that dying in one's dreams, or experiencing the coming back of one who has died in one's dreams, is what really prepares one for death in this life. Now I've heard you indicate that just dreaming itself—dreams themselves, and becoming more lucid/aware in our dreaming itself—will prepare us for what's going to happen at death.

JW: Being a lucid dreamer will prepare you to consciously act *out of your body.* When you die, that's just what you are—you're out of your body. That's what meditation is all about.

KK: Exactly! And in a sense then, lucid dreaming, meditation, and near-death experiences are really varieties of the same reality, of the same kind of thrust.

JW: Well if we can knock down the borders for a second, you'll get a much better picture of the situation: all of them contribute to what life is, which is motion, transformation, and transcendence. I've found the meaning of life and now I'm getting a job. OK, and people think I am joking. Believe me, when I'm joking, I'm most serious. That's basically what life is about.

And if that's what life is about, let's reason from that premise. What is death about? What are dreams about? It all fits.

KK: Back to what you said earlier. Literally what life is about is dying, and the whole point of it has to be that we have to bring death into life, and that we have to be dying regularly, continually, all the time . . . dying, dying, dying.

JW: I die daily.

KK: So then, to just focus on this particular kind of dream is beside the point.

JW: But that's the way you have to do it. There is an important point to those types of dreams. When you die in your dream, and when you experience someone coming back, that is all meant to help your conscious mind cope with the idea of death—in waking, as in preparation for dying. Because what's going to happen when you die? You are going to have an experience similar to the one you had dreamed before you died, plus you are going to see some people that you knew before.

So how does that add up? It's a great thing for the death experience, but how does that affect you in your waking life? Don't fear it. If you ever ask anyone who died (i.e. has had a near-death experience), the first thing they'll tell you is that it's painless; it's nothing . . . OK? Woody Allen summed it up. I was actually going to write a book, and the chapter on death was gonna be started with this quote: "I'm not afraid of dying, I just don't want to be there when it happens."

COMMENTARY

In this chapter—set in the context of a remark made by William James that normal waking consciousness is surrounded by many entirely different potential forms of consciousness of which we are largely unaware—we have suggested that certain altered states of consciousness, near-death experiences and out-of-body experiences are analogous to certain types of death dreams. For example, Charles Tart pointed out that an impressive number of similarities exist between experiences of so-called altered states of consciousness, such as reduced exteroceptive stimulation, increased motor activity, increased mental involvement, deep relaxation, and alterations in body chemistry and emotional climate.

Closely associated with these experiences of death and rebirth is what has been called the near-death experience. According to Raymond Moody, there are three categories of such experiences: persons who were resuscitated after being pronounced clinically dead, persons who came close to physical death for whatever reason, and persons who reported their experiences of dying as they died. Typical of such experiences is: a peaceful feeling, hearing a noise, traveling down a dark tunnel, seeing a light at the end of the tunnel, being out of the body and meeting friends and relatives. The most common element in these experiences is the bright light at the tunnel's end which at first appears very dimly, and then grows dazzlingly brilliant.

We then spoke about out-of-body experiences, and more especially of Robert Monroe's work. He details experiences he and others have had of bi-locating such that their bodies are in one place, their consciousness in another. Arguments were raised to disassociate these types of experiences from dreams, yet, given recent research in lucid dreaming, there may be more similarities than was at first thought.

Being lucid in dreams, we suggested, meant being aware that one is dreaming while maintaining the dream state. Being in a dream, and outside of it at the same time, may have significant implications for death dreams. As John Williamson indicated in his interview, "experiencing death and coping with death in a lucid dream would be a great prelude to lucid dying." He further suggested that one reason for this is that "being a lucid dreamer will prepare you to consciously act 'out of your body'."

Applying the comparativist's approach to our subject, we have noted the following: (1) that for ancient peoples dreams of the dead were not unreal fantasies, but indications of the spirit-filled nature of reality (e.g. that souls transmigrate from this life to the next and, in turn, influence this life through dream appearances) (Chapter 3); (2) that for peoples of eastern religious traditions, death dreams were viewed negatively (as illusory images), as well as positively (as a yogic practice pointing to enlightenment), and that, in either case, spiritual death (dying to one's ego before dying physically) was an existentially necessary life-realization (Chapter 4); (3) that according to the western, monotheistic faiths, death dreams were either demonically inspired temptations, or the revelation of a divine message, and that in the latter case, they were usually accompanied by the dreamer's receiving a new identity, or new name (Chapter 5); (4) that from the standpoint of the philosophical tradition, attention was focused less on locating the final meaning of dreams than on the process of the investigation itself, for example on discovering the "family resemblances" between all death dreams, and on being meaningfully engaged by the death dreams (Chapter 6); (5) that from the standpoint of the physiological tradition, a major concern was the cause (or origin) of death dreams which, depending on the theorist, varied widely (e.g. psychosomatic disturbances, sensory stimulation, repressed conflicts, illness, grief, or a spiritual quest), and that just as Jung challenged Freud's reduction of death dreams to wish-fulfillments, Buber challenged what he called Jung's gnostic deification of the self in place of faith in the wholly other (Chapter 7); (6) that from the standpoint of the literary tradition, the unconscious and the imagination intersected to draw readers into a deep dialogue with the author and the text through the detailed intricacy of death dreams descriptions yet without providing any final interpretation (Chapter 8).

In a way, elements of each of these six summations can be applied to the material in this chapter, that is, as long as one is convinced by the close connection between these analogous experiences and death dreams. From our point of view, what has been said of death dreams can also be said about many of these analogous experiences, namely that death is both a problem and the solution to that problem. While the threat of physical death challenges one's existence to the roots, at the same time such a near death may trans/form one's attitude toward death and life. Death dreams, like these analogous experiences, may awaken the possibility of being released from the dread of death, if not activate a trans/formed sense of self in the process.

NOTES

[1]San Jose State University student in a "Psychology & Religious Experience" class 1989.

[2]William James, *The Varieties of Religious Experience* (New York: Random House, 1902),378– 379.

[3]Charles T. Tart, "Introduction," in *Altered States of Consciousness,* edited by Charles T. Tart (New York: John Wiley & Sons, Inc., 1969), 2.

[4]Similarities (and differences) are reported in Arnold M. Ludwig's "Altered States of Consciousness," in *Altered States of Consciousness,* edited by Charles T. Tart, 13–18.

[5]*Ibid.,* 74.

[6]*Ibid.,* 172. Tart uses the term "high" rather than "psychedelic" to imply a positive and valued experience, and to avoid associations with the term "psychedelic." "The primary shift in this dream," Tart writes, "is the great intensification of sensory qualities and the dropping out of ordinary intellectual activity, to the point where the dreamer no longer experiences the usual split between the knower and the known" (172).

[7]Thomas de Quincy, *Confessions of an English Opium Eater* (New York: Heritage Press, 1950), 63.

[8]David Loumer, "The Near-Death Experience: Cross-Cultural and Multi-Disciplinary Dimensions," in *Perspectives on Death and Dying: Cross-Cultural and Multi-Disciplinary Views,* edited by Arthur Berger, *et al.* (Philadelphia: The Charles Press, 1989), 256. Loumer points out that opinion is split as to the interpretation of

the experience—"whether it should be taken at face value, or as a psychological compensation, or as a sign of a malfunctioning brain resulting from cerebral anoxia or hypercarbia."

[9]Raymond Moody, Jr., *Life After Life* (New York: Bantam; 1975), 21–22.

[10]Raymond Moody, Jr., *Reflections on Life After Life* (Atlanta: Mockingbird Books, 1977), 62.

[11]*Ibid.*

[12]Reported by Maria Elena Gonzales, a student at San Jose State University.

[13]Raymond Moody, Jr., *The Light Beyond* (New York: Bantam, 1988), 148–149. When trying to discover a psychological explanation for NDEs, he finally retreats to William James' description of mysticism (mentioned earlier in this chapter), and notes: "It is, pure and simple, an experience of light" (150).

[14]Kenneth Ring, *Life at Death* (New York: Quill, 1982), 82–83. To carry out the investigation scientifically, there were four criteria used: (1) the survivor had to come close to death or have been resuscitated from clinical death as a result of a serious illness, accident, or suicide attempt; (2) the survivor had to be sufficiently recovered from the near-death incident to be able to discuss it coherently; (3) the survivor had to speak English well enough for an interview to be conducted in that language; (4) the survivor had to be at least eighteen years old. These investigations took place in several large hospitals in central Connecticut, smaller hospitals in Connecticut, and one hospital in Maine.

[15]Charles T. Tart, "Introduction," in Robert A. Monroe's *Journeys Out of the Body* (New York: Anchor Books, 1977), 8–9.

[16]*Ibid.,* 28.

[17]Quoted by Rosalind Heyword in "Attitudes to Death in the Light of Dreams and Other 'Out-of-the-Body' Experiences," in *Man's Concern with Death,* edited by Arnold Toynbee, *et al.* (New York: McGraw-Hill Book Company, 1968), 197–198.

[18]Quoted by S. Smith in *The Enigma of Out-of-the-Body Travel* (New York: Helix Press, 1965), 22. Hemingway wrote about this experience in Chapter Nine of *A Farewell to Arms.*

[19]Jan Currie, *You Cannot Die* (New York: Methuen, 1978), 78.

[20]Recently, meditators from various traditions have allowed themselves to be monitored, while meditating, by means of an

electroencephalograph (EEG) attached to the scalp to measure brain waves. The significance of these studies is that a change in the EEG is one of the reliable ways we have to access states of wakefulness or sleep. From the EEG point of view, alpha waves in meditation slowed from 1-2/second to 7-8/second and theta waves slowed to 6-7/second. These changes "could not be clearly differentiated from those seen in the hypnagogic state or the hypnotic sleep, though the changes during Zen meditation were more persistent and did not turn into a deeper sleep pattern." See Akira Kasamatsu and Tomio Hirai, "An Electroencephalographic Study on the Zen Meditation (Zazen)," in Charles T. Tart's *Altered States of Consciousness, op. cit.,* 501.

[21]See Frederik Willems van Eeden, "A Study Of Dreams," in *Proceedings of the Society for Psychical Research* (Vol. 26, 1913), 431–461.

[22]Stephen La Berge, *Lucid Dreaming* (New York: Ballentine Books, 1985), 155–156.

[23]Gackenbach and Bosveld, *op. cit.,* 128.

[24]At this point John gave the following example. "One day, many years ago, I was watching my yogi's body and he was giving me a play-by-play account of a plane in Japan, and that they were unable to keep it up, and that it was gonna crash, and that there were a number of people there who were working with him—both those who were still alive and those who were not. They were trying to ease the situation, and speak to the pilot, and calm everyone aboard, because it was inevitable that they would crash and many would pass over. And his job, if not saving the plane—which has happened—was to help those across. I said, 'Were there survivors?' He said, 'Yes. There's one man who's walking around in circles, and who's quite dazed. He has a head injury, and I've told him to sit down and stay put. But there's a girl in the tree, and I've calmed her down and told her, "Help is on the way." ' It was two days later that they found the girl in that tree in Japan. I had already documented the incident before the rescuers even made it to her."

CONCLUSION: REINVENTING DEATH

The dream is never intellectual [Bergman adds, extending his thought]. But when you have dreamt, it can start your intellect. It can start you intellectually. It can give you new thoughts. It can give you a new way of thinking, of feeling. . . . It can give you a new light for your inner landscape. And it can give you, suddenly, a little bit of a new way of handling your life.[1]

With Ingmar Bergman we would say that a dream is never merely intellectual and yet, once dreamt, it can ignite one's intellect by generating new ways of thinking and feeling. To his final line—that dreams can provide a new way of handling one's life—we would add "and death." The dreams that we have examined in this text (e.g. dreams of dying, dreams of the dead returning, dreams in which the dreamer continues to live after death, and dreams of total extermination, whether non-lucid or lucid) have opened pathways into previously unexplored territory. Like a flashlight beam in the night, they illumine regions beyond the newly opened door, as well as provide impetus and courage to explore the twists and turns in the new paths. More than anything else, these dreams have taught us that the journey is ours, and ours alone, and that for those who push ahead, the rewards are beyond what can be imagined. Serving both as a look back over our shoulder, as well as a look ahead, we will conclude by commenting specifically on those death dreams which speak most directly to the possibility of what can be called a fundamental human trans/formation (i.e. being grasped ontologically and existentially by a new life-perspective).

DREAMWORLD TRANSLATIONS

One of the concerns which has been implicit in this investigation is the question: What do death dreams teach us, metaphysically so to speak, about the process of dying? For us, there

258

can be no simple answer, for death dreams in all their variety—
i.e. dreamer dies (43%), other dies (30%), the dead returns (17%),
mass death (5%), death personified (3.5%), and animal death
(1.4%)—present configurations which may affect the dreamer
both negatively and positively. With regard to those dreams
which shall be our primary concern here—dreams in which the
dreamer dies—we have seen that while almost half of all such
dreams end with the dreamer's death (49%), in almost half the
dreamer continues to experience some form of consciousness
(51%).

Let us recall here some of the earlier mentioned statistics
(see Chapter 2, Tables 2.6a and 2.6b). In the 700 dreams collected,
with regard to the dreamer's response to death, we found basically three possibilities: 14% were positive (or negative to positive),
almost 70% were negative (or positive to negative), and 16% were
neutral. Why, one might wonder, did almost 70% of the dreamers
respond negatively to their own death? While this figure may at
first seem high, when we reflect upon possible explanations, our
initial perception may be altered. The following list is not meant
to be exhaustive, but rather suggestive:

- since 91% of deaths occurring in dreams are from violent,
  or overwhelmingly sudden, causes (e.g. homicide, 33%
  and accidents, 19%), the dreamer's response may be in-
  stinctively negative;
- since dreams often reflect life-situations, some, if not
  many, of the negative dream responses may simply reflect
  prevalent cultural attitudes toward death (e.g. anxiety,
  dread, denial, anger, fear);
- since the statistics are drawn primarily from student-aged
  (and therefore younger) dreamers, they may reflect a more
  innately primal resistance to death;
- since this may be for some dreamers the first "real" encounter with a death experience, its newness is bound to
  be frightening;
- because of already existing guilt feelings associated with
  the death of a family member, or a loved one, dreaming of
  one's own death may evoke similarly negative emotions.

Given the weight of these possibilities, it may now strike the reader as all the more significant that 14% of dreamers responded positively to their dreamed death. In what follows, we will focus our attention solely on death dreams in which the dreamer's emotional response to the death event is either initially, or eventually, positive. Our discussion is not offered as a definitive interpretation or analysis; it is rather a descriptive *translation* of dream configurations into waking words through an interdisciplinary and comparative disposition. Reflection at this level does not intend to separate one from the dreamworld, or to turn personal dreams into symbolic figures. Instead, this particular translation seeks only to reflect ways in which death dreams image the possibility of a fundamental human trans/formation which arises when the dreamer, having died in the dream, is able to look back at the pre-death body and realize that one's authentic consciousness not only is independent of that body, but has emerged into new life.

TRANS/FORMATIONAL CONFIGURATIONS

Death dreams (in all forms) are both natural and even necessary. Cultural anthropologists, historical philosophers, and scholars of ancient religions (east and west) corroborate this fact in their studies of rituals, myths and sacred texts. One way that various cultures and peoples have expressed the nature of a spiritual trans/formation is by delineating a fundamental life-problem—e.g. ignorance (Hindu), suffering (Buddhist), original sin (Christian)—which inhibits that trans/formation, and then by pointing to a fundamental solution—e.g. *moksha* (liberation), *nirvana* (extinction of ego), *metanoia* (repentance and renewal)—which overcomes the problem.

The predicament of human life, no matter how expressed, is nowhere more dramatically evident than when facing death, not as an abstract image but in a personal way. Death threatens life in a way that is total and final. Yet the problem of death, for some, points toward a religious solution, namely a spiritual death and rebirth experience (a dying to one's attachments to life, in life, such that death itself is trans/formed in the process).

Ironically, overcoming the fear of death is accomplished by those who have willingly surrendered, wholly and completely, to the dying process itself, only to realize that who they *truly* are cannot die.

When we look at the way death dreams mirror this vantage point, what emerges is a twofold process—a *de-formation* of the dreamer's pre-death identity, and a *re-formation* of a post-death identity in life. When viewed as trans/formational configurations, death dreams confront dreamers with the necessity of each process (i.e. the de-formation of embodied consciousness, and the re-formation of an unembodied, or spirit-bodied, awareness). As if looking into a mirror partially covered with dust, when one looks closely at the symbols found in trans/formational death dreams, elements of the spiritual death process emerge. In uncanny ways, these elements (e.g. a suspension of time and space, a freedom from the effects of causation and gravity, the disappearance of fear, anxiety and addictive mechanisms, and an enlivened perspective toward one's new wakefulness) parallel, and point to, what philosophers, theologians and psychologists have described as components of a renewed attitude toward death.

But this is not a simplistic activity. When death comes in a dream it often throws the dreamer into a confused, frightened state. Depression, fear, anger, sorrow, frustration and deep sorrow are emotions often mentioned along with responses of peace, happiness, beauty, pleasure and contentment. Many times these are intermixed in the same dream. One student reports:

> The other night I had a dream where my mother had died. I didn't know how or when. I just knew she was gone. There were my relatives surrounding me, comforting me. However, I was basically ignoring their gestures (although they didn't catch on) because I was confused by it all. "When did this happen? How? Why don't I feel sad?"—all these thoughts raced through my mind. My lack of grief bewildered me and I realized these people (my relatives) were suffocating me— I *had* to leave. I ran for what seemed to be forever, stopped and sat down. I was at peace.[2]

At times, the actual occasion of death is described in very colorful, if non-human, terms. A student reports that when she died, she saw "a space shaped like the front of a crown." It was huge (like space) and it was the most glorious royal blue. I said "It is regal! I am regal?" She woke feeling wonderful.

Other dreamers report their own dying in more specific detail.

> I am in a small field hospital near a battle zone somewhere. I don't know exactly where the field hospital is, but I can hear the sounds of incoming mortars and feel the concussion of the rounds as they hit near the tent I am in. At present I am in the operating room preparing a couple of seriously wounded soldiers for emergency surgery, when suddenly there is an enormously strong force pushing me across the room and down on the floor. I try to get back up but something is stopping me. I can't determine just what is preventing me from getting back up; the loud ringing in my ears seems to be preventing me from hearing what the people around me are saying. I am lying face down and am calling for help, but I'm not sure if anyone can hear me because I can't tell if they are answering my call for help. I can see movement out of the corner of my eye. I am a little scared because I should be in some kind of pain after being thrown to the ground in the way I was. Instead, I don't feel anything at all except a tingling sensation that is present about half-way down my neck. The ringing in my ears is beginning to fade, and I can make out a few words of someone nearby. The words are "hopeless," and "he never knew what hit him," and I wonder for a second who the person is talking about. I feel my body being lifted and I am turned over, but the room doesn't get any brighter. Strange, I ought to at least feel something and I don't. I wonder if it's me that person was talking about. It's getting darker in here, but not the scary darkness you see in the movies. There is a presence that makes me feel safe and secure like the darkness, so I'm not afraid. I know now that I am dying, but it's not like I pictured it at all. The last thing I remember is reaching into the darkness for the presence I feel is there. Then I wake up and it's usually morning. I am not tired; in fact I usually feel pretty good.[3]

The dreamer's dying experience combines explosive mortar shells with an enormously strong force which he tries to resist. Usually the dying dreamer will resist the agent of death and yet, in the process, be left helpless. Though scared, he is surprised not to be in pain. Often dreamers report that they do not experience actual pain in their dying circumstance. While the encroaching darkness of death frightens him, he senses a presence in the darkness which reassures him. As we see here, dreaming of one's own death often elicits emotive responses from both ends of the spectrum.

Even more striking are dreams in which the dreamer dies more than once. Consider the dream of a university student who had just been involved in an emotionally-trying break-up with his fiancée.

I was in a hospital room where everything was white on white. Soft light glowed about the room and it was warm. I could feel the air circulate around me like a springtime breeze. I looked down to see my body (through my eyes) shrouded in a white gown in a bed with white sheets. Everything was pure white.

Suddenly a form appeared at the end of the bed. I actually noticed an earthy smell (kind of like the redwoods after a rain) first. The figure was shrouded and hooded in a raggy burlap robe. I could not see its face or hands. The figure smoothly glided around to the side of my bed. At that moment I felt its arms beneath me, lifting. My sensation was one of acceptance, longing and desire. I could also feel my soul and body being separated—there was a "staticy" feeling, velcro-like, as they parted.

While in the arms of death—I identified it as such—I then felt a warm blanket being wrapped around my face and I could see my body in the bed. I wanted this—I really did! I wanted to go!

But at that moment I saw another figure at the end of the bed. It was an angel—neither male or female. It had long, wavy golden hair and white robe. It pointed to me and spoke, "Death comes in many forms." At that instant I felt my "soul" slammed back into my body! The distance didn't look far but the fall was incredibly long and terrifying. I screamed all the way, "Noooooooo!"

I hit the core of my body with a tumultuous crash. It was loud, painful and hard.

I shot straight up at that moment, wide awake and sweating. My body was numb as if I had been dipped in a tub of novocaine.

I was scared, disappointed, hurt and I cried. I have never been the same since.[4]

While this dream occurred several years ago, it was so realistic for the dreamer that it could have actually just happened. In his dream, the room is alive with visual, tactile and olfactory sensations. As he acceptingly surrenders himself to the figure of death, he begins to feel the commonly reported separation of body and soul. However, unlike near-death experiences, in which one chooses to return to life, in this dream he is forced to return by an angel. "Death comes in many forms," it says. Indeed, this is his second death—a death to death, so to speak, a death back into life. Soul and body are rejoined. Ironically, while he does not resist his first death, he is terrified of the second death which is loud, painful and hard. Two deaths in one dream—no wonder he reports never being the same after that dream.

POST-DEATH BODY

One of the more common characteristics associated with dreaming of one's own death—that is, when the dream does not end with death—is the separation of the dreamer's consciousness from the dreamer's now-dead body. If the death experience can be said to be the de-formation of earth-bound consciousness, this separation of consciousness re-forms the dreamer's identity. Sometimes this trans/formation is quite literal. One student reports that at death in some dreams his soul left his physical body in "a peaceful passing through different passages," while in other death dreams it was "sad and mortifying." Another student reports that she died in a plane crash in front of her parents' home:

> I was lying on my side and I was trying to speak, but it was extremely difficult to do so. Then a strange sensation came over me. I can only describe it as a "good" feeling. It was like a release in my body . . . my body releasing itself, but it frightened me and I started to awaken. I think it was my own voice which woke me. I was asking someone if they were all right.[5]

Her feeling good was triggered by her body releasing itself into death. Acting of its own accord, it was as if her bodily release occurred naturally, had a will of its own, and thus led her into a trans/formation process beyond conscious achievement. Another dreamer describes her post-death experience as the feeling of her flesh being passed through her, like through a fine strainer.

One example of this separation between the pre-death body and post-death consciousness is reported by a student who dreamed he was at the edge of a racing freeway under a pedestrian bridge that joined two areas beyond the freeway. Afraid that the devil had come for him, he decided to step in front of a car.

> The pain in my gut is unbearable from the fear and anxiety about my death decision. In the same second, I feel my fear of dying leave my body and I leave with it. I step out of my body and watch while it is run over by a car. Then it is as before. The devil is gone, and I wait for something to happen. I care not to look at my remains because that is not me. I am me, the one looking around and having nothing to do. But I can float and instantly I am viewing the skyscrapers of San Francisco.[6]

How is this trans/formation described? Here pain is experienced as a function of fear and anxiety but, in the same second, it leaves his body as "he" leaves it. His dead body is no longer who "he" is. His post-death identity is free from the claims of gravity and can transport itself (at will?) in an instant (of thought?). The fundamental question of the dream, and others like it is: Who is the I who steps out of the dead body?

Curiously, there is often a degree of unanimity in the "physical" descriptions of the post-death body. It becomes lighter, and/ or full of light. One student reports that at death she "was only a shadow—I remember skirting across a wall like a shadow." Everything in the dream was black and white except a bouquet of red flowers. Her already-deceased father, and her husband, were seated at a table discussing her in the past tense.

> I remember trying to pull out of my "shadow stall" and communicate with them, but I could only listen. They were exploring their concept of me to each other. They both disagreed and argued. I remember shouting "it doesn't matter," but they could not hear me. I then felt like I just slipped out the window. I don't recall there being anything outside the room—just a lot of light.[7]

In her post-death body, which is shadow-like, the dreamer transcends characterizations of her earthly identity. Interestingly, those living can reach no agreement about who they think she is. She attempts to communicate with them but, as is commonly reported, the living cannot hear the messages of those who have just died. It seems as though a period of time must first intervene before the dead can be heard.

One student reports that at death she felt herself "drifting, becoming lighter." No longer feeling pain, she was aware that she was looking at herself from high above—very pleased, very peaceful. Another student reports that he felt "weightless."

> Amazingly, I was able to direct myself left and right, up and down. I was also able to see all around me, but I could not see myself in my bed. That did not seem to bother me. In fact I thought nothing of it. As I was gliding over mountains, trees, etc., I felt compelled to go in a certain direction. Then I came

to a clearing. It seemed to me like it was an overhead view of a cemetery.[8]

As we have seen, a fairly common characteristic of the post-death body is its ability to glide, or fly, or slip from one space to another, effortlessly. Along with this "physical" ability, one usually gains the advantage of an overhead perspective which allows the person to see more comprehensively than when alive. For instance, one dreamer reports:

> I am falling down a cliff. In the dream, I know if I hit the bottom I will die. (I've been told by dream "experts" that this is so.) I hit the bottom—my body is splattered on the ground, but "I" am floating through the air thinking "How strange! I'm supposed to be dead! But I'm alive and free."[9]

We have suggested that when a death dream is trans/formational, one's old identity de-forms and is replaced by a re-formed, desubstantialized identity which often is no longer attached to a body, or limited by time, causality or gravity. In the following dream examples, the beginnings of the dreamer's new identity becomes the focus of the dream. In the first, the dreamer becomes, after death, a rose.

> I guess I'm dead now.
>
> I never thought it would be like this. Where is the pain? Where is the loneliness?
>
> Ah, I see my funeral. There's my parents and my family. Bernard, Nancy, Anita, Dave . . .
>
> I see them cry. But now they laugh. Good. This passing is a good thing.
>
> The gardener comes to me. He calls me a red rose taken from his garden. He takes me into his house and tenderly puts me in a crystal vase filled with crisp, clean water. I am his beautiful flower, put on display.

Thank you, dear gardener, for watering me and keeping me trimmed. I am glad to be in your house now. It's about time. It was so cold at night outside. Thank you for cultivating me. Your house is where I want to be—my Lord.[10]

In the second dream, the dreamer is aware that someone she loves is trying to kill her. She is chased all over the house and repeatedly hides from the killer whose sex continues to change, as does hers. While there are other people in the house, no one helps her. She reports:

One time, I remember I tried to hide in a box that highly resembled a coffin, except it was very shallow and had a separation in the middle. It was too small, so I got out. Anyway, I remember some guy came over and he was going to save me. I was very relieved to see him. He set up a projector (a film projector), and there was a red beam coming from it shining on the wall. He told me when the killer wasn't around (because he/she didn't know where I was, or what was going on), to stand in front of the beam, and that my soul would be released from my body, and I would be free from the killer. So, I did it. When I got in the beam's pathway, my body collapsed to the floor and my spirit was floating in the room. I felt so relieved and safe. I still wanted to get away, so I left the house and went into the woods behind it. I was going to go to my mom's house. All of a sudden, I was trapped in a body—the body that I really have—and I couldn't float anymore; but I still felt like I was "dead." I started walking through some mud which was very deep, and I was feeling as though my body was a great burden. I didn't want it because it was weighing me down. Finally, I got through the mud and was on a path surrounded by trees. I said to myself, "Why am I walking? I'm dead, and I'm only a spirit. I can fly." So, I started flying very low to the ground. I could see people walking all around the area, but they couldn't see me. Then I started walking again.[11]

What is most remarkable about this dream, aside from the mechanism introduced to enable her to disappear from her body, so to speak (i.e. the film projector's red beam), is the fact that she is aware of her post-death powers. Feeling relieved and safe after her body separates from her spirit, she is able to float in the house. It is only when she goes outside to further distance herself from the killer in the house (i.e. a post-death attachment to her pre-death situation) that she is again trapped in her body. Remembering that she is dead, that she is a spirit, she begins to fly again. (This seeming confusion reflects *The Tibetan Book of the Dead* which states that immediately after death, one tends to think that he or she is still alive.) It takes a "conscious" awareness of her situation to free her of pre-death (karmic) attractions. Typically, the post-death dreamer is able to see others who, in turn, are not able to see her. Then she becomes an invisibly, life-like walking spirit.

In the third dream, a Sikh woman is being chased in a dark city by people in dark cars and is, at the same time, chasing them. Before they shoot her, she is required to shoot them through their third eye (the eye of spiritual wisdom).

> I notice that after shooting a blond woman through the third eye, she does not die. The bullet stops her from pursuing me and puts her in a trance state.
>
> After that, I notice that this is what is happening to everyone I shoot. They didn't die. I just stop them in their tracks.
>
> Eventually, I too am shot in the third eye—seven times. I experience myself going into a trance-like state knowing that I actually am not going to die. EVEN THOUGH I DIE FROM THE SEVEN BULLETS IN MY HEAD, I WAS ALIVE AND WOULD CONTINUE TO LIVE THOUGH I WOULD BE PERMANENTLY ALTERED . . .[12]

The dreamer is aware that she needs to die in order to be released from ordinary waking consciousness. She sees herself as permanently altered. It is as if she needs to be shot in her third eye (her spiritual awareness), to die while alive, in order to be trans/formed in and through death. As well, the dreamer is aware that the dream may indicate that she must surrender (die to) even her notions of the third eye in order to be alive in a post-death (altered) state.

NEWLY ALIVE

While as varied as the range of emotions experienced by
dreamers at death, a common result of trans/formational death
dreams is a renewed sense of aliveness. After viewing her own
funeral, one dreamer reports that she "woke up feeling empty
inside and confused" and that the "dream made me feel more
alive." And in another dream, after dying, a student discovered
that her body had changed into that of a wolf, and that she could
see through the wolf's eyes. When she awoke, she reported feeling "more alive than ever before." It is with this sense of being
more alive in-and-through death than in life that we will conclude.

If it can be said, as we have suggested, that trans/formation-
al death dreams reflect characteristic elements of the spiritual
death experience, are there any motifs or images which seem to
appear more often than others?[13] Ironically, the answer lies in
the dreamer's "waking up" after dying, while yet in the dream.
While dreaming, to discover that one is no longer identified with
the pre-death body is to become alive to a completely new, post-
death, life possibility. In this sense, dying without dying is analogous to realizing, within the dream, that from the perspective of
the post-death aliveness, one's entire reality (including one's self-
identity) has undergone an enormous flip-flop. Time and causality no longer hold their pre-death associations. That which
used to evoke responses of anxiety and fear is now seen in a new,
expanded context in which death itself has died. A new awareness, a new life-possibility, a renewed structure of meaning
and value take shape, from the perspective of which one's old,
pre-death self-understanding is realized to be inadequate, even
laughable.

One dreamer reports it this way.

I am in a totally enclosed, tiled room with no doors, no windows, nothing except a drain-looking device at the bottom, in
the center of the floor. Water begins to emerge rapidly up
from the drain. Quickly, the room is filling with water. Soon I
am floating and treading water in order to keep breathing. As
the water rises, I realize that there is a limited amount of air

left in the chamber. I struggle to keep my head above the rising water and yet I am aware that very soon there will be no
air left.

I am quite anxious. What the hell am I going to do!

At the last minute, when my head touches the ceiling, I dive
toward the dead center of the water. It is thicker the deeper
I dive. The pressure increases rapidly. The drain, the drain!
With desperation, I dive toward the drain. The darkness of it
and the all-out effort is instantaneously transformed, and I
am in outer space. Infinite air! I suddenly see myself still
swimming to get air and realize that I don't have to continue
with the incredible effort. It was humorous to see myself.[14]

In the midst of his fear and panic, when it appears that he will
suffocate against the ceiling, he dives through the drain, through
the darkness and, *instantaneously,* he is in infinite air. Body-less,
he is able to see himself (his body) still attempting to swim (as he
had before he died). But from his trans/formed perspective, his
old, untransformed, activity is laughable. *He* no longer needs to
exercise all-out effort. A new mode of being—more alive in-and-
through death than ever—is born.

As in other such dreams, this shift from fearing death to
laughing at it, from struggling against life's situations to being at
peace, from feeling trapped by events beyond one's control to
feeling released, is trans/formational. Underneath the various
images and symbols appearing in these dreams, a fundamental
shift in the dreamer's perspective is evoked, that is, from an embodied body to a bodiless body. It is not that the soul is contained
within the body, but vice-versa—the body is contained within a
soul whose boundaries are "infinite air!"

Such dreams, while they do not automatically reconfigure
the dreamer's wakened consciousness do, however, *inform* the
wakened dreamer of a way to respond to life's fundamental
predicament—death (i.e. to learn to die, while alive, and in the
process to out-live or unlearn, the fear of dying). To the extent
that the dream information is reliable, and applicable, at least
one thing is clear: by passing through the doorway of death one

can become more alive, more self-aware, and less afraid of death, in life, than could ever be dreamt.

NOTES

[1]Ingmar Bergman, Radio TV Reports, Inc., Public Broadcast Laboratory, WNDT-TV, New York City, 9.

[2]Paul R., a student in "Death, Dying, & Religions" class at San Jose State University, 1989.

[3]Jeffrey H., a student at San Jose State University, 1990.

[4]Erich G., a student in "Death, Dying, & Religions" class at San Jose State University, 1992.

[5]Anonymous student.

[6]Anonymous student.

[7]Lydell S., a student at San Jose State University.

[8]Adam D., a student at San Jose State University.

[9]Joan C., a multiple death dreamer.

[10]Anonymous student.

[11]Jennifer W., a student in "Death, Dying, & Religions" class at San Jose State University, 1992.

[12]Kamlapati Khalsa, formerly a student in the "Death, Dying, & Religions" class and an avid dreamer and dream interpreter.

[13]While we have focused on death dreams which are more obviously trans/formational in their content, one could argue that most, if not all, death dreams provide the dreamer with information which may help him or her to resolve life-conflicts, to replace ignorance with new insights and even to transfigure the dreamer's self-understanding. Though not at first obvious, these other death dreams may contain trans/formational signification beneath their manifest content.

[14]Lee Roser, a teacher of English at Temple University in Japan, 1991.

GLOSSARY

ABATON:
Greek for "the place which is not to be entered uncalled." It was the innermost sanctuary in ancient dream temples where incubants slept in order to receive a dream message.

ARCHETYPAL:
The original pattern, or idea, of which other representations are copies.

ASC:
Initials stand for "altered states of consciousness" in which normal awareness is temporarily suspended, or replaced, by a qualitatively different state of consciousness.

ATMAN:
Sanskrit for the *true self,* that which is unborn and undying; one's true identity.

AVIDYA:
Sanskrit for beginningless ignorance; a not knowing of the true self such that one does not know that one does not know.

BARDO:
A state, or gap, between two modes of being; *The Tibetan Book of the Dead* focuses upon the gap between death and rebirth.

BRAHMA:
Sanskrit for the creator of the cosmos who is worshiped along with Vishnu (The Perserver), and Shiva (The Destroyer).

CHALON:
Hebrew for "to see" which is translated in the Hebrew scriptures as "to dream." It is to be distinguished from the words *khazon* and *mar'eh* which mean a vision.

COLLECTIVE UNCONSCIOUS:
A Jungian term for the reservoir of pre-historic, mythic, symbolic images shared with all of humanity and which are manifested in archetypal patterns in dreams.

EEG:
Initials stand for electroencephalograph, the measurement of the brain's electrical activity in waves.

EKG:
Initials stand for electrocardiograph, the measurement of the heart's rhythms.

EMG:
Initials stand for electromyogram, the measurement of muscle tone and movements.

EOG:
Initials stand for electroculogram, the measurement of retina and cornea movements.

HUN:
Chinese for the spiritual soul of a human being. See PO.

HYPERMNESIC:
Vivid recall of the past, at times occasioned by the dead appearing in dreams to convey forgotten information.

HYPNAGOGIC:
The state of drowsiness just before sleep when the conscious mind slips into the beginnings of unconsciousness.

HYPNOPOMPIC:

The state of semi-consciousness preceding waking when one is in a kind of twilight state of consciousness.

JIVA:

Sanskrit for an individual's consciousness, or the embodied soul.

KHAZON:

See CHALON.

KOAN:

A conceptual puzzle, or contradictory question, presented by a Zen master to a student in order to awaken the student from ignorance.

LATENT CONTENT:

A Freudian term for dream content which is repressed or denied expression, and which, therefore, is not consciously recalled.

LOGOS:

Greek for Word, or Purpose, or Reason, or Wisdom which, in the New Testament, is an attribute of Christ.

LUCID DREAMING:

Dreaming in which the dreamer is aware that he or she is dreaming and, at times, may refer to exercising control over the direction of the dream.

MALAK:

Hebrew for "angel" or "messenger," and is used in the Hebrew scriptures to indicate one of God's methods of communicating with humans.

MANIFEST CONTENT:

A Freudian term for dream content which is consciously remembered.

MAR'EH:

See CHALON.

MAYA:

Sanskrit for the illusory effect or the fragmented appearance of the objective world.

NDE:

Initials stand for "near-death experience" and describe those conscious experiences which continue even though a person almost dies, or dies clinically, only to be revived. Common to such experiences are reports of a dark tunnel, being outside of one's body and a bright light.

NREM:

See REM.

OBE:

Initials stand for "out-of-the-body experiences" in which one's consciousness separates from the physical body and moves independently of it.

ONAR:

Greek for "that which is seen in sleep and then remembered"; in the New Testament it is usually translated with the word "dream."

PHG:

Initials stand for phallograph which monitors penile activity in dreams.

PO:

Chinese for the physical soul of a human being. See HUN.

PRAJAPATI:

Sanskrit for the Lord of Creatures who, once born, is identified with all creatures; he is both the universe and its life force, both death and immortality.

PURUSHA:
Sanskrit for the cosmic male; in later Hindu thought it came to mean the eternal, spiritual essence of an individual.

REM:
Initials standing for rapid eye movement during sleep which marks periods of dream activity. NREM means non-rapid eye movement, or periods of reduced dream activity.

RIG VEDA:
The earliest sacred texts of India composed in Sanskrit and containing the *Upanishads* (philosophical treatises, or secret teachings, composed between 800–600 BCE).

SAMSARA:
Sanskrit for the endless cycle of births, deaths and rebirths which involves human suffering, and from which one must awake.

SAT:
Sanskrit for Being, or awakened Being—*Sat-chit-ananda* (Being-Consciousness-Bliss—the realization of the Self.)

SHIVA:
See BRAHMA.

TANTRA:
A non-Vedic form of esoteric yoga (spiritual practice) which emphasizes the erotic, the forbidden, the unknown.

VISHNU:
See BRAHMA.

YANG:
The male, positive, heavenly force in the universe. In popular religion it is associated with goodness.

YIN:
The female, negative, earthly force in the universe. In popular religion it is associated with evil.

BIBLIOGRAPHY

Abe, Masao. "Transformation in Buddhism." *Buddhist-Christian Studies,* Vol. 7 (1987), 15–24.

Ali, Abdullah Yusuf, trans. *The Holy Qur'an.* New York: McGregor & Werner, Inc., 1946.

Allinson, Robert E. *Chuang-Tzu for Spiritual Transformation: An Analysis of the Inner Chapters.* New York: State University of New York Press, 1989.

Artemidorus of Daldis. "A Soothsayers's Dream Book." *The New World of Dreams.* Eds. Ralph L. Woods and Herbert B. Greenhouse. New York: Macmillan Publishing Co., Inc., 1974.

———. *The Interpretation of Dreams.* Trans. Robert J. White. New Jersey: Noyes Press, 1975.

Beckett, Samuel. *Waiting for Godot.* New York: Grove Press, 1954.

Bergson, Henri. *Dreams.* New York: B.W. Huebsch, 1914.

Buber, Martin. *Eclipse of God.* New York: Harper Torchbooks, 1952.

Bulfinch, Thomas. *Bulfinch's Mythology.* New York: Avenel Books, 1979.

Campbell, Joseph. *The Hero with a Thousand Faces.* Princeton: Princeton University Press, 1949.

———. *The Mythic Image.* Princeton: Princeton University Press, 1982.

———. *Myths, Dreams, and Religion.* New York: E.P. Dutton & Co., 1970.

Campbell, Joseph, and Bill Moyers. *The Power of Myth.* New York: Doubleday & Company, Inc., 1988.

Carlyon, Richard. *A Guide to the Gods.* New York: Quill/William Morrow, 1981.

Castaneda, Carlos. *Journey to Ixtlan.* New York: Simon and Schuster, 1972.

———. *The Eagle's Gift.* New York: Washington Square Press, 1987.

———. *Tales of Power.* New York: Simon and Schuster, 1974.

Chang, Garma C.C., trans. *The Six Yogas of Naropa.* New York: Snow Lion Publications, 1963.

278

Chidester, David. *Patterns of Transcendence: Religion, Death and Dying.* Belmont: Wadsworth Publishing Co., 1990.

Cousineau, Thomas. *Waiting for Godot: Form in Movement.* Boston: Twayne Publishers, 1990.

Coxhead, David and Susan Hiller. *Dreams: Visions of the Night.* New York: Crossroad, 1976.

Crane, John Kenny. "Crossing the Bar Twice: Post-Mortem Consciousness in Bierce, Hemingway, and Golding." *Studies in Short Fiction,* 6 (1969), 361–370.

Currie, Jan. *You Cannot Die.* New York: Methuen, 1978.

Currie, Mary M. "The Way of Dreams." *The Nineteenth Century,* 1903.

de Quincy, Thomas. *Confessions of an English Opium Eater.* New York: Heritage Press, 1950.

Descartes, René. *Discourse on Method.* Trans. John Veitch. Chicago: Henry Regnery Co., 1949.

Dostoyevesky, Fyodor. *The Dream of a Queer Fellow.* London: George Allen & Unwin, 1961.

Durant, Will. *The Story of Civilization: Part II, The Life of Greece.* New York: Simon and Schuster, 1966.

Edinger, Edward. *Ego and Archetype.* New York: Putnam's Sons, 1972.

Eliot, T.S. *The Complete Poems and Plays: 1909–1950.* New York: Harcourt Brace Jovanovich, 1980.

Evans, Christopher. *Landscapes of the Night.* New York: Pocket Books, 1985.

Evans-Wentz, W.Y., trans. *The Tibetan Book of the Dead.* London: Oxford University Press, 1960.

Faraday, Ann. *The Dream Game.* New York: Perennial Library, 1974.

Felman, Shoshana. "To Open the Question." *Yale French Studies,* Number 55/56 (1977) 5–10.

Foucault, Michel. "Dreams, Imagination, and Existence." *Dream & Existence.* Ed. Keith Moeller. (A special issue from *The Review of Existential Psychology & Psychiatry,* Vol. XIX, No. 1)

Freud, Sigmund. *The Interpretation of Dreams.* New York: The Modern Library, 1950.

Fromm, Erich. *The Forgotten Language.* New York: Grove Press, 1951.

Gackenbach, Jayne and Jane Bosveld. *Control Your Dreams.* New York: Harper & Row, 1989.

Garfield, Patricia L. *Creative Dreaming.* New York: Simon and Schuster, 1974.

Graham, A.C. *Chuang Tzu, The Inner Chapters.* London: Unwin, 1981.

Grof, Stanislav and Joan Halifax. *The Human Encounter with Death.* New York: E.P. Dutton, 1977.

Guenther, Herbert V., trans. *The Life & Teaching of Naropa.* Oxford: Oxford University Press, 1963.

Hadfield, J.A. *Dreams and Nightmares.* Baltimore: Penguin Books, 1954.

Hall, Calvin S. *The Meaning of Dreams.* New York: McGraw-Hill, 1953.

Hall, Calvin and Vernon J. Nordby. *The Individual and His Dreams.* New York: Mentor Books, 1972.

Hall, James A. *Clinical Use of Dreams.* New York: Grune & Stratton, 1977.

Hemingway, Ernest. *The Short Stories of Ernest Hemingway.* New York: Charles Scribner's Sons, 1938.

Herzog, Edgar. *Psyche and Death.* New York: G.P. Putnam's Sons, 1966.

Heyword, Rosiland. "Attitudes to Death in the Light of Dreams and Other 'Out-of-the-Body' Experiences." *Man's Concern with Death.* Ed. Arnold Toynbee, *et al.* New York: McGraw-Hill Book Company, 1968.

Hillman, James. *The Dream and the Underworld.* New York: Harper & Row, 1979.

Hobbes, Thomas. *Leviathan.* London: George Routledge & Sons, 1885.

Hobson, J. Allan, and Robert W. McCarley. "The Brain as a Dream State Generator: An Activation-Synthesis Hypothesis of the Dream Process." *The American Journal of Psychiatry,* 134:12 (December 1977).

Hull, R.F.C., trans. "Wirklichkeit der Seele," 1934. *The Meaning of Death.* Ed. Herman Feifel. New York: McGraw-Hill Book Company, Inc., 1959.

James, William. *The Varieties of Religious Experience.* New York: Random House, 1902.

Johnston, William. *The Still Point.* New York: Harper & Row, 1970.

Jowett, Benjamin, trans. *Plato, The Republic.* New York: The Modern Library, 1941.

Jung, Carl G. *Dreams,* Trans. R.F.C. Hull. Princeton: Princeton University Press, 1974.

———. *Collected Works,* Vol. 4. Trans. R.F.C. Hull. Princeton: Princeton University Press, 1961.

———. *Memories, Dreams, Reflections,* Trans. Richard and Clara Winston. New York: Vintage Books, 1965.

———. *Collected Works,* Vol. XI. Trans. R.F.C. Hull. New York: Pantheon Books, Bollingen Series, 1958.

Kalweit, Holger. "Dreamtime and Inner Space." *The World of the Shaman.* Boulder: Shambhala Publications, Inc., 1984.

Kapleau, Philip, ed. *The Wheel of Death.* New York: Harper Torchbooks, 1971.

Kelsey, Morton T. *God, Dreams and Revelation.* Minneapolis: Augsburg Publishing House, 1968.

King, Horatio. "On Dreams." *The New England Magazine,* 2, No. 3 (1890), 329.

Kramer, Kenneth Paul. *The Sacred Art of Dying: How World Religions Understand Death.* Mahwah: Paulist Press, 1988.

Kubose, Gyomay M. *Zen Koans.* Chicago: Henry Regnery Co., 1973.

Kundera, Milan. *The Unbearable Lightness of Being.* Trans. Michael Henry Heim. New York: Harper & Row, 1984.

La Berge, Stephen. *Lucid Dreaming.* New York: Ballantine Books, 1985.

Lincoln, Jackson Stewart. *The Dream in Primitive Cultures.* London: Cresset Press, 1936.

Loewe, Michael, and Carmen Blacker. *Oracles and Divination.* Colorado: Shambhala Publications, Inc., 1981.

Loumer, David. "The Near-Death Experience: Cross-Cultural and Multi-Disciplinary Dimensions." *Perspectives on Death and Dying: Cross-Cultural and Multi-Disciplinary Views.* Ed. Arthur Berger, *et al.* Philadelphia: The Charles Press, 1989.

Mackenzie, Norman. *Dreams and Dreaming.* New York: Vanguard Press, 1965.

Maddock, Kenneth. *The Australian Aborigines: A Portrait of Their Society.* London: Allen Lane/Penguin Press, 1972.

Meier, C.A. *Healing Dream and Ritual: Ancient Incubation and Modern Psychotherapy.* Switzerland: Daimon Verlag, 1989.

Monroe, Robert A. *Journeys Out of the Body.* New York: Anchor Books, 1977.

Moody, Jr. Raymond. *Life After Life.* New York: Bantam, 1975.

———. *Reflections on Life After Life.* Atlanta: Mockingbird Books, 1977.

———. *The Light Beyond.* New York: Bantam, 1988.

Müller, Max, trans. *The Upanishads.* New York: Dover Publications, 1884, 1962.

Mullin, Glenn. *Death and Dying: The Tibetan Tradition.* Boston: Arkana, 1986.

O'Flaherty, Wendy Doniger. *Dreams, Illusions and Other Realities.* Chicago: The University of Chicago Press, 1984.

Parker, K.L. *The Euahlayi Tribe: A Study of Aboriginal Life in Australia.* London: A. Costable, 1905.

Pascal, Blaise. *Pascal Pensées.* New York: E.P. Dutton & Co., 1958.

Poe, Edgar Allan. *Edgar Allan Poe.* Eds. Margaret Alterton and Hardin Craig. New York: Hill and Wang, 1935.

Priest, John F. "Myth and Dreams in Hebrew Scripture." *Myths, Dreams and Religion.* Ed. Joseph Campbell. New York: E.P. Dutton & Co., 1970.

Radcliffe, C.B. "A Speculation About Dreaming." *The Contemporary Review,* 40 (1881).

Ratcliff, A.J.J. *A History of Dreams.* Boston: Small, Maynard & Co., 1923.

Ring, Kenneth. *Life at Death.* New York: Quill, 1982.

Ross, W.D., trans. *The Works of Aristotle.* Oxford: The Clarendon Press, 1908.

Rupprecht, Carol S. "Dreams and Literature: A Reader's Guide." In Jayne Gackenbach's *Sleep and Dreams: A Source Book.* New York: Garland, 1986.

Saliba, David R. *A Psychology of Fear: The Nightmare Formula of Edgar Allan Poe.* Maryland: The University Press of America, 1980.

Sandars, N.K., trans. *The Epic of Gilgamesh.* New York: Penguin Books, 1960.

Sanford, John A. *Dreams: God's Forgotten Language.* San Francisco: Harper & Row, 1968.

Smart, Ninian, and Richard D. Hecht, eds. *Sacred Texts of the World: A Universal Anthology.* New York: Crossroad, 1982.

Smith, S. *The Enigma of Out-of-the-Body Travel.* New York: Helix Press, 1965.

Speiser, E.A. *The Anchor Bible: Genesis: Vol. 1.* New York: Doubleday & Company, 1979.

Spence, Lewis. *Myths and Legends Series: Egypt.* New York: Avenel Books, 1986.

Starhawk. *The Spiral Dance: A Rebirth of the Ancient Religion of the Great Goddess.* San Francisco: Harper & Row, 1979.

Stewart, Kilton. "Dream Theory in Malaya." In Charles T. Tart's *Altered States of Consciousness.* New York: John Wiley & Sons, Inc., 1969.

Tart, Charles T. *Altered States of Consciousness.* New York: John Wiley & Sons, Inc., 1969.

———. "From Spontaneous Event to Lucidity: A Review of Attempts to Consciously Control Nocturnal Dreaming." *Conscious Mind, Sleeping Brain: Perspectives on Lucid Dreaming.* Eds. Jayne Gackenbach and Stephen La Berge. New York: Plenum Press, 1988.

———. "Introduction." In Robert A. Monroe's *Journeys Out of the Body.* New York: Anchor Books, 1977.

Taylor, Sir Edward B. "A Primitive View of Dreams." *The New World of Dreams.* Ed. Ralph L. Woods and Herbert B. Greenhouse. New York: Macmillan, 1974.

Thompson, Lawrence G. "Dream Divination and Chinese Popular Religion." *The Journal of Chinese Religions,* No. 16 (Fall 1988), 73–82.

Tredennick, Hugh, trans. *Plato: The Last Days of Socrates.* New York: Penguin, 1954.

Van de Castle, Robert. *The Psychology of Dreaming.* New York: General Learning Press, 1971.

van Eeden, Frederik. "A Study of Dreams." *Proceedings of the Society for Psychical Research.* Vol. 26, 1913.

———. "A Study of Dreams." In Charles T. Tart's *Altered States of Consciousness.* New York: John Wiley & Sons, Inc., 1969.

Vande Kemp, Hendrika. "The Dream in Periodical Literature:

1860–1910." *Journal of the History of the Behavioral Sciences,* 17 (1981), 88–113.

von Franz, Marie-Louise. *On Dreams and Death.* Trans. Emmanuel Kennedy and Vernon Brooks. Boston: Shambhala, 1987.

Wheelwright, Jane Hollister. *The Death of a Woman.* New York: St. Martin's Press, 1981.

Whitman, Walt. *Leaves of Grass.* New York: Signet, 1980.

———. *The Portable Walt Whitman.* Ed. Mark van Doren. New York: Viking Press, 1945.

Whyte, Lancelot Law. *The Unconscious Before Freud.* New York: Basic Books, Inc., 1960.

Wiesel, Elie. *Messengers of God: Biblical Portraits and Legends.* New York: Random House, 1976.

Woods, Ralph L., and Herbert B. Greenhouse. *The New World of Dreams.* New York: Macmillan Publishing Co., Inc., 1974.

Zachner, R.C., trans. *Hindu Scriptures.* New York: E.P. Dutton, 1966.

INDEX